Letters Between a Catholic and an Evangelical

Fr. John R. Waiss
James G. McCarthy

HARVEST HOUSE™ PUBLISHERS

EUGENE, OREGON

Cover by Koechel Peterson & Associates, Inc., Minneapolis, Minnesota

LETTERS BETWEEN A CATHOLIC AND AN EVANGELICAL

Copyright © 2003 by John R. Waiss and James G. McCarthy
Published by Harvest House Publishers
Eugene, Oregon 97402

Library of Congress Cataloging-in-Publication Data

McCarthy, James G., 1952-
    Letters between a Catholic and an evangelical / James G. McCarthy, John R. Waiss.
      p. cm.
    Includes bibliographical references and index.
    ISBN 0-7369-0989-3 (pbk.)
    1. McCarthy, James G., 1952---Correspondence. 2. Protestants--United States--Correspondence. 3. Waiss, John R., 1957---Correspondence. 4. Catholic Church--United States--Clergy--Correspondence. 5. Evangelicalism--Relations--Catholic Church. 6. Catholic Church--Relations--Evangelicalism. I. Waiss, John R., 1957- II. Title.
    BR1643.M33 A4 2003
    280'.042—dc21   2002010024

Printed in the United States of America

03 04 05 06 07 08 / DP-MS / 10 9 8 7 6 5 4 3 2 1

Contents

How to Enrich Your Reading of This Book

The authors suggest you begin by reading the Authors' Prologue. It will help you understand who they are, their purpose in writing, and the format of this book. You then have two choices: You can read the book straight through, following the events in their lives during the two years during which the book was written. Or, if you prefer, you can begin with those topics that are of greatest interest to you. The table of contents will help you in your selection. On crucial issues, take the time to look up references to the Bible and the *Catechism of the Catholic Church* and read them in context. Finally, each time you pick up this book, begin with prayer, asking God to help you to know the truth. Pray also for the authors, that they may resolve their doctrinal differences and come to worship the one Lord together.

References to the Bible and the *Catechism of the Catholic Church*

Except where otherwise indicated, all Scripture quotations are from *The Holy Bible*, Revised Standard Version (RSV), a translation accepted by Protestants and Catholics. References to the Bible are in the form Genesis 1:3, meaning the book of Genesis, chapter one, verse three. In this book, bracketed text within Bible quotations indicates a comment added by one of the authors. Text in *italics* indicates added emphasis.

Though both Protestants and Catholics recognize the same 27 books of the New Testament, there is some disagreement concerning the books of the Old Testament. The Catholic Church recognizes seven additional books in the Old Testament (Tobith, Judith, First and Second Maccabees, Wisdom, Sirach, and Baruch). The Catholic Church refers to these as the Deutero-Canonical books. Protestants refer to them as the Apocrypha and do not consider them part of Scripture.

This book is also cross-referenced to the *Catechism of the Catholic Church*. It is an official guide, authentic reference text, and sure norm of the Roman Catholic faith. References to the numbered paragraphs of the *Catechism* are in brackets. For example, [CCC 830] refers to numbered paragraph 830 of the *Catechism of the Catholic Church*.

Authors' Prologue

John *(the Catholic priest)*

At the Last Supper, Jesus prayed:

> I do not pray for these only, but also for those who
> believe in me through their word, that they may all be
> one; even as thou, Father, art in me, and I in thee, that
> they also may be in us, so that the world may believe
> that thou hast sent me.
>
> JOHN 17:20-21

Though essential to our Christian witness, unity has eluded
Catholics and evangelicals. It is quite challenging to dialogue char-
itably with another who strongly believes he is in the truth. However, it is possible.

Jim and I have spent hours together discussing our faiths. With
God's help, we never argue. Occasionally something is said that
triggers intense emotions, as though one were being personally
attacked. However, after listening calmly, we have found that the
Holy Spirit enlightens us to the real issues along with the necessary light to respond. Our discussions remain friendly and civil,
largely due to our mutual love and respect for Scripture and our
desire to seek, find, and witness to the truth. This unites us and is
the foundation of our exchange.

Jim *(the evangelical minister)*

Our dialogue began in the early 1990s. I was leading an evangelical ministry called University Christian Fellowship at the University of California, Berkeley. It was there that I met Dave, a history student with a keen mind. He was also an enthusiastic Catholic. Dave and I discussed some of the differences between Catholics and evangelicals, such as the place Mary has in the lives of God's people. Since I was in the process of writing a book on Catholicism, later published as *The Gospel According to Rome,* I asked Dave for his opinion of the chapter on Mary.

John

At the time, I was the Catholic chaplain for Garber House, a Berkeley residence of Opus Dei that helps college students integrate their faith into their daily life. After reviewing Jim's manuscript with Dave—a Garber House resident—I suggested he might invite Jim over to talk. Frankly, I didn't expect Jim to accept, but to my delight he did.

Thus began our series of discussions, held at Garber House or at Jim's home over dinner. There I met his wife, Jean, and their three daughters—Elizabeth, Faith, and Grace. Often Jim's friends and colleagues would join us for our discussion.

Jim

Though now living miles apart, we have maintained our friendship through letters and occasional visits. Presently, John serves as the chaplain of an Opus Dei center for men and another for women near the University of California, Los Angeles. I am an elder of an evangelical church in San Jose, California, serving in pastoral and teaching ministry. It was during a visit to our home in the summer of 1999 that I first suggested to John the writing of this book. What I had in mind was that we would restart our discussions and put them in writing through an exchange of letters. John was immediately interested, having been thinking of something similar.

John

Long before we began this project, it had been my hope and prayer to bring Jim and his family home to the Catholic Church. Whether this happens or not, perhaps our exchange can benefit others—Catholics and evangelicals—and help us not only to understand what each other believes, but to learn to listen to opposing beliefs with respect and charity, praying and growing in love for one another.

I welcome this opportunity to explain Catholic teaching, to show its unique and complete consistency with Scripture, while dispelling any misconceptions or stereotypes of Catholicism. Jim, in turn, will try to show the exclusivity of his interpretation of Scripture. Without a common recognized authority to authenticate one interpretation over another, this seems the most respectful way to treat our differing beliefs; may it bear fruit in leading us to the truth.

In addition, I want to apologize ahead of time if I have offended Jim or any readers; pride can be a barrier, preventing me from fully listening, understanding, or respecting Jim or his beliefs. This opposes true Christian dialogue. Also, forgive me for times I do not fully challenge Jim with a proper account of my faith, either by my behavior or inadequate explanation. My dialogue with Jim has taught me a lot; may I continue to learn, especially to love as Christ loves. I trust the Holy Spirit will overcome our inadequacies and lead us to truth (2 Thessalonians 2:13) and unity in Christ (Ephesians 4:3).

Jim

I also welcome the opportunity this book provides for John and I to discuss our faiths in the public arena. We hold some beliefs in common, as our letters will reveal. We strongly disagree on others, some foundational to the Christian faith. Though at times our debate has grown intense, I have always found John to be a gentleman, soft spoken, and a patient listener. Though we remain on opposite sides of a dispute of great importance, I have grown in my respect for him and value his friendship.

I will be presenting my beliefs as an evangelical Christian. Evangelicals attend a variety of churches but share a common core of beliefs:

- There is one God, eternally existing in three persons— Father, Son, and Holy Spirit.

- Man is sinful, fallen from God's favor and under divine condemnation.

- Jesus Christ is the incarnate Son of God, born of the virgin Mary. He lived a sinless life on earth, died on our behalf on the cross, rose on the third day, and is coming to judge the living and the dead.

- Through personal faith in Jesus Christ one is spiritually reborn and receives eternal life. Salvation is through faith alone by God's grace alone.

- The Holy Spirit indwells each believer, enabling him or her to live a holy life.

- Scripture is the inspired Word of God, the supreme guide to the Christian faith.

- It is the responsibility of every Christian to tell others the good news of salvation through Jesus Christ.

A recent study by the Barna Research Group estimates that eight percent of Americans are evangelicals. That is about 14 million people. Worldwide, there are reportedly 214 million people who identify themselves as evangelicals. Most of these are in Protestant churches linked to formal evangelical alliances such as World Evangelical Fellowship.

John

I will present the Catholic position. *Catholic* (a Greek term meaning *universal)* was added to *Christian* when heretical sects developed *particular* beliefs differing from the *totality* of what

Christians had believed in *every time* and *place*. By the early second century, *Catholic* became a common term for all orthodox Christians: "Where there is Christ Jesus, there is the Catholic Church" [CCC 830].¹

A Catholic must believe, at least implicitly, *all* (universal) that the Catholic Church teaches, as detailed in the *Catechism of the Catholic Church*. A true Catholic cannot be a "cafeteria" Christian, picking and choosing what he wants to believe. Such a Catholic, as well as one who ceases going to church or living out his faith, has begun losing his *Catholic* identity.

Approximately half of the two billion Christians worldwide identify themselves as Catholics, and about 60 million of these individuals reside in the United States. For a *Catholic*, I am fairly *evangelical* in my approach, turning to Jesus Christ and His gospel (*evangelium*) for the roots of Catholic teaching. If we were to remove the words *alone* and *supreme* from Jim's list of core evangelical beliefs, I could agree with every one of them: God's grace saves us through Christ's crucifixion, is accepted by faith, and is applied to us by baptism and manifested in works.

Jim

The format we designed for this book emphasizes the positive presentation of our beliefs. We address six topics, each a major area separating Catholics and evangelicals. We exchanged ten letters on each topic, and limited the length of the letters to keep things moving. This means we were unable to respond to every issue raised. We also conducted two tape-recorded conversations on each topic in which one of us asked questions of the other. A portion of these questions were submitted to the other in advance.

February 2000—after refining the format of this book—we began our correspondence. Neither of us realized at the time the direction our discussions would take us. This much we did know: Each of us was going to try to convert the other—in a friendly way, of course.

TOPIC 1
God's Word

*Is it found in
Scripture alone
or in Scripture
plus Tradition?*

Letter 1

Dear John,

I miss the long discussions we enjoyed when you lived nearby in Berkeley, and look forward to resuming them now through our letters. Hopefully our friendship will deepen and our understanding of one another's faith will increase.

At the heart of our differences is the subject of authority. We disagree on basic questions, such as, How has the revelation received from Christ been preserved? Who has the authority to interpret and to teach the Christian faith? How is Christ's church to be governed?

Probably the most basic question is this: What is the Word of God? Evangelical Christians answer:

> The written Scriptures are the inspired, authoritative, and trustworthy Word of God. They are the supreme norm or standard to which Christians must submit, the final court of appeals in matters of doctrine and morals. In the Bible we find all truth essential for salvation and Christian living. The Scriptures have no equal on earth, for they alone are the Word of God.

Let me know how you see it. Include any questions you have about my position. I'll do my best to respond.

In Christ's love,

Jim

Letter 2

Dear Jim,

How are you, Jean, and the girls doing? I keep you often in my prayers. I hope to stop by after Easter, if you are home.

I often think of you. As I read Scripture, passages pop up that make me think, *How I'd like to share this with Jim.* What a joy it is to resume our discussions. May they move us toward fulfilling Christ's prayer "that they may be one" (John 17:11).

Now you should know that good Catholics take Scripture seriously and read it regularly:

> The Church "forcefully and specifically exhorts all the Christian faithful...to learn the surpassing knowledge of Jesus Christ, by frequent reading of the divine Scriptures. 'Ignorance of the Scriptures is ignorance of Christ.'"
>
> [CCC 133]

Scripture is God's Word, inspired of His Spirit [CCC 135]. It is authoritative, trustworthy, and error-free because God is its author. Therefore, no doctrine, council, creed, declaration, or tradition may contradict an authentic interpretation of Scripture. Truly the Bible has "no equal on earth." On this point we seem to agree.

Is Scripture the Sole Source of Truth?

However, Catholics do not believe that Scripture is our *sole* source for the truth and certainty of God's revelation. Do you? Does the Holy Spirit entrust us with sound and authoritative doctrine *only* through Scripture? Where does Scripture claim this?

The Supreme, Final Court of Appeals?

There are some scattered references in the Bible that speak to its inspiration and authority, but where does it teach that it is "the supreme norm or standard to which Christians must submit"? Or where does Scripture call itself the "final court of appeals?" How does it resolve contradictory interpretations and when an interpretation is from the Holy Spirit or not?

The Canon of Scripture

How does Scripture resolve whether a passage or book, like Paul's letter to Philemon, is canonical? Can Scripture *alone* answer such disputes?

Salvation Communicated *Only* Through the Bible?

You also say, "In the Bible we find all truth essential for salvation." Does a person need scholarly qualifications to interpret the Bible correctly? Did God intend to communicate salvation *only* by individuals reading the Bible? Where does Scripture say that?

I hope these concerns are just stereotypical misunderstandings. To me, *Sola Scriptura* leads to doctrinal and ecclesiastical anarchy. If a Protestant disagrees with his pastor's interpretation, is he compelled to go off and start his own church? So many have. If each can interpret Scripture himself, why do we need a church at all?

I look forward to your always thoughtful response.

Yours in Christ,

John

Letter 3

MONDAY, APRIL 17, 2000

Dear John,

Thanks for your letter. Jean, the girls, and I are well. You'll be surprised how much Faith (16) and Grace (almost 15) have grown. They are now taller than Jean, and have become aspiring athletes, recently joining the high school swim team. Elizabeth (20) is in her second year of college. She is majoring in English.

I hope you can visit when you are in the Bay Area at Easter. It's been almost a year since you were in our home. That was when we first spoke about this exchange of letters. It's good to have finally begun.

I am thankful for the common ground we hold. Most important is our shared belief that the Bible is the inspired, authoritative, and trustworthy Word of God, as you state in your last letter. I also share your hope that someday we might enjoy the unity for which the Lord Jesus prayed in John 17:11 and 21. His petition, however, includes another request for His disciples. Jesus asked the Father to "sanctify them in the truth" (John 17:17). He then added, "thy word is truth" (John 17:17). So it is with us. We will be united only when we embrace together the true teachings of Christ as found in God's Word.

Unfortunately, we do not even agree on what *is* the Word of God. Evangelical Christians, such as I, hold that God has preserved the revelation received from Christ in the inspired writings of Scripture. Your church says that the Christian faith is

18

contained in Scripture and Tradition. Together they make up the
Word of God. Looking to different sources, we have come to significantly different understandings of the Christian faith. As such
we are divided, and will remain so until this matter is resolved.
With that goal in mind, I will begin by trying to answer the questions in your last letter and to explain my position more fully.

God's Supreme Standard

You asked, "Where does the Bible teach that it is the 'supreme
norm or standard to which Christians must submit'?" I find this
throughout the Scriptures. Over 100 times we read that "the Word
of the Lord came to" divinely appointed prophets. Over 400 times
we read, "Thus says the Lord." This communicates divine inspiration and supreme authority. Judaism's greatest confession of
faith, the *Shema,* also expresses the unparalleled position of these
Scriptures as the supreme standard of truth for the Jews
(Deuteronomy 6:4-7). Once every seven years, God ordered the
nation of Israel to assemble, both adults and children. The Levites
were then to read the first five books of the Bible to the people,
exhorting them to carefully obey the Scriptures (Deuteronomy
31:11-13). Joshua echoed this command, warning Israel, "Be very
firm, then, to keep and do all that is *written* in the book of the law
of Moses, so that you may not turn aside from it to the right hand
or to the left" (Joshua 23:6 NASB). God commanded the Jewish
king to keep a personal copy of the Scriptures and to obey them
diligently (Deuteronomy 17:18-20).

Similarly, the New Testament proclaims its divine authorship
and supreme authority throughout its pages. For example, in the
Sermon on the Mount, Jesus taught the supremacy of God's
written Word (Matthew 5:18-20). Peter describes how it was
recorded:

> First of all you must understand this, that no
> prophecy of scripture is a matter of one's own inter-
> pretation, because no prophecy ever came by the

> impulse of man, but men moved by the Holy Spirit
> spoke from God.
>
> 2 PETER 1:20-21

Here Peter tells us that the apostles and prophets who wrote the Scriptures did not simply record their "own interpretation" of the events they had witnessed. Rather, the Holy Spirit "moved" or *carried* them along in their writing. The same Greek word is used in Mark 2:3, where some men *carried* a paralyzed man to Jesus, hoping He would heal him. Similarly, the Holy Spirit carried along the writers of Scripture so that they precisely recorded that which God wanted communicated.

John, you affirm God as the author of the Bible, yet you ask, "Where does it teach that it is 'the supreme norm or standard to which Christians must submit'?" Is it not self-evident? If "all scripture is inspired by God" (literally *God-breathed,* 2 Timothy 3:16), then must it not be the supreme norm or standard to which Christians must submit?

God's Unique Record of Revelation

You ask if I believe that the Scriptures are our *sole* source for the truth and certainty of revelation. Yes, I know no other. Their place in Judaism, as we have seen, was unique. God established them as the supreme norm for Israel. With the passage of time, however, the Jews strayed. They came to hold the oral tradition of the elders, the teaching of the scribes and the Pharisees, and the Sanhedrin (the high court of the Jews) as authoritative sources of truth. Jesus, by contrast, rejected all three. He never appealed to any authority as supreme other than God's Word. He taught His disciples to do likewise.

This is not to say that all other sources are wrong. We can find sound doctrine in some of the creeds, confessions, documents of the councils, and the writings of early Christians. The Holy Spirit, however, tells us to "test everything; hold fast what is good" (1 Thessalonians 5:21). We must judge the writings of men by Scripture. We should consider them true and authoritative only to the extent that they accurately communicate the truths of God's Word. Never should we put them on a par with Scripture.

You ask, What does treating the Scriptures as the final court of appeals mean in practice? It means that as Christians we should turn first and foremost to the Bible for truth, knowing it to be "inspired by God and profitable for teaching, for reproof, for correction, and for training in righteousness, that the man of God may be complete, equipped for every good work" (2 Timothy 3:16-17). Should a controversy arise in the church as to some aspect of our faith, God, through His written Word, should have the final say.

The Lord Jesus modeled this approach to truth. When the Sadducees challenged Jesus with a question about a woman widowed seven times, Jesus answered, "You are wrong, because you know neither the scriptures nor the power of God" (Matthew 22:29). He then quoted Exodus 3:6, ending the debate. The Jews of Berea also serve as an example. When Paul and Silas came to their city and preached the gospel to them, the Bereans "received the word with all eagerness, examining the scriptures daily to see if these things were so" (Acts 17:11). So should it be with us. We should examine all teaching carefully to see whether it is in agreement with Scripture.

John, one of your follow-up questions relates closely to this point. You asked how using Scripture as the final court of appeals resolves contradictory interpretations.

Interpretation can be a problem. "The law of the LORD is perfect" (Psalm 19:7), but, as your question implies, our understanding may be lacking. I find that most errors involve a failure to interpret a passage in its context. When we take the time to study each book of the Bible as a whole, our ability to interpret it accurately increases significantly. Another well-proven rule of interpretation is to use Scripture to interpret Scripture. What this means is that we should use those passages of the Bible that are clear and readily understood to interpret those parts that are difficult to understand. Fortunately, the Bible is clear when it teaches the primary doctrines of the Christian faith.

—

21

Recognizing a Book as Scripture

You also asked how Scripture can resolve the canonicity of a book. Can Scripture *alone* answer such disputes? Again, I answer yes. It should be stated at the outset that a book is part of the canon—that is, rightly a part of the list of books making up the Bible—not because we decide to put it there, but because the Holy Spirit inspired it in the first place. God's people only *recognize* a book as Scripture. The writings are largely self-authenticating, demonstrating by their source, integrity, and dynamic character that God is their author.

The first factor is source: Who wrote it? If the answer was a trusted apostle or prophet, God's people took notice. Another hallmark of divine origin is integrity. A book had to be in full agreement with the doctrinal and moral teachings of already-recognized Scripture. One error was enough to disqualify a work from inclusion. A third factor is what some describe as the *dynamic power* of the Scriptures. An inspired book should speak with moral force and authority. The Bible says, "The word of God is living and active, sharper than any two-edged sword, piercing to the division of soul and spirit, of joints and marrow, and discerning the thoughts and intentions of the heart" (Hebrews 4:12). When we read Scripture, it should commend itself to us as inspired.

God's people applied these factors in differing degrees to the various books of the Bible. The Jewish nation did this with respect to the Old Testament, and the early Christians with respect to the New Testament. The Holy Spirit oversaw the process, guaranteeing the outcome. We believe that as God has faithfully communicated divine revelation through inspired writings, so He has safeguarded their assemblage as the Bible. Thus the process of recognizing the canon was both natural and supernatural.

I hope this helps you to understand better my position. Give me a call and we can discuss these matters more.

In Christ's love,

Jim

Conversation 1

John: Thanks again for having me over for dinner two weeks ago. I enjoyed the meal and the visit with your family. That night's discussion brought out the urgency of our present exchange.

Jim: We enjoyed having you over, John.

Is *only* God's written word authoritative?

John: Jim, I agree with so much of what you wrote. You did a good job of showing how Scripture gets its authority from God as inspired by the Holy Spirit. Our real difference is in the word *alone*. Is *only* Scripture inspired and authoritative? What about the unwritten words of David (2 Samuel 23:2) and Elizabeth (Luke 1:41)? Doesn't the Holy Spirit give authority to speech (Matthew 10:19-20), or is that *unique* to Scripture? Am I missing something? Must God's Word be written down to be authoritative?

Jim: I don't think you are missing anything, but rather seeing something that isn't there. When evangelical Christians such as I say that God's written Word is authoritative, we are not implying that someone has to write down God's words for them to become authoritative. The inspired words of a true prophet—such as David, Isaiah, or Paul— are authoritative because they are God-breathed. Spoken or written, God's words are equally authoritative.

—

We agree that the standard of truth is the revelation God gave through Christ, the apostles, and the prophets. Where we differ is in our answer to the question, How has God preserved and transmitted that revelation to us who live almost 2000 years later?

Your answer, as I understand the Roman Catholic position, is Scripture and Tradition. Together they are the Word of God and contain the truths Christ revealed. My answer, and that of millions of Christians like me, is that God has preserved and transmitted to us the teachings of Christ in the Bible. When contrasting our position with that of Rome's, however, we express this belief with specific emphasis, saying *the source and standard of truth is God's written Word alone.* Here we use two qualifiers for the sake of clarity: *written* and *alone.* Catholic theologians, as you are aware, say that revelation is contained in the *written* Word of God (Scripture) and the *unwritten* Word of God (Tradition). We use the Latin phrase *Sola Scriptura,* Only Scripture, or Scripture Alone, to distinguish our belief from Rome's. It is for us both the proclamation of Scripture as our supreme source and standard of truth as well as a denial of Rome's assertions for Tradition. Properly speaking, we must understand *Sola Scriptura* in this context. It is also important to note, however, that over time the term has taken on a wider meaning among evangelical Christians. Today we often use *Sola Scriptura* simply to express our confidence in the Bible as the supreme source of truth. In this more general sense, it does not necessarily contain the denial that is historically attached to it. For many, *Sola Scriptura* simply means "we just stick to the Bible," as my daughter Elizabeth likes to express it.

John: Our two positions do differ. I say that the Holy Spirit's authority is *necessarily* found in Scripture, whereas *Sola*

Scriptura claims that the Holy Spirit's authority is *only* found in Scripture. Would you agree?

Jim: I'm not sure that I agree with that. The Holy Spirit is authoritative whenever He speaks.

John: You say that writing the New Testament fulfills John 14:25-26 and 16:12-13, wherein the Holy Spirit teaches the apostles all truth. Yet only two apostles wrote Gospels —Matthew and John—and only three others wrote letters—Peter, James, and Jude. Didn't our Lord make this promise to all twelve?

Jim: Yes, I am not saying that the Holy Spirit didn't also give prophetic utterances to others. The book of Revelation, chapter 11, tells us of two prophets still to come.

Is Scripture *alone* profitable?

John: We too believe that Scripture is "inspired by God and profitable for teaching, for reproof, for correction" (2 Timothy 3:16-17). But is Scripture *alone* profitable? Can oral teaching strengthen and bless a Christian too (Romans 16:25; Revelation 1:3)? Can Paul reprove and correct Peter *only* with Scripture (Galatians 2:11-14)?

Jim: I am not aware of a conflict between the apostles' oral and written teachings. The first generation of Christians "devoted themselves to the apostles' teaching" (Acts 2:42), undoubtedly finding it of great profit whatever its form.

Where is "the final court of appeals"?

John: Jim, you fail to quote a single passage for Scripture as "the final court of appeals." The closest reference I find to a final court of appeals is Deuteronomy 16:18-20; 17:8-13, where God commands Moses to appoint judges over the people, with priests handling the more difficult cases. Moses was "the final court of appeals" for cases that others could not resolve (Exodus 18:13-27). If Scripture really is "the final court of appeals," why is this never mentioned explicitly?

Jim: Please review the many scriptures in my last letter. These demonstrate 1) that Scripture is the Word of God; 2) that it speaks with supreme authority; and 3) that the Jews, the first Christians, and even Christ Himself used Scripture as the standard of truth to judge disputes of doctrine and morals. If we agree on these three points, then I say let's not let the term *final court of appeals* be an obstacle. If, on the other hand, you don't agree with one or more of these principles, then let's discuss that.

John: But you seem to be avoiding my question and those passages that do describe a final court of appeals.

Jim: John, I think you are taking the metaphor too literally. I treat the Bible much the same way that the Supreme Court treats the Constitution. They settle disputes by referring to the written document. That is what we need to do as Christians.

John: But doesn't Jesus describe the Church as a final court of appeals for resolving disputes?

> If your brother sins against you, go and tell him his fault, between you and him alone....But if he does not listen, take one or two others along with you....If he refuses to listen to them, tell it to the church; and if he refuses to listen even to the church, let him be to you as a Gentile and a tax collector.
>
> MATTHEW 18:15-17

Jim: Scripture is our chief authority, but we recognize that it delegates authority to the church, to parents, to governments. However, even the church—in the case of discipline, as we see here in Matthew 18—must use Scripture as its standard. That is what we mean when we say Scripture is "the final court of appeals."

Is Scripture sufficient to contain God's Word?

John: John concludes his Gospel with these words: "There are also many other things which Jesus did; were every one of them to be written, I suppose that the world itself could not contain the books that would be written" (John 21:25). Doesn't this show that the Scriptures cannot contain all God's words?

Jim: No, I don't believe it does. In the passage you quote, John refers not to what Jesus taught, but what "Jesus did" (John 21:25). He is saying that the life of the Lord Jesus was too wonderful to describe fully in any number of books. He is not commenting on the general purpose of Scripture or its alleged inadequacy to communicate revelation. In addition, just a few verses earlier John wrote:

> Jesus did many other signs in the presence of the disciples, which are not written in this book; but these are written that you may believe that Jesus is the Christ, the Son of God, and that believing you may have life in his name.
>
> JOHN 20:30-31

Now, if John can promise in his short book—less than 3 percent of the total Bible—that his readers will find the truths necessary for salvation, need we doubt that the Bible in its entirety is sufficient to contain everything God wants us to know at this time?

John: But Christ also says, "Man shall not live by bread alone, but by every word that proceeds from the mouth of God" (Matthew 4:4). Can we ignore unwritten words that proceed from God's mouth?

Jim: God's words are authoritative whether written or spoken. The question before us, however, is how do we know what the Word of God is *today*? The Scriptures are the only inspired record we have of the prophetic utterances of Christ, the apostles, and the prophets.

John: Yet Paul says that we not *only* need to "stand firm and hold to the traditions which you were taught...by letter" but also by those traditions taught "by word of mouth" (2 Thessalonians 2:15). Shall we not follow these indications?

Jim: What Paul means by "traditions" in 2 Thessalonians 2:15 are those things that he had received from God and passed on to the church—that is, *revelation*. We have no objection to the things that were taught by word of mouth or by letter from Paul and the apostles. Indeed, that is what we consider the New Testament to be, an inspired record of those things passed down by them.

Is assistance needed to understand Scripture correctly?

John: The eunuch needed Philip's authoritative assistance to understand Isaiah (Acts 8:26-38). Our Lord also corrected the "Scripture experts" regarding the resurrection of the dead (Matthew 22:23-30). If others using *Scripture alone* can get it wrong, how can anyone be certain that his interpretation is doctrinally sound?

Jim: *Sola Scriptura* is the principle that Scripture alone is our authority. It is not the belief that we can understand Scripture alone. To comprehend God's Word we need the assistance of the Holy Spirit. He helps us directly and also indirectly through gifted teachers. Philip's explanation of Isaiah to the Ethiopian official is one example.

Neither does the principle of *Sola Scriptura* teach that Christians are immune to error when they study the Bible. Some things in the Scriptures are difficult to understand. We cannot be absolutely certain of their meaning. God has chosen not to fully reveal them to us at this time. The Bible plainly teaches, however, the foundational doctrines of the Christian faith.

Did Jesus go beyond Scripture *alone?*

John: Our Lord taught with authority, using Scripture. Yet Jesus did more than just elaborate on the Old Testament (John 10:34-35). His teaching was radically new, going beyond the Scripture, fulfilling it, without contradicting it. Would you agree?

Jim: Yes, I think we agree here. Jesus came both to fulfill the Law (Matthew 5:17) and to bring "a new commandment" (John 13:34).

John: Do you agree, then, that Jesus did not rely on Old Testament Scripture *alone?*

Jim: Jesus was not limited to the revelation of the Old Testament. His is a greater revelation.

What is the historical evidence for *Sola Scriptura?*

John: Historically, John Wycliffe invented *Sola Scriptura* in the fourteenth century. Prior to that, we find no evidence of it—neither in the 2000 years of the Old Covenant nor in the first 1400 years of the New. Do you see *Sola Scriptura* in the early Christian writings?

Jim: John Wycliffe, the great University of Oxford professor of medieval England, rejected Rome's assertions about Tradition. He championed the Bible as the sole test of sound doctrine, but he hardly invented this principle. He found it in many of the same verses that I have quoted for you.

The writings of Augustine (354-430), Bishop of Hippo, also influenced Wycliffe. These provide convincing evidence of the principle of *Sola Scriptura* in the fifth-century church. Augustine speaks of "the doctrine of Scripture, the sum of Christian knowledge."[2] He considered the Bible the perfect source of divine revelation, writing:

> This Mediator [Christ Jesus], first through the Prophets, then by His own lips, afterwards through the Apostles, revealed whatever He considered necessary. He also inspired the Scripture, which is regarded as canonical and of supreme authority and to which we give credence concerning all those truths we ought to know and yet, of ourselves, are unable to learn.[3]

Cyril (c. 315-386), Archbishop of Jerusalem, is a witness to belief in the unmatched supremacy of Scripture in the fourth-century church. For example, he wrote this in his lectures to new believers preparing for baptism:

> For concerning the divine and holy mysteries of the Faith, not even a casual statement must be delivered without the Holy Scriptures; nor must we be drawn aside by mere plausibility and artifices of speech. Even to me, who tell thee these things, give not absolute credence, unless thou receive the proof of the things which I announce from the Divine Scriptures. For this salvation which we believe depends not on ingenious reasoning, but on demonstration of the Holy Scriptures.[4]

John: This shows that early Christians believed in the necessity of Scripture. Augustine also wrote:

> But in regard to those observances which we carefully attend and which the whole world keeps, and which derive not from Scripture but from Tradition, we are given to understand that they are recommended and

ordained to be kept, either by the Apostles themselves
or by plenary councils, the authority of which is quite
vital in the Church.[5]

Do you think this teaches *Sola Scriptura?*

Jim: I am not familiar with this quotation. Augustine refers to
Scripture in the first quotation as the *supreme* authority to
which we give credence concerning *all* those truths we
ought to know.

John: Jim, if you were to discover that the *Sola Scriptura* doctrine
is historically just a man-made tradition, would you reject
it as Christ advised the Jews to reject the traditions and
precepts of men (Mark 7:6-13)?

Jim: No, John, my confidence in Scripture is not based on history, but upon the Word of God itself.

John: I am not questioning Scripture, but *Sola Scriptura* as a
man-made doctrine.

Jim: In answering that, I would refer you back to my reply to
your first question. Properly speaking, *Sola Scriptura* is a
response to the assertions of Rome for Tradition which
were developed during the middle ages. The Council of
Trent (1553), the First Vatican Council (1870), and the
Second Vatican Council (1965) developed the doctrine of
Tradition further. We should not expect to find a response
to a sixteenth-century controversy in a first-century document such as the New Testament—and we don't.

How do we authenticate true Scripture?

John: You say that we can recognize the canonicity of a book
because it is self-authenticating. Luther used this argument to exclude the book of James. The Mormons and
others use this argument to authenticate their "scriptures."
You also make a big deal about wording such as, "Thus
says the Lord…," "And God said…," and "The word of the
Lord came to…." But the *Book of Mormon* contains many

similar passages. Is that enough? Does that kind of language guarantee something is canonical?

Jim: I certainly would hope not. In the first centuries of the church there were scores of fraudulent books circulating, some 300 by one count. These included more than 50 false gospels, with titles such as the Gospel of Thomas, the Gospel of Peter, and the Gospel of James. The early Christians rejected them all, finding them lacking in true apostolic authorship, doctrinal integrity, and the dynamic character of Scripture.

As for Luther, he rejected the book of James because he thought it taught justification by works. He also doubted that its authorship was apostolic. Luther was wrong on both counts, as even Lutherans will tell you. The historic Lutheran confessions bear this out, quoting the book of James as Scripture.

Where is *Sola Scriptura* explicitly found?

John: Jim, you don't quote any passage that explicitly says Scripture is our *sole source* for truth and certainty of revelation. Do you agree, then, that the *Sola Scriptura* doctrine must be deduced from other texts?

Jim: I think we need a recount! How many sources of truth did God establish through Moses for the Jewish nation (Deuteronomy 6:4-7; 31:11-13)? How many sources did God tell the Jewish king to copy, to keep, and to read all the days of his life (Deuteronomy 17:18-20)? How many did Jesus say would outlast the heavens and the earth (Matthew 5:18-20)? How many did He appeal to in His disputes with the ruling Jews (Matthew 22:15-46)? How many sources does Paul say are "inspired by God and profitable for teaching, for reproof, for correction, and for training in righteousness, that the man of God may be complete, equipped for every good work" (2 Timothy 3:16-17)? How many did the Bereans examine daily to see if what they were being told was true (Acts 17:11)? By my count, the answer to each of these questions is one, explicitly one, Scripture alone.

John: Well, I'd like to ask you more questions, but we agreed to end here. You clarified many things for me. Let me mull them over and get back to you, summarizing my concerns over *Sola Scriptura* in a letter.

Jim: I look forward to receiving it.

Letter 4

Dear Jim,

Please wish Jean a happy Mother's Day. I kept her in my prayers. You and she seem to be doing a fine job raising those marvelous *gifts* God has entrusted to you. Please continue your good work.

Common Ground

Jim, I am amazed how fruitful and productive our exchange has been. We agree on so many points: that God authors and inspires Scripture, making it a source and standard of truth, "profitable for teaching...reproof...correction..." making us "complete, equipped for every good work" (2 Timothy 3:16-17). Oral teaching, too, is profitable for teaching (Acts 2:42; Romans 16:25-27) and church authority for reproof and correction (Matthew 18:15-17; Acts 16:4-5; Galatians 2:11-17; 2 Timothy 2:24-26), because God's grace equips us for good works (Hebrew 13:20-21) through Scripture and through apostles, prophets, evangelists, pastors, and teachers (Ephesians 4:11-12).

We both believe God's Word is preserved and transmitted by Scripture, which is—by definition—the only *inspired* record of prophetic utterances. Yet, God's spoken word (oral tradition) is equally authoritative. Scripture's authority derives from being *from God,* not from being written; thus Scripture is *of* or *from* supreme authority.

No teaching can contradict Scripture that is properly interpreted, for Scripture—and any authentic teaching—cannot contradict itself. Yet we can misunderstand Scripture and err by ourselves. We need the Holy Spirit's assistance through means other than Scripture.

Amazingly, we both hold that *Sola Scriptura* was established in response to and as a denial of the Catholic Church's teaching on Scripture, Tradition, and Magisterium.

Differences

Jim, our difficulty seems to lie in terminology. If *Sola Scriptura* just referred to a general confidence in the Bible, we would agree. The word *sola* confuses things. Or, if "final court of appeals" simply meant Scripture is a standard of truth that cannot be contradicted because it is God's Word, then we would agree completely. Your Supreme Court analogy, comparing the Scriptures to the Constitution, exemplifies the confusion, implying the Constitution can be interpreted by each individual *alone* without reference to the courts, their past decisions, or the writings of our country's founding fathers. Try telling that to the police the next time they stop you for a traffic or parking violation!

The terms *supreme authority, norm,* or *standard* seem to supplant God—who is the *only* supreme authority. I know you don't mean that.

You found excellent Bible quotes proving our points of agreement. However, *you failed to quote a single Bible passage* that backs up the uniquely *Sola Scriptura* claims:

- Scripture is the *only* source of truth;

- something is true and authoritative *only* to the extent that it does not contradict Scripture;

- Scripture is the *only* reliable witness of prophetic utterances;

35

- Scripture needs no authentic interpreter, anybody's interpretation can definitely resolve every significant church controversy;

- Scripture (not God) is the supreme authority and the "final court of appeals";

- Scripture "delegates authority to the church, to parents, to governments."

Jim, why is it so hard to admit there are no Bible passages that unambiguously make these claims? They just don't follow logically from the passages you quoted. For example, to deduce that Scripture is the *only* source of truth, you must show how Scripture affirms that all other sources are false.

The Canon of Scripture

When it comes to the canon—that is, which books belong to the Bible—we agree this is a question of divine authorship. You admit Scripture cannot be self-authenticating, that wording such as "Thus saith the Lord..." and so on does not authenticate a book as God's Word. Apostolic authorship (for New Testament Scripture), doctrinal integrity (Scripture cannot contradict itself), and acceptance by the Church are, you admit, the criteria for authenticity. These are the same criteria for authentic Tradition (we'll explore this next).

Jesus fulfilled the Law using Scripture to teach and correct, but His *new law* was not limited by an Old Testament *Sola Scriptura*. Paul and the Bereans (Acts 17:11) were also not limited to Old Testament *Sola Scriptura*. The Bereans began with Old Testament scriptures and found that Paul's gospel was consistent with them, yet his gospel went much further. Philip taught the eunuch, and "beginning with this scripture he told him the good news of Jesus" (Acts 8:35). All begin with Scripture without limiting themselves to the written word.

Jim, we are both pursuing the truth and not some teaching of men. Let's ask the Holy Spirit for light. If *Sola Scriptura* is merely human tradition, then His light will reveal this along with the truth that will set us free (John 8:32).

I await the opportunity to explain how the Holy Spirit leads us to the truth with Scripture and Tradition.

May the Holy Spirit bless you and your family,

John

Letter 5

TUESDAY, MAY 30, 2000

Dear John,

I appreciate your efforts to find common ground in our beliefs. Your last letter, however, overstates our areas of agreement. Even more troublesome is that you often misstate my position. Case in point: You define six principles you call "the uniquely *Sola Scriptura* claims." None fairly represent the evangelical position. Nevertheless, you challenge, "Jim, why is it so hard to admit that there are no Bible passages that unambiguously make these claims?"

Consider the first item on your list: "Scripture is the *only* source of truth." You call this illogical, writing, "To deduce that Scripture is the *only* source of truth, you must show how Scripture affirms that all other sources are false, which it doesn't." John, my position is that Scripture is the only *inspired* source of truth. I do not believe that "all other sources are false," as you ask me to prove. In response to a question you asked earlier, I wrote, "This is not to say that all other sources are wrong. We can find sound doctrine in some of the creeds, confessions, documents of the councils, and the writings of early Christians."[6]

Your fifth item is equally off target: "Scripture (not God) is the supreme authority." In the previous paragraph you wrote, "The terms, *supreme authority, norm* or *standard* seem to supplant God—who is the *only* supreme authority." You immediately add, "I know you don't mean that." Why then do you list it as one of my beliefs?

38

In another place you say I "admit Scripture cannot be self-authenticating." In fact, I asserted the opposite: "The writings are largely self-authenticating, demonstrating by their source, integrity, and dynamic character that God is their author."[7]

So where are we? I say the Bible is the sufficient and supreme norm or standard of the Christian faith; you say it is not. You write that Scripture is insufficient to contain all God's words and that treating Scripture as supreme seems "to supplant God."[8] Let's refocus the discussion with some definitions.

Important Definitions

Evangelical Christians define *revelation* as God-given truths that we could not discover by ourselves. We believe that God revealed through Christ and His apostles everything He wants us to know, requires us to do, that binds our consciences, and is necessary for salvation. We call this *normative revelation*. God completed this revelation before the passing of the last apostle (Galatians 1:8-9; Ephesians 2:20; Revelation 22:18-19). Christianity, therefore, is "the faith which was once for all delivered to the saints" (Jude 3).

Where Catholics and evangelicals disagree is on the way that God chose to safeguard revelation from being lost or corrupted and how He passed it down through the centuries. Evangelicals believe that, first for the Jews and now for the church, God has preserved and transmitted normative revelation in inspired writings.

By *inspiration* we mean "a supernatural influence exerted on the sacred writers by the Spirit of God, by virtue of which their writings are given Divine trustworthiness."[9] The result is *written revelation,* perfectly communicated "in words not taught by human wisdom but taught by the Spirit" (1 Corinthians 2:13), "God-breathed" words (2 Timothy 3:16 NIV). To enable us to understand the Bible, God then sent the Holy Spirit to teach us and enlighten our minds. This we term *illumination.*

—

39

The Embodiment of Knowledge and Truth

We hold that in Scripture the Holy Spirit has restated all normative revelation previously received and enlarged upon it, providing greater detail. It is "the embodiment of knowledge and truth" (Romans 2:20). Consequently, we dare not add to it nor take from it, as John warns in the last chapter of the Bible (Revelation 22:18-19). The Bible contains every truth necessary for salvation and Christian living. Paul testifies of this to his disciple Timothy, writing, "…from childhood you have been acquainted with the sacred writings which are able to instruct you for salvation through faith in Christ Jesus. All scripture is inspired by God and profitable for teaching, for reproof, for correction, and for training in righteousness, that the man of God may be complete, equipped for every good work" (2 Timothy 3:15-17).

This is why we hold the Bible to be sufficient. It is why we turn to it to tell us what is true and false, what is right and wrong, to answer our questions, to settle our disputes, to judge us when we are in sin. We see no tension, as you allege, between the supreme authority of God and His Word. What God says, the Bible says. The Scriptures are "the oracles of God" (Romans 3:2). When we submit to them, we submit to Christ, our living head, giving Him the final say. He speaks to us through Scripture, for unlike any other document, "the word of God is living and active, sharper than any two-edged sword" (Hebrews 4:12). The Bible assures us that it is "able to judge" (Hebrews 4:12 NASB).

That's how I see it, John. If you would like a formal summary of the evangelical position, refer to the Chicago Statement on Scripture, published in 1978 by the International Council on Biblical Inerrancy. Some 300 scholars signed it, representing almost every major evangelical organization. It is widely available on the Internet.

The time has come for you to present your position. I will respond with the issues I would like you to clarify.

In Christ's love,

Jim

—

Letter 6

THURSDAY, JUNE 1, 2000

Dear Jim,

Thank you for your latest letter. First, may I apologize for misrepresenting your position; that wasn't my intent. Also, thank you for clarifying your stance. I don't know whether you share these letters with Jean or Elizabeth (please do if they are interested), but if so, I hope I did not offend you, them, or anyone else.

Although my summary missed the point, it should help you appreciate how Catholics may read your words. Catholics and Protestants really do speak different languages. This dialogue helps us appreciate that difference, challenging us to express our beliefs in ways understandable to the other's religious culture and tradition.

Now let me summarize the Catholic Church's teaching about Sacred Scripture and Tradition:

> We believe God communicated his Word to the apostles by the Old Testament Scripture and Tradition, but especially by Jesus Christ himself: in his spoken words, his way of life, his works, and later—prompted by the Spirit—in his disciples. The same Spirit transmitted the Gospel through the apostles in two ways: in writing and by their spoken word, example, and the institutions they established. We accept, honor, and obey both Sacred Scripture and Sacred Tradition as

—

coming from the same supreme authority, God's Spirit, who cannot contradict himself.

The Church's position should be clear and positive. However, before I explain it in detail, please tell me how you and evangelicals perceive and understand it. Then I can address the issues that most concern you.

May Christ's Spirit continue to enlighten us,

John

Letter 7

WEDNESDAY, JUNE 14, 2000

Dear John,

Thank you for your gracious apology. Understanding one another is indeed a challenge. At times we will fail.

Now to my concerns about Tradition.

Definition

Given Tradition's importance in the Roman Catholic Church, official explanations of it seem surprisingly brief. What exactly is Tradition? A full and precise definition would be a good starting point.

Reliability

Church documents emphasize that Tradition has its origin in the oral teaching of Christ and the apostles. They say little about how this teaching was reliably passed down in unwritten form for the next 2000 years. Could you explain how this was accomplished?

Accessibility

Where is Tradition today? Is it tangible? If so, where can I examine it? If not, how can I trust it?

Content

Could you provide a list of the ten most important teachings of Christ essential for salvation that Rome finds in Tradition, but not in Scripture?

Validity

Earlier you asked me to prove the validity of *Sola Scriptura*. Now I ask you to do the same for Tradition. Your church says that "…both Scripture and Tradition must be accepted and honored with equal feelings of devotion and reverence."[10] Can you demonstrate in some objective way that God has placed Tradition on par with Scripture?

As you present your case for Tradition, consider the relationship of our two positions. Rome says that Scripture is the *written* Word of God, and Tradition is the *unwritten* Word of God.[11] The Church says it "has always regarded, and continues to regard the Scriptures, taken together with sacred Tradition, as the supreme rule of her faith."[12] The evangelical position is that Scripture alone is the Word of God and standard of truth. I have represented these two positions in Figures 7:1 and 7:2.

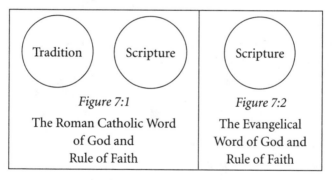

Figure 7:1
The Roman Catholic Word
of God and
Rule of Faith

Figure 7:2
The Evangelical
Word of God and
Rule of Faith

Examining these figures, it appears that I don't need to prove anything, for the evangelical position is a subset of the Catholic position. Consequently, within the context of our discussion we can consider the authority of Scripture a given.

Now, in a court of law, the burden of proof lies with the one who asserts a particular point, not the one who denies it. It appears, then, that it is you who must prove the claims for Tradition, rather than I who must show that Scripture is the *sole* rule of faith, as you have insisted in your letters. In addition, should you

—

be unable to prove that God has established Tradition as the Word of God, your position reduces to Scripture alone, *Sola Scriptura*.

I trust this is a fair evaluation of the matter before us. Thank you again for your willingness to address my concerns.

In Christ's love,

Jim

Letter 8

MONDAY, JULY 3, 2000

Dear Jim,

How are your summer plans shaping up? I bet Jean is eager for a vacation, especially since you won't have the girls around much longer for family vacations. Later this month I will go to Valparaiso, Indiana, to teach a philosophy course. I also hope to visit my alma mater, Notre Dame, while there.

Jim, you've outlined a daunting task. Each of your concerns could be its own topic. So, pardon me if my answers seem abbreviated.

Before beginning, let's remember we are dealing with things of faith, not the wisdom of men (1 Corinthians 2:1-5), as would be found in a "court of law."

Definition

Before defining *Tradition,* let's clarify what we mean by *revelation* (since you seem to like visual aids, I will use some diagrams to illustrate this). For Catholics:

> Christ, the Son of God made man, is the Father's one, perfect and unsurpassable Word. In him he has said everything; there will be no other word than this one.

[CCC 69]

—

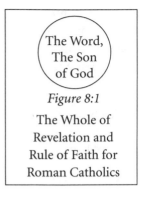

Figure 8:1

The Whole of Revelation and Rule of Faith for Roman Catholics

The Old Testament is revelation because it points to Christ and His body, the Church. The New Testament is, by communicating words and actions of Christ and His body, the Church.

Generically, *tradition* ("handing down") refers to teachings, practices, customs, or writings passed down from generation to generation. Family traditions—often preserved for many generations—may include how family members decorate their house and celebrate Christmas. Spoken and written language are other human traditions. Scripture is the written form of handing down God's Word.

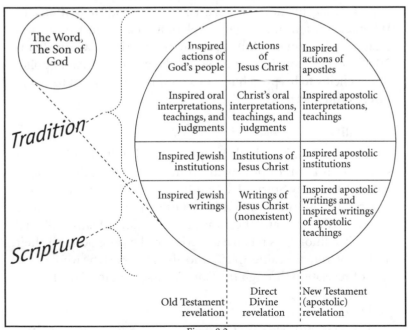

Figure 8.2
Where Revelation (the Word) Is Found

When inspired by the Holy Spirit, tradition becomes sacred [CCC 83]. Apostolic Tradition *(Tradition* with a capital "T") consists in the apostles' oral teachings, practices, and institutions inspired by the Holy Spirit, including art and implements of worship, as Scripture attests:

> The LORD said to Moses, "See, I have called by name Bezalel...and I have filled him with the Spirit of God...to devise artistic designs, to work in gold, silver, and bronze."
>
> EXODUS 31:1-4

Old Testament traditions—important precedents for transmitting revelation by apostolic Tradition—are sacred to the extent that the Spirit inspires them. Notice how Scripture encompasses just a small piece (subset) of the "inspirational" pie, which would hypothetically include Christ's own writings, had He written any. Whether written or spoken, revelation consists in words "not taught by human wisdom but...by the Spirit" (1 Corinthians 2:13), as you quoted earlier.[13] Notice, however, that Paul applies this explicitly to his preaching (1 Corinthians 2:1-5), not to Scripture, as you inferred.

Reliability

The Spirit authors both Scripture and Tradition. We cannot say, "Jesus is Lord" or pray with confidence to the Father, "Abba," without the Holy Spirit (1 Corinthians 12:3; Galatians 4:6), the source of "wisdom...knowledge...faith...prophecy.... All these are inspired by one and the same Spirit" (1 Corinthians 12:8-11).

So, Tradition is as reliable as Scripture, because both get their authority from the same Spirit, who also preserves the whole content of revelation through the Church (more on this later).

Validity

Let's start by looking at Old Testament Tradition. Jim, in letter 3 you described how God's people used Scripture to transmit revelation from one generation to the next. Yet prior to that, many promises and oaths were transmitted orally for generations. For example, God's covenant with Adam and Eve (Genesis 2–3), and His promises to Noah (Genesis 6:11-22; 9:8-17), Abraham (Genesis 12:1-3), and Isaac (Genesis 26:1-5). This shows that God's unenscripturated words contain inspired truth handed down for generations.

God remembers His oral words (Exodus 2:24; 6:5) and expects His people to remember and obey them. God punished Adam and Eve for disobeying His oral command (Genesis 2:16–3:24), and blessed Noah for fulfilling an oral command (Genesis 6:13–7:16).

God commanded Abraham to circumcise himself and his household (Genesis 17:9-27; 21:4). Those who refused to abide by this Sacred Tradition were cut off from God's people (Genesis 17:9-14) and from the Passover sacrifice (Exodus 12:43-49). Circumcision was enscripturated some 400 years after the Oral Tradition began! We too must obey and teach all God's commandments, whether Oral Tradition or the written Law, as Matthew 5:18-20 states.

God introduced Scripture only after His people refused to listen to Him directly (Exodus 19–20, especially 19:10-11; 20:20-21). When the people refused to approach God, Moses went up alone, returning with the first written covenant (Exodus 24:1-11). God desired direct communication; His people refused out of fear and lack of faith. Paul mentions this in his letter to the Galatians:

> Now the promises were made [orally] to Abraham and to his offspring....This is what I mean: the law [Scripture], which came four hundred and thirty years afterward, does not annul a covenant previously ratified by God [and handed down by Tradition], so as to make the [oral] promise void. For if the inheritance is by the law, it is no longer by promise; but God gave it to Abraham by a promise. Why then the law [Scripture]? It was added because of transgressions, till the

offspring [Christ] should come to whom the promise
had been made....Is the law then against the promises
of God? Certainly not; for if a law had been given
which could make alive, then righteousness would
indeed be by the law.

GALATIANS 3:16-22 (INSERTIONS ADDED)[14]

The oral promise preceded the Law by some 430 years. Scripture does not contradict or abolish God's Oral Tradition. Scripture is the written testimony against those who disbelieve or transgress God's oral testimony, since "faith comes from what is heard" (Romans 10:17).

The New Testament attests to many Old Testament events found only in Sacred Tradition. For example, 1 Corinthians 10:1-4 mentions how the rock followed the Jewish people through the wilderness to provide water. Second Timothy 3:8 names the two magicians of Pharaoh, Jannes and Jambres of Exodus 7:11. These facts are found in rabbinical tradition expounded in Jewish targums, but nowhere in the Old Testament itself. Jude mentions how Michael and Satan struggled over Moses' body (Jude 9), a tradition found in the non-canonical book *The Assumption of Moses*. Jude also quotes the prophetic oracle, Enoch (Jude 14-15), a tradition handed down from the seventh generation from Adam until enscripturated in the non-canonical book of *Enoch* around 100 B.C. Paul also quotes Christ's words communicated orally and not by any written Gospel (Acts 20:35). Both Paul and Jude mention these traditions as accepted truths, not some novelty.

Paul makes explicit references to Tradition, urging Timothy, for instance, to teach and pass on to others what he heard from Paul:

Be strong...what you have heard from me before
many witnesses entrust to faithful men who will be
able to teach others also.

2 TIMOTHY 2:1-2

—
50

Paul urges the Corinthians to maintain the traditions that he had delivered to them:

> I urge you, then, be imitators of me. Therefore I sent to you Timothy…to remind you of my ways in Christ, as I teach them everywhere in every church….
>
> 1 CORINTHIANS 4:16-17

> Be imitators of me, as I am of Christ. I commend you because you remember me in everything and maintain the traditions even as I have delivered them to you.
>
> 1 CORINTHIANS 11:1-2

If we are to imitate Christ, then Christ's deeds—which go mostly unreported in Scripture—are also part of God's revelation (remember John 21:25?).[15] Tradition includes Paul's example, including deeds witnessed to by others. Clearly, Scripture is insufficient to contain all Christ's and the apostles' words and deeds, often describing Christ's preaching without reporting what He said (Luke 5:1-4, for example). Yet none of God's revelation is ever wasted (Isaiah 55:10-11).

We too must stand firm in the gospel transmitted to us by oral and written tradition:

> God chose you from the beginning to be saved… through our gospel, so that you may obtain the glory of our Lord Jesus Christ. So then, brethren, stand firm and hold to the traditions which you were taught by us, either by word of mouth or by letter.
>
> 2 THESSALONIANS 2:13-15

Content

A few important teachings found in Tradition are the proper interpretation of:

51

- "unless one is born of water and the Spirit, he cannot enter the kingdom of God" (John 3:5). Earlier I quoted Augustine referring to Tradition on the applicability of this passage to infant baptism;[16]

- "unless you eat the flesh of the Son of man and drink his blood, you have no life in you" (John 6:53). This refers to Christ's body and blood as the New Testament Passover lamb.

- John 20:22-23, which mentions the giving of power to forgive sins to the apostles and their successors;

- how Christians are to fulfill Mary's prophesy "all generations will call me blessed" (Luke 1:48).

Perhaps the best example of the essentiality of Tradition is the canon of Scripture [CCC 120]. You mentioned in our conversation how "true apostolic authorship" is necessary to validate a book as scriptural.[17] Yet, Scripture never mentions the authors of Matthew, Mark, Luke, John, Acts, Hebrews, and 1 John through 3 John. Only Tradition tells us who authored these nine books, and two of the writers (Luke and Mark) are not even apostles. However, Tradition resolves this, telling us that Luke wrote on behalf of Paul and Mark for Peter. Without Tradition we would have only 18 books in the New Testament and no Gospels.

Jim, aren't these issues pretty essential for salvation? There are more, such as the full doctrine of the Trinity—not explicitly found in Scripture—the New Testament priesthood, the infallibility of Peter's office, the succession of bishops, and so on.

Accessibility

If Tradition were inaccessible, it would severely limit the Holy Spirit's power to the writings of just five apostles. If the omnipotent Holy Spirit truly authors Tradition and still enlightens the Church, then it must be accessible.

Perhaps you are really asking, where is Tradition found? It is found wherever inspired actions, interpretations, teachings, judgments, and institutions of the Old Testament people, of Jesus Christ, and those of the apostles are recounted.

Examining early Christian writings, art, and artifacts, one finds a pletheora of expressions of Tradition. Sorting out human from inspired tradition is key, yet Vincent of Lerins describes how the early Church did just that:

> In the Catholic Church herself, every care must be taken that we may hold fast to that which has been believed everywhere, always, and by all. For this, then, is truly and properly Catholic....This general rule will be correctly applied if we pursue universality, antiquity, and agreement. [Universality,] confessed by the whole Church throughout the whole world; antiquity...those interpretations which, it is clear, our holy predecessors and fathers solemnized; and likewise agreement...the definitions and theses of all or certainly of almost all priests and teachers.
>
> *COMMONITORIA*, WRITTEN IN 435[18]

Churches founded by Thomas the apostle in Sudan and India were isolated from Rome for hundreds of years. Yet they essentially have the same beliefs and practices as we do today. Only the Spirit could preserve apostolic Traditions in independent churches over such a long period. There are dozens of such churches—seemingly small and insignificant—but persevering in the same traditions as received from the apostles.

Ireneus wrote of this in about A.D. 180:

> It is possible, then for everyone in every Church, who may wish to know the truth, to contemplate the tradition of the Apostles which has been made known throughout the whole world....For the Apostles, like

a rich man in a bank, deposited with her [the Church] most copiously everything which pertains to the truth....What then? If there should be a dispute over some kind of question, ought we not have recourse to the most ancient Churches in which the Apostles were familiar, and draw from them what is clear and certain in regard to that question? What if the Apostles had not in fact left writings to us? Would it not be necessary to follow the order of tradition, which was handed down to those to whom they entrusted the Churches?

ADVERSUS HAERESES, 3.3.1; 3.4.1[19]

Jim, early Christianity clearly points to Tradition, not *Sola Scriptura*. If you'd like, I'll give you more references from the early Christians, or you can read them for yourself. A handy book for finding Tradition is Jurgens' book *The Faith of the Early Fathers.*[20] It has thousands of quotes from early Christian writers cross-referenced to practically all the Catholic teachings, including Tradition.

Please pray about this with an open mind. At least you have to admit that there is a scriptural case for Tradition. Please call me to discuss the issues that I haven't answered satisfactorily.

As always, I am keeping you and your family in my prayers.

Yours in Christ,

John

Conversation 2

SUNDAY, JULY 9, 2000

Jim: Thanks, John, for your explanation of Tradition. I found it interesting, especially the two figures. I know you're about to take off for Indiana, so I'll try to keep this brief. We're leaving tomorrow also for a family vacation in Yosemite.

John: Jim, I hope you have a great vacation. Yosemite is one of my favorite places to hike and camp.

Jim: There we agree. We're really far apart, however, on the topic of authority. Either we find revelation in Scripture, as evangelicals hold, or in Scripture and Tradition, as taught by the Roman Catholic Church. Of course, this explains why we have such a different understanding of the Christian faith.

John: Our individualistic culture makes it hard to understand the Catholic position. Individualism teaches us to seek God all by ourselves, independent of any church or group. But that's not how God intended it. He established a people, entrusting them His revelation to transmit it to others.

Look at how Jews approach Scripture, and you'll feel much more comfortable with Catholicism. God's people and religious Jews today don't interpret Old Testament Scripture individualistically, but reach trustworthy interpretations through rabbinical tradition.

What's an inspired action and what's not?

Jim: In your definition of Tradition, you list more than a dozen sources as inspired by the Holy Spirit. These include the actions, teachings, institutions, and artworks of God's people and the apostles. "God's people," however, have done some horrific things down through the centuries. I think of Israel's apostasy during the time of the divided kingdom (931-586 B.C.) and the crusades initiated by Pope Urban II at the Council of Clermont (A.D. 1095). Even the apostles made grave errors. Peter, for example, was guilty of hypocrisy in not being "straightforward about the truth of the gospel" (Galatians 2:14). As you state yourself, sorting out human traditions from inspired traditions is key. This being the case, how is one to know which actions down through history are inspired of God and which are merely of men?

John: You make a good point: God doesn't inspire every action in Scripture and Tradition, nor should we imitate everything there. We must sort out what God approves and what He condemns. Peter stopped eating with Gentiles to avoid offending the Judaizers; Paul rightly condemned this. Scripture recounts many immoral acts (like Israel's apostasy). Discerning interpreters can sort out actions inspired by God from those that are not. This can be done with Tradition too.

If you cannot, then how can you meet the criteria for New Testament books being Scripture, especially those books whose authors aren't even mentioned? These criteria are fulfilled with information from Tradition and confirmed by the Church's Magisterium.

Jim: I don't see how in this case you can compare Tradition with Scripture. The Bible is a written document containing a limited amount of material. We can read and study it carefully, examining every sentence in detail. But how could anyone sort through the countless actions, teachings, works of art, and institutions of history and recover from them the minute portion that you call Sacred Tradition?

John: Certainly Tradition and Scripture differ. But Luke compiled his gospel account and the Acts of the Apostles by sorting through the Tradition available to him:

> Inasmuch as many have undertaken to compile a narrative of the things which have been accomplished among us, just as they were delivered to us by those who from the beginning were eyewitnesses and ministers of the word, it seemed good to me also, having followed all things closely for some time past, to write an orderly account...that you may know the truth concerning the things of which you have been informed.
>
> LUKE 1:1-4

Obviously, Tradition helped Luke and the early Christians.

Jim: John, you seem to speak of the writing of Scripture as nothing more than the recording work that a historian would do: collecting data, compiling it, and writing it down. In this way you justify your concept of Tradition. But isn't Scripture inspired by the Holy Spirit, a supernatural revelation of information to the writer?

John: Yes, but that doesn't eliminate Tradition. When Paul mentions that Scripture is inspired, he says to Timothy:

> As for you, continue in what you have learned and have firmly believed, knowing from whom you learned it and how from childhood you have been acquainted with the sacred writings....
>
> 2 TIMOTHY 3:14-15

Paul reminds Timothy of the Tradition he learned from him and the sacred writings studied in youth. Scripture and Tradition go hand in hand:

Sacred Tradition and Sacred Scripture, then, are bound closely together, and communicate one with the other. For both of them, flowing out from the same divine well-spring, come together in some fashion to form one thing, and move towards the same goal....

[CCC 80]

How was oral tradition passed down?

Jim: In my previous letter I asked how Tradition could transmit revelation reliably in unwritten form for 2000 years without it becoming lost or corrupted. You answered, "Tradition is as reliable as Scripture, because both get their authority from the same Holy Spirit."[21] I don't see how this answers the question. Authority and reliability are two different issues. Specifically, how has the oral teaching of the apostles allegedly been passed from generation to generation without becoming lost or corrupted?

John: If you were to ask, "Why is Scripture reliable?" I would answer, "Because it is inspired by the Holy Spirit, whose supreme authority makes it reliable." If you were to ask, "Why is Scripture credible or worthy of belief?" then I'd point to prophetic predictions that have come to pass, and to miracles (works of the Spirit, see Galatians 3:5) carried out by its writers or protagonists. I'd also point to their holiness and how their writings have inspired others to be holy throughout the ages.

Regarding Tradition, the same supreme authority of the Spirit makes it reliable. Regarding its credibility, look at early Christian witnesses to Tradition: many worked miracles, some were martyred for the faith they preached and wrote, living holy lives and inspiring others to do the same. These are proofs of sure faith. As James tells us, trials prove our faith, making us "perfect and complete, lacking nothing" (James 1:2-4), just like Scripture (2 Timothy 3:15-17).

Martyrdom is the ultimate trial, pretty good "proof" of the Holy Spirit confirming the Tradition and scriptural teachings that the early Christians died defending. As Christ said, "When they bring you to trial and deliver you up, do not be anxious beforehand what you are to say; but say whatever is given you in that hour, for it is not you who speak, but the Holy Spirit" (Mark 13:11).

Regarding the holiness of early Christian writers, Jude advises us to fight for the faith—for the Tradition—delivered to us by the saints, by holy men and women (Jude 3).

Ultimately, reliability is a matter of faith—of believing that the Spirit can preserve apostolic teachings through the churches the apostles founded.

Jim: You still haven't answered my question. What I want to know is the method by which oral Tradition was passed down for the past 2000 years. Does one generation of bishops recite oral Tradition to the next?

John: As the Holy Spirit inspired the writers of Scripture, He also guides proper interpretation. Any inspired interpretation must be consistent with Scripture and previous interpretations guided by the Spirit [CCC 89-90]. So, we discern authentic Tradition by seeing how the teaching or artwork or other manifestation of Tradition is consistent with Scripture and with interpretations from previous generations. This is especially true for practices of worship. "Liturgy is a constitutive element of the holy and living Tradition" [CCC 1124].

Jim: I am not asking about interpretation. I'm asking about the *mechanism* by which oral Tradition was passed down from Christ to us today. Can you explain how oral Tradition can be passed on year after year without becoming lost or corrupted?

John: We live in a culture of written information. In our Lord's time, most people were illiterate and did not possess written materials. They told stories, however, reciting things they had heard. And if someone got something wrong while repeating a story, someone else would correct him. In this way people of that era passed on the information.

Jim: In Letter Four you wrote, "We both believe God's Word is preserved and transmitted by Scriptures, which are—by definition—the only *inspired* record of prophetic utterances."[22] How can Tradition be as reliable as Scripture if only Scripture preserves revelation as an inspired record?

John: The Holy Spirit gives Scripture a special guarantee, but His authority is not limited to this. As Paul says, "While we preached to you the gospel of God...the word of God which you heard from us, you accepted it not as the word of men but as what it really is, the word of God" (1 Thessalonians 2:9,13). Obviously the Thessalonians accepted Paul's preaching, not Scripture, as God's Word because it was Spirit-inspired, as were Paul's later scriptural writings. There's the reliability we seek.

Where is Tradition today?

Jim: In response to my question, "Where is Tradition today?" you answered, "It is found wherever inspired actions, interpretations, teachings, judgments, and institutions of the Old Testament people, of Jesus Christ, and those of the apostles are recounted."[23] This begs the question. Where is this "wherever"? Is there a complete list of the doctrines contained in Roman Catholic Tradition? Where can I examine it?

John: I'm sorry, Jim, my answer is broad to avoid limiting our perspective of Tradition. Specifically it can be found and examined in Christian art from the second century Roman catacombs; in earlier Christian funeral inscriptions; in church fathers describing apostolic teachings and practices;

in early descriptions of Christian worship. We learn, for instance, that Christians worshiped on Sunday, not Saturday, as required by Old Testament Scriptures. Seventh Day Adventists condemn Sunday worship with *Sola Scriptura;* fortunately, the early Christians had it clear from the apostles which day to worship on.

Even biblical translations carry Tradition. For example, the Hebrew text of Isaiah 7:14 says, "a young woman [not 'virgin'] shall conceive and bear a son..." (comment added). Yet when translated into Greek, the translators producing the Septuagint incorporated the tradition indicating the Messiah would be born miraculously from a virgin. Matthew 1:23 confirms that tradition.

Jim: John, again I asked a specific question that you didn't answer. Where can I obtain a complete list of the doctrines contained in Roman Catholic Tradition?

John: There is no complete list of doctrines contained in Tradition. However, the *Catechism of the Catholic Church* is a great place for references to these doctrines and where they are found in both Scripture and Tradition.

Jim: The predecessor to the *Catechism of the Catholic Church* (1997) was the *Roman Catechism* (1566), also called the *Catechism of the Council of Trent.* There is no dogma in it related to papal infallibility, the Immaculate Conception of Mary, or the Assumption of Mary, three doctrines based largely on Tradition. How can I know what dogmas will be in the next version based on Tradition, since I can't find the complete list of dogmas in the present version?

John: That's a good point. This is true of many doctrines, including that of the Trinity. Most dogmatic statements are developed and refined after being attacked. The dogmas most frequently attacked in the first five centuries of the church include the Trinity and Christ's divinity, humanity, and incarnation. Dogmatic statements make explicit what Scripture and Tradition contain.

Jim: In asking me to accept Roman Catholic Tradition, then, you are asking me to accept teachings that haven't been formally defined 2000 years after Christ! That seems unreasonable.

John: The Bible is not a dogmatic textbook, but more like a family history—or even love letters—containing few dogmatic statements. However, when someone attacks the dogmas underlying the letters and history, then the Church needs to intervene to explicitly condemn error and proclaim truth.

Does Scripture need Tradition?

Jim: Let's say you were to carefully study an important chapter of the Bible—say John 6. You begin with prayer, asking the Holy Spirit to guide you. Next you examine the historical setting, context, grammar, and the meaning of each word. Finally, interpreting each sentence and paragraph in its normal, usual, and customary manner, you arrive at what you believe to be the true interpretation intended by the Holy Spirit. Now, let's say that someone then informs you that according to Roman Catholic Tradition, your conclusions about John 6 are all wrong. The proper interpretation, explains this person, is essentially the opposite of what you came to through your study. Which of the two interpretations would you accept as the true one?

John: Let's say someone who picked up the *Book of Mormon*—praying to the Holy Spirit for guidance—determined, after careful reading, that it was from God. Then he picks up a Christian author who condemns Mormonism. Whom shall he follow?

It is not which approach is more acceptable, but whom do you trust. Do you trust yourself, your own wisdom, or do you trust witnesses to the Truth who died defending the interpretation from Tradition? Personally, I fear trusting myself. I wouldn't want to end up like Solomon, even with all his wisdom.

Moreover, we never approach Scripture with a blank slate, but bring with us our personal history. Our cultural heritage—how we were taught and raised, our experiences with family and friends—affects how we interpret Scripture. Also, how we were taught the Christian faith, our experience of worship, and the example of other Christians affect how we read the Bible. Add to that the particular religious and cultural slant of the translators and biblical commentators, the sources for the historical context (more human traditions), plus human error and moral weakness…no wonder there are so many contradicting scriptural interpretations and above all, fallible human judgments.

In establishing or condemning biblical interpretations, the Catholic Church checks to make sure those interpreted with the rest of Scripture are consistent with the early Church's interpretation and practice, as well as, with official teaching declarations [CCC 95].

What is the validity of Tradition not found in Scripture?

Jim: In presenting your case for the validity of Tradition, you argue that prophecies and commandments were transmitted orally before being written down by Moses. You cite as examples God's instructions to Adam and Eve, Noah, Abraham, and Isaac. You conclude that God expects His people to remember and obey His unwritten word, too.[24] All of these examples, however, relate to people who lived in the era before God gave the Scriptures. Your argument, therefore, cannot be used to prove that once God provided the Jews with the Old Testament that He expected them to submit also to an additional

—

unwritten set of commandments—what you call Tradition. Further, the Scriptures that came through Moses were the inspired written record of the covenant between God and Israel. It was a written contract, the very nature of which demands that all binding terms be contained within the document. The terms of the contract were proposed by God, agreed to by Israel, and formally ratified (Exodus 19:3-8; 24:3-8). Likewise, the New Testament is the inspired record of the teachings of Christ and His apostles, the New Covenant between God and mankind. What proof do you offer to substantiate your claim that God expected the Jews of the Old Covenant and expects Christians of the New Covenant to submit to actions, teachings, interpretations, and judgments not required by the Scriptures?

John: Nowhere does Scripture abrogate God's oral promises and commandments. On the contrary, Paul insists on the validity and importance of oral tradition over the written law.[25] Moreover, Jude mentions the tradition regarding Enoch[26]—much older than any Old Testament Scripture—as still valid and true. In fact, he gives it the same importance as the scriptural accounts of Cain and Abel, Balaam's error, and Korah's rebellion.

In Matthew 19:1-9, the Pharisees used Scripture (Deuteronomy 24:1-4) to defend divorce. But our Lord corrects them with the creation story, a tradition that had been handed down orally before being written down in the Pentateuch. By this our Lord shows us how a teaching from Tradition can take precedence over literal interpretation of the written Mosaic law.

Jim: In a previous letter you seemed to agree with me, writing, "Truly, the Bible has 'no equal on earth.'"[27] In your last letter, however, you placed Tradition on equal footing with Scripture, if not above it, saying Tradition determines the proper meaning of Scripture. You do that again here. Do we agree that the Bible has no equal, or do we not?

John: The Bible has no equal because it is the inspired record of God's Word. But we venerate Tradition to recognize the Spirit's inspiration behind it. Since Tradition does contain God's Word, we ought to venerate it as such.

> This living transmission [of apostolic preaching], accomplished in the Holy Spirit, is called Tradition, since it is distinct from Sacred Scripture, though closely connected to it.
>
> [CCC 78]

Jim: Even if Tradition, for the sake of argument, originated from the inspiration of the Holy Spirit, if it is not passed on in inspired forms from one person to the next, how can we consider it inspired today?

John: Consistency is the key. As we read early Christian writings, we see how they are consistent with Scripture. They orient our scriptural interpretation. We carry all sorts of historical, cultural baggage that affects our interpretation. Tradition allows us to transcend our particular cultural and historical situation to understand God's Word in the context in which it was written and first interpreted.

Jim: Jesus harshly rebuked the Jews for treating Tradition as authoritative and placing it alongside Scripture (Mark 7:1-23). How is what Rome has done with Tradition any different?

John: Jesus condemns the "tradition of men" (Mark 7:8) as does Paul in Colossians 2:8, not Spirit-inspired Tradition. Jesus rebukes the Jews for their human interpretation of Scripture with similar harshness: "You know neither the scriptures nor the power of God" (Mark 12:24).

Our Lord condemns human tradition and interpretation that contradicts what the Spirit inspires, whether oral or written. May Jesus not criticize either of us as He did Jews who relied only on Scripture:

> You search the scriptures, because you think that in them you have eternal life; and it is they that bear witness to me; yet you refuse to come to me that you may have life.
>
> JOHN 5:39-40

Jim: Well, as I said earlier, we're really far apart on this subject. I'll consider what you've said and send you my response. Thanks for giving me this opportunity to ask these questions.

John: I hope this conversation helps alleviate some of your concerns. I pray that His Spirit may enlighten us in our search for the Truth.

Letter 9

FRIDAY, AUGUST 4, 2000

Dear John,

Our trip to Yosemite was perfect. The weather was clear and mild; the mountains spectacular. Our girls enjoyed drifting down the Merced River. Jean and I spent our time exploring the valley and visiting friends who vacation there each year at this time. We returned home refreshed and inspired by God's creation.

How did your trip to Indiana and Notre Dame turn out? It must have brought back many memories. It's a beautiful campus. I visited there once to meet with Kevin and Dorothy Ranaghan, two of the early leaders of the Catholic Charismatic movement. It was fascinating hearing about its beginnings at Notre Dame in the late 1960s. Did you have contact with them or that movement while a student there?

I'm grateful for the time you have given to presenting your church's position on Tradition. I want you to understand, however, why I cannot accept this position.

Questionable Assertions for Tradition

Your appeal to the Catholic martyrs as "pretty good proof" of Tradition is unconvincing. All faiths have their martyrs, including my own. I think of John Huss, Catholic priest and professor of theology at the University of Prague. Rome burned him at the stake in 1415 for preaching that Scripture was the ultimate religious authority. I don't think you would accept his martyrdom as proof of *Sola Scriptura*.

We didn't seem to connect on my question as to how oral Tradition has been passed from Christ to us. You pointed out that in biblical times people were good at reciting stories. My question, however, pertains to recent centuries, not just the time of Christ. I haven't been able to find an explanation regarding the preservation of Tradition in church documents either. They speak almost exclusively of the *origins* of Tradition, glossing over the hard questions of transmission and reliability.

You speak of the Bible as a remedial form of communication that God introduces "only after His people refused to listen to Him directly." You quote Galatians 3:16-22 to support this point, omitting some of Paul's words and inserting others of your own in brackets.[28] You conclude, "Paul insists on the validity and importance of oral tradition over the written law."[29] John, I believe your modification of the text reflects your sincere understanding of it as a Catholic. Nevertheless, you have altered its meaning. There is no emphasis on the priority of *oral* communication over *written* in the original text of that passage.

Your free use of references to preaching in the Gospels and epistles as support for Roman Tradition is also unjustified. You quote, for example, Paul's exhortation "stand firm and hold to the traditions which you were taught by us, either by word of mouth or by letter" (2 Thessalonians 2:15). Here Paul is speaking of truths he received from God and then handed down *in person* to the Thessalonians. This cannot be equated with Roman Tradition, a complex and vague concept that even most Catholics can't define. The *Catholic Encyclopedia* says that Tradition "...is not, properly speaking, an assemblage of doctrines and institutions consigned to books or other monuments....it must be represented as a current of life and truth coming from God through Christ and through the Apostles to the last of the faithful who repeats his creed and learns his catechism."[30] The Vatican says that Tradition is "written principally in the Church's heart rather than in documents and records" [CCC 113]. Certainly this is not what Paul is referring to in 2 Thessalonians 2:15.

Evolving Dogmas

You have said that "...there is no complete list of the doctrines contained in Tradition."[31] What then prevents the gradual introduction of new doctrines? Could not a pious comment by a Pope in one century—say about Mary or the power of the papacy—spread and become widely known in the next century, a generally held belief in the third, and a dogma in the fourth or fifth? With no written record of what is contained in Tradition, who's to say what's in and what's not? The Church of Rome says that its bishops—and they alone—can identify true Tradition and interpret its correct meaning. But doesn't this make faith in Tradition ultimately faith in a group of men?

This scenario is not mere speculation. Consider how the Catholic Church has used Tradition in recent years. Some 2000 years after Christ gave us "the faith which was once for all delivered to the saints" (Jude 3), the Popes are still declaring new dogmas. You defended this practice in our recent conversation, saying that "dogmatic statements are developed and refined after being attacked." I don't believe history supports your argument with respect to two dogmas I cited: the Immaculate Conception (that Mary was conceived without sin, declared dogma by Pope Pius IX in 1854) and the Assumption of Mary (that she was taken body and soul into heaven at the end of her earthly life, declared dogma by Pope Pius XII in 1950). The Catholic Church formally pronounced these doctrines not because of attacks by opponents, but because of lobbying by proponents. In the 1940s, for example, 32,000 priests, 50,000 nuns, and more than eight million lay Catholics sent formal requests to Rome asking Pope Pius XII to declare the Assumption a dogma of the Church. Today an international campaign is being waged to petition the Pope to proclaim as dogma that Mary is the Co-Redeemer of the human race. Whether it is successful or not, I still must ask: What's next?

—

Traditions of Men

Finally, your remarks about the similarities between the Catholic and Jewish approaches to Scripture are telling. As you point out, first-century Jews relied on rabbinical tradition to interpret Scripture. Similarly, Catholics today look to the Church's Tradition for the proper interpretation of the Bible. Jesus, however, condemned Jewish reliance on rabbinical tradition. You have said that He was only criticizing the "tradition of men,"[32] for He calls them such in Mark 7:8. But what Jesus calls the "tradition of men" (Mark 7:8) was revered by the Jews as "the tradition of the elders" (Mark 7:3). This is a reference to the teachings of the great rabbis—most notably Hillel the Elder and Shammai the Elder. The context of Mark 7 is a question the Pharisees asked Jesus: "Why do your disciples not live according to the tradition of the elders, but eat with hands defiled?" (Mark 7:5). Jesus answered with a rebuke: "You leave the commandment of God, and hold fast the tradition of men....You have a fine way of rejecting the commandment of God, in order to keep your tradition!" (Mark 7:8-9). Sadly, I believe the Roman Catholic Church is guilty of the same.

John, I appeal to you to prayerfully reconsider your reliance on Tradition. Let God's holy Scriptures speak to you unhindered. Only then will you be able to understand their true meaning.

In Christ's love,

Jim

Letter 10

THURSDAY, AUGUST 10, 2000

Dear Jim,

I'm glad you enjoyed Yosemite. What a gorgeous place!

I enjoy teaching, challenging young people to think, and they challenging me. And you're right: Notre Dame is a beautiful campus, and my visit aroused many fond memories. Although the Charismatic movement was big at Notre Dame when I was there, I was never involved.

Jim, your last letter raised many interesting questions. I wish they had come up in earlier conversations where I could have responded to them at greater length. So forgive me if my reply seems a bit abbreviated. For example, I'd like to show how the dogmas related to Mary are rooted in the Bible and ancient Tradition. The papal pronouncements you described are an exercise of the Catholic Church's magisterial role, which we will discuss in our next topic. So, please raise the topic of Mary again after that.

No Unhindered Reading

Accepting the Catholic position on Scripture and Tradition is hard; it is a matter of faith—faith in the Holy Spirit (1 Corinthians 2:14). One can easily read Scripture with eyes of human logic filtered by current American culture and prejudiced by 500 years of Protestant tradition. No wonder you see things so differently. In fact, *it is impossible to read Scripture unhindered* as you propose, unless you're a computer. Thus, to read Scripture

---

through the eyes of those to whom it was written, and not through mere human eyes, Tradition is indispensable.

Your particular predisposition tends to equate God's Word with Scripture. In defending *Sola Scriptura* and critiquing Tradition you reference some 40 passages: four mention God's Word in general (spoken and written, excluding the 100+ "the Word of the Lord came to…"); 18 mention His spoken words or deeds (excluding the 400+ "Thus says the Lord…"); only 12 specifically mention written Scripture—but three of these criticize improper scriptural interpretation, such as Romans 2:17-21 (you quote only verse 20[33]). Yet you indiscriminately equate *God's Word* exclusively with Scripture. Is not the word that is "living and active, sharper than any two-edged sword…,"[34] the "good news…they *heard*… with faith in the *hearers*…, 'when you *hear* his *voice*…'"(Hebrews 4:2,7)? Equating Scripture with *God's Word* confuses the issues and your "unhindered" read of Scripture.

Now we could investigate the complex historical question: What did Huss die for? But ignoring or cheapening the witness of those "slain for the word of God" (see Revelation 6:9-11) would malign the Spirit. Christ's own obedience unto death witnessed to His authority (John 8:28; Philippians 2:5-11).

Scriptural Context

You challenge my use of two Scripture quotes. There isn't room here for a detailed defense, but let me remind you, they were presented in the context of some 80 biblical passages—passages affirming Scripture's value for making us complete,*[‡] in a unity* of truth* based on faith, not human wisdom.* Christian teachings begin with Scripture,* but aren't limited to Scripture,** which is *not alone* in perfecting and equipping us for doing good.**

The Spirit authenticates oral teaching** and sacred art* with miracles,* holiness,* and endurance in trials,* especially martyrdom.*

---

‡   A single * indicates statements or affirmations supported by Scripture from a single
    passage that I cite in previous letters and conversations; double ** indicate statements
    supported by multiple passages.

We need Tradition* because Scripture cannot contain all Christ's words and actions,** yet, every word is important,** never wasted.* Scripture witnesses to New* and Old** Testament Traditions, treating Tradition equally** or even preeminently.** Luke fashions his Gospel using Tradition;* Matthew uses Tradition recorded in the Greek Old Testament translation.* Tradition *alone* reliably transmitted revelation for centuries; God introduced Scriptures because Israel refused His direct revelation** (including Galatians 3).

We should reject both *human* interpretations* and traditions,** but defend Traditions the saints delivered orally,* because they are God's Word.* God makes** and keeps faithfully** oral covenants and promises, expecting obedience to both* (2 Thessalonians fits here), and to oral** and written* commandments. Disobeying oral commandments severs us from God.** Christians must listen to Paul's preaching, imitate his action,** and teach this to others.* This oral gospel is profitable for teaching** and reproof,** with church authority being the "final court of appeals,"** not Scripture.

God commands us to transmit His word orally* because faith comes from hearing,* not reading. Without faith, Scripture becomes hard to understand,** distorted,* and inadequate to achieve eternal life.* Fortunately, God does not leave us alone with *Scripture alone.*

I could cite more Scripture, but to what affect? I feel like the children sitting in the marketplace: "We piped to you, and you did not dance; we wailed, and you did not weep" (Luke 7:32).

We define oral Tradition (which you find vague) as the Holy Spirit behind the letter of the law, guiding interpretation throughout history. At times you seem to recognize oral Tradition's authority and inspiration: "The inspired words of a true prophet...are authoritative because they are God-breathed. Spoken or written, God's words are equally authoritative."[35] But then you retreat back into the preconceived box of *Sola Scriptura,* saying, "Scripture is the only inspired source of truth."[36]

Where is *Sola*?

The word *only* is what divides us, since we both believe Scripture is inspired. Yet, where does Scripture say *only?* I searched all your citations; nowhere could I find *only, alone, exclusive, exclusively, singular, sole, solely, solitary, unique,* or *uniquely.* Perhaps I missed one.

You keep mentioning how Christ condemned the tradition of the rabbis, yet ignore His condemnation of human interpretations, the source of their human traditions. You suggest I reject sacred Tradition as "tradition of men." Reject what early Christians believed was necessary to interpret Scripture and discern the canon of Scripture? Reject it for a *Sola Scriptura* doctrine that you admit developed during the middle ages in response to Tradition? Reject what Scripture clearly confirms is from the Holy Spirit? I'll continue to listen the Holy Spirit: "He who is of God *hears* the words of God; the reason why you do not *hear* them is…" (John 8:47).

Jim, I thoroughly enjoyed your letters. You've challenged me to think and to solidify my faith. I sincerely thank you for that. I have tried to present compelling scriptural arguments, but these are matters of faith. Please pray over them. Please do investigate the details of Huss' death and, while you do, go a little deeper into *Sola Scriptura*'s historical roots.

Shortly, I'll send you another letter stating what Catholics believe regarding church authority, but I'll give you some time to digest all this first. As we get into other doctrines and differences of scriptural interpretation, I firmly believe that you will better see not only how Tradition works, but also how it is necessary for Christ's Church.

You and your family are in my prayers daily. Please keep me in yours.

May He keep you in His peace,

John

TOPIC 2
Teaching and
Ruling Authority

Who has it?

Letter 11

Dear Jim,

I hope you are enjoying the last days of summer. I've had a number of extra activities that have made this month busy but enriching. I was chaplain for a camp for girls and then gave married members of Opus Dei a ten-session course on the history of Christianity (by the way, I included all the scandals).

I hope you had a chance to mull over my last letter. You may not agree with my Catholic interpretation; I hope now you see the extensive biblical basis for Tradition. You raised some important issues that should be addressed, namely: how do we know that a particular tradition is of the Holy Spirit and how do Popes today still declare dogmas? Our answer is magisterial or teaching authority.

Catholics believe Christ instituted teaching authority to serve the Word, safeguarding it with authoritative interpretation. Jesus replaced Jewish elders and priests with apostles, gracing them with His own authority. These apostles communicated their teaching authority to their successors, the bishops. Everyone ought to read Scripture, yet bishops receive the grace and responsibility to interpret and teach God's Word with authority, and to resolve disputes. Acting together, the bishops can infallibly interpret Scripture; as Peter's successor, the Pope possesses this gift in a special way, confirming his brother bishops in the faith.

This teaching must be difficult for you. But let us continue to ask the Holy Spirit to enlighten our minds and soften our hearts to the fullness of Christ's gospel truth.

With His love,

John

Letter 12

THURSDAY, SEPTEMBER 28, 2000

Dear John,

The summer is past and we are again at the start of another academic year. Like you, I am busy launching various ministries. In addition to our regular programs, this year I will be teaching in an internship for men preparing for ministry. The program is a cooperative effort shared by two churches here in the Santa Clara Valley. To keep up with the increased workload, I may need to spread out our correspondence a bit.

The summary of your position concerning teaching and ruling authority in your last letter was helpful. Here are the issues I would like you to clarify.

Succession

You say that the bishops of your church are the successors of the twelve apostles. What is the biblical basis for this belief?

Teaching Authority

In the Bible I find everyday Christians studying and interpreting God's Word. You say, however, that although anyone can read the Bible, only the bishops of your church have the right to interpret and to teach it with authority. I don't see such claims in the Scriptures. Nor do I find a council of men called bishops claiming the exclusive right to interpret the Scriptures for everyone else.

The Papacy

I was surprised how little you said in your letter concerning the ruling authority of the Pope. Rome makes such grandiose claims in this area. The bishops of the First Vatican Council (1870) stated:

> ...the Roman pontiff is the successor of blessed Peter, the prince of the apostles, true vicar of Christ, head of the whole church and father and teacher of all Christian people. To him, in blessed Peter, full power has been given by our Lord Jesus Christ to tend, rule and govern the universal church.[37]

One would think that if such claims were part of the original teachings of Christ and His apostles we would find them throughout the New Testament. Yet nowhere do we read of a "Roman pontiff." I realize that many of the teachings of your church are based upon Tradition. But surely if Christ and the apostles taught these doctrines and considered them foundational to the church, they would have included them in their writings. Can you explain this omission?

The Title of "Pope"

Jesus said, "Call no man your father on earth, for you have one Father, who is in heaven" (Matthew 23:9). I am interested in knowing how you can address a man as *Pope,* meaning "father," and how you yourself accept the title of Father as a Catholic priest.

Infallibility

Jesus rebuked Peter for trying to persuade Him not to die on the cross (Matthew 16:21-23). Later, Peter denied the Lord three times (Matthew 26:69-75). Still later, Paul publicly rebuked Peter for leading people astray with regard to the gospel (Galatians 2:11-21). What makes you think Peter, allegedly the first Pope, was incapable of teaching error?

I greatly appreciate this opportunity to discuss these doctrines. Frank, honest, and yet friendly dialogue has been missing between our two sides for too long.

I spoke about our correspondence with Carolyn McCready, head of the editorial department at Harvest House Publishers. She expressed considerable interest and asked for a review copy. I'll let you know her response as soon as I hear something.

In Christ's love,

Jim

Letter 13

MONDAY, OCTOBER 2, 2000

Dear Jim,

Thank you for taking the initiative with potential publishers. I appreciate how busy you are. With classes starting, UCLA students are back seeking spiritual guidance. Moreover, last weekend I was up in Seattle preaching at a retreat to women.

Jim, you started our exchange by reviewing how God used Scripture to transmit revelation throughout salvation history. Since New Testament authority didn't develop in a vacuum but in its Old Testament context, I'd like to examine it along the same line.

Old Testament Authority

The Old Testament exemplifies God's plan for Church authority. For example, God gave the ancient patriarchs authority to establish traditions and confer blessings (Genesis 27 and 48). He also gave prophets authority (in fact, *prophecy*—Hebrew *naba*—means "to speak or teach"; *Magisterium*—from the Latin *magister*, teacher—means "authoritative teaching"). Yet the paradigm of authority is Moses, proto-Pope and prophet, with whom God shared His own authority (Exodus 4:10-12).

Moses exercised his God-given authority in many ways. He exercised priestly authority, consecrating the tabernacle and offering sacrifices (Numbers 7), and interceding and atoning for sin (Exodus 32; 34:9). He appointed and anointed other priests, including the chief priest, pontiff, Aaron (Leviticus 8) and his successor-son, Eleazar (Numbers 20:22-28; Deuteronomy 10:6), and established conditions for their successors (Leviticus 21:10-24).

God also made Moses judge:

> Moses sat to judge the people..."Because the people come to me to inquire of God; when they have a dispute, they come to me and I decide between a man and his neighbor, and I make them know the statutes of God and his decisions."
>
> EXODUS 18:13,15-16

Hence the term "Moses' seat" (Matthew 23:2). Later, Moses appointed several levels of judges and leaders, deciding difficult cases himself as *the final court of appeals* (Deuteronomy 1:9-18; Exodus 18:21-26). Later, priests would resolve the more difficult cases (Deuteronomy 16:18-20); those who disobeyed their decisions were executed (Deuteronomy 17:8-13).

Moses often taught through elders (Exodus 3:16; 4:29-31). God shared Moses' prophetic authority with seventy elders (the Sanhedrin):

> The LORD said to Moses, "Gather for me seventy men of the elders....and I will take some of the spirit which is upon you and put it upon them; and they shall bear the burden of the people with you....Then the Lord... took some of the spirit that was upon him and put it upon the seventy elders; and...they prophesied.
>
> NUMBERS 11:16-17, 25;
> see also EXODUS 24:1-11

Irresolvable questions in the Law were brought to Moses, who consulted God to clarify matters that Scripture could not (Numbers 9:1-14; 27:1-11; 36). Disbelief in Moses meant disbelief in God (Numbers 14:11). Despite this, God continue shepherding His people through Moses' successors (Deuteronomy 18:15-19).

—

God chose Joshua to be Moses' first successor. Moses laid hands upon him (Numbers 27:12-23), investing him with wisdom, power, and supreme authority (Deuteronomy 3:28):

> Joshua the son of Nun was full of the spirit of wisdom,
> for Moses had laid his hands upon him; so the people
> of Israel obeyed him.
>
> DEUTERONOMY 34:9

Moses and Joshua's authority had to be infallible, since God required everyone to obey their leadership and interpretation. But infallibility does not mean sinlessness. Moses could still sin (see, for example, Numbers 20:10-13). Nor does it guarantee Moses' private opinions or requests (Deuteronomy 3:23-29). The infallible teachings or writings do not imply perfection of their prophets or authors.

Transition to the New

This Old Testament model of authority continued until our Lord's time. Scribes and Pharisees legitimately sat on Moses' seat; Jesus required all to obey them (Matthew 23:1-3). The chief priest had special prophetic authority (John 11:49-52). However, their authority had to end. The new wine of Christ's gospel would burst the wineskins of Old Covenant authority (Matthew 9:17). God would transfer authority from the evil tenants and entrust it to the apostles (the new wineskins):

> "There was a householder who planted a vineyard...
> and let it out to tenants....When the season of fruit
> drew near...the tenants took his servants and beat one,
> killed another, and stoned another....But when the
> tenants saw the son...they took...and killed him.
> When therefore the owner of the vineyard comes...
> [he] will put those wretches to a miserable death, and
> let out the vineyard to other tenants who will give him

the fruits in their seasons...." When the chief priests
and the Pharisees heard his parables, they perceived
that he was speaking about them.

See MATTHEW 21:33-45

With new church leadership, obedience to the priests and
Pharisees now meant obeying man rather than God (Acts 5:29).
Paul and Apollos were God's new vineyard "workers" (1 Corinthians 3:1-9), with authority to make "demands as apostles of
Christ...like a father with his children" (1 Thessalonians 2:6,11),
which Christians must obey (2 Corinthians 2:9; 2 Thessalonians
3:4,14).

All authority comes from the Father (Romans 13:1), who
shares it with His Son (Matthew 28:18; Colossians 2:10), and He
with the apostles (Matthew 10:1). God confirms Christ's authority
with miracles, or works of the Father (John 5:36; 10:32-38), and
the apostles would do greater works (John 14:10-12). Peter (Acts
3:1-16; 5:1-15; 9:32-42) and Paul (Acts 14:9,10; 28:1-8) worked
such miracles, confirming that their teaching authority came from
Christ (Acts 4:10). This authority united the early Christians (Acts
2:42-45) into one heart and soul (Acts 4:32-33). Authority serves
unity (Ephesians 4).

Figures of Authority

Like authority, all fatherhood comes from the Father (Ephesians 3:14-15, Greek) who makes us His children (Galatians 4:1-
7; Ephesians 5:1). Yet the Father shares His paternity with
Christ—making us Christ's children (Hebrews 2:10)—and with
the apostles: Peter calls Mark his son (1 Peter 5:13); John calls
Christians his little children (1 John 2:1); and Paul calls believers
his beloved children (1 Corinthians 4:14-15). Likewise, *Pope* (from
the Greek *papas,* or "father") indicates spiritual paternity. All early
Church bishops were called *papas.* Does this surprise you? Were
not Moses and the judges called gods, sons of the Most High

85

(Psalm 82:6; John 10:34-35) and patriarchs (from the Latin *pater,* "father") because God bequeathed His own authority to them?

Similarly, God shepherds His people (Psalm 23), but also delegated His pastoral authority to Moses (Isaiah 63:8-13), Joshua (Numbers 27:17), David (2 Samuel 5:2), and even to bad Old Testament pastors (Ezekiel 34). Christ is *the* Good Shepherd (John 10:1-30), yet the apostles and church elders (Greek *presbuteros,* whence the English word *priest*) are too (Acts 20:17-18,28; Ephesians 4:11; 1 Peter 5:1-4). Christ especially calls Peter to feed His lambs and sheep (John 21:15-17).

The term *watchman* (overseer or bishop) also expresses authority. Christ is the overseer or guardian of our souls (1 Peter 2:25; Greek *episkopos*), as is Matthias, the first successor of an apostle (Acts 1:20; Greek *episkope*). Timothy and Titus too were episcopal successors to Paul (1 Timothy 3:1-7; Titus 1:5-9).

Rock also indicates authority. God is our Shepherd and Rock (Genesis 49:24). Christ is *the* rock the builders rejected (Matthew 21:42), the source of living waters (Romans 10:4). The Church, the pillar of truth (1 Timothy 3:15), is built upon the foundation of Christ and the 12 apostles (Ephesians 2:19-22; Revelation 21:9-14). But again, Peter is preeminently called "rock" by Christ (Matthew 16:18), called to confirm his brother apostles and bishops in their faith (Luke 22:32). Peter's primacy is similar to Moses' and Joshua's as head of all God's people (Deuteronomy 3:28). The Pope is Christ's vicar, as Moses was God's; God commissioned Moses to be "God" to his brother Aaron (Exodus 4:16) and to Pharaoh (Exodus 7:1).

Notice that all figures of authority primarily refer to God or Jesus, and secondarily to Old Testament authorities, apostles, and their successors, because Christ speaks through them (2 Corinthians 13:3).

Transmission of Authority

New Covenant authority is transmitted by the laying on of hands, as with Timothy:

> Do not neglect the gift you have, which was given you
> by prophetic utterance when the elders laid their
> hands upon you....Do not be hasty in the laying on of
> hands, nor participate in another man's sins....Hence
> I remind you to rekindle the gift of God that is within
> you through the laying on of my hands.
>
> 1 TIMOTHY 4:14; 5:22; 2 TIMOTHY 1:6

Exercise of Authority

Like Moses, the Church has authority to resolve controversies. As our Lord advised:

> If your brother sins against you, go and tell him his
> fault, between you and him alone....But if he does not
> listen...tell it to the church; and if he refuses to listen
> even to the church, let him be to you as a Gentile and
> a tax collector.
>
> MATTHEW 18:15-17

Church authority can resolve difficult interpretations and applications of Scripture. When certain Jewish converts required that non-Jewish converts be circumcised—opposing Paul with Scripture (Acts 15:5)—the Holy Spirit guided Peter and the apostles to resolve the matter with their authority:

> The brethren, both the apostles and the elders, to the
> brethren who are of the Gentiles....Since we have
> heard that some persons from us have troubled you
> with words, unsettling your minds...it has seemed
> good to us in assembly....it has seemed good to the
> Holy Spirit and to us to lay upon you no greater
> burden than these necessary things: that you abstain
> from what has been sacrificed to idols...and from

—

unchastity. If you keep yourselves from these, you will do well. Farewell.

ACTS 15:23-25,28-29

Notice they don't use Scripture to convince the churches, but exercise their own apostolic authority from the Holy Spirit. We must obey this authority: "Obey your leaders and submit to them; for they are keeping watch over your souls" (Hebrews 13:17).

Infallibility

Obedience to the Church requires that it have ultimate and infallible authority. As our Lord addressed the apostles: "whatever you bind on earth shall be bound in heaven, and whatever you loose on earth shall be loosed in heaven" (Matthew 18:18). Peter received this authority in a singular way (Matthew 16:19). We obey the Pope and bishops united to him because our Lord says, "He who hears you hears me, and he who rejects you rejects me, and he who rejects me rejects him who sent me" (Luke 10:16).

Peter has "the prophetic word made more sure…as to a lamp shining in a dark place" (2 Peter 1:19). This authority is from God. Supreme, pontifical authority goes to the holder of keys, Christ (Revelation 1:18). Nevertheless, as a king delegates the keys of supreme authority to his prime minister (Isaiah 22:1-25), Christ does to Peter (Matthew 16:13-20).

Early Church Authority

How did the early church exercise authority? Extradited to be martyred in Rome, Ignatius of Antioch (†110) tells us:

> Give ear to the bishop and to the presbytery with an undivided mind…show [the bishop] all reverence in consideration of the authority of God the Father…. Indeed, when you submit to the bishop as you would to Jesus Christ…do nothing without the bishop…be

subject also to the presbytery, as to the Apostles of
Jesus Christ.

LETTERS TO THE EPHESIANS, 20.2;
MAGNESIANS, 3.1; *TRALLIANS*, 2.1[38]

Ignatius also acknowledges the Roman Church's primacy or
presidency, to whom he writes: "the Church beloved and enlightened after the love of Jesus Christ, our God...because you hold the
presidency of love, named after Christ and named after the
Father."[39]

Earlier, Clement, bishop of Rome—martyred in A.D. 101—
exercised his primacy, resolving a dispute against the priests in
Corinth. He wrote them of apostolic succession and episcopal
authority:

The Apostles received the gospel for us from the Lord
Jesus...and they appointed their earliest converts,
testing them by the spirit, to be the bishops and deacons of future believers.

LETTER TO THE CORINTHIANS, 42.1[40]

When he received Pope Innocent's letter confirming the
council decrees of Carthage and Hippo against the Pelagians
(including the canon of Scriptures), Augustine declared "case
closed: *causa finita est.*"[41] Also, please read Augustine's sermon on
Church authority.[42]

You see, Jim, there is quite a case for Church authority in
Scripture and Tradition. And if you, as a knowledgeable evangelical minister, can only offer fallible Scripture interpretations, how
can you demand that I—or anyone else—obey those interpretations? Are they not just "traditions of men?" *Good* interpretations
make *good* fallible traditions of men, but that's it. Please study
these Scripture passages with a heart open to the full infallible
truth found in Scripture, Tradition, and Church authority.

—

Please give my greetings to Jean and the girls. I know you are the spiritual leader in that family and they all look to your leadership in discerning the truth. So, my prayers extend beyond you to them and to the people you minister to.

In Christ's truth and love,

John

Conversation 3

Jim: Thanks, John, for your last letter. Your presentation of Catholic ruling and teaching authority was well written and interesting. Several arguments were new to me.

John: Thank you for the compliment. These ideas principally sprang from my Scripture reading, hopefully through the Holy Spirit's guidance and not my own invention. If they don't correspond to God's Word, then I'm not interested in them.

I've tried presenting the "big picture" of authority in the Bible, while avoiding simplistic "proof-texting."

Are your Popes and bishops qualified?

Jim: You say Matthias was "the first successor of an apostle," implying that there were others. The Bible, however, mentions only him. The first disciples selected Matthias to replace Judas Iscariot. Peter said that "one of the men who have accompanied us during all the time that the Lord Jesus went in and out among us, beginning from the baptism of John until the day when he was taken up from us— one of these men must become with us a witness to his resurrection" (Acts 1:21-22). The disciples put forward two candidates who qualified: Joseph Barsabbas and Matthias (Acts 1:23). They drew lots, and Matthias was selected. My question is this: How can your Pope and bishops claim to be the apostles' successors if none of them can meet the qualifications put forth by Peter?

John: Jim, what qualifications does your church require to ordain preachers, teachers, and other ministers? Do they need to be male, know Scripture, and be commissioned, or can anyone be ordained? Do they need to have a personal relationship with Jesus Christ? Do they need to have witnessed John's baptism and our Lord's resurrection?

The Catholic Church requires priesthood candidates to be male, of proven character and sound doctrine, with a minimum five years of philosophical and theological studies.[43] In addition, an episcopal candidate needs to have solid faith, good morals, piety, zeal for souls, an ecclesiastical doctorate, and be ordained a priest five years.[44]

The Holy Spirit could have replaced Judas with anyone off the street, guiding him "into all the truth" (John 16:13). But the Spirit directed Peter—as head of the apostles—to seek someone who had a personal relationship with Jesus Christ and good knowledge of His gospel. Someone who had witnessed Jesus' life from His baptism to the resurrection would most aptly fulfill that requisite.

These general requirements will always remain, while the specific criteria to discern them will change, as it had when Paul commissioned bishops (1 Timothy 3:1-7; Titus 1:7-9), presbyters (Titus 1:5-6), and deacons (1 Timothy 3:8-13).

Jim: Evangelical ministers do not claim to be the successors of the apostles. Neither did Paul. In Galatians 1:1 and elsewhere he says that God personally appointed him an apostle. Your bishops, on the other hand, say they have the authority of the apostles because they are their successors. Should we not require them, therefore, to meet the qualifications set by Peter and the apostles for succession?

—

John: I think we'd both agree that the general requirements for a successor—having a personal relationship with Jesus Christ and good knowledge of His gospel—are indispensable for exercising church authority. Obviously, the specific criteria that Peter detailed can no longer be met. Besides, Paul gave much different criteria when commissioning bishops.

Jim: You say, "Timothy and Titus too were episcopal successors of Paul."[45] You cite 1 Timothy 3:1-7 and Titus 1:5-9 as support. These verses make no mention of Timothy or Titus being Paul's successors. How do you draw your conclusion from these passages?

John: Like Matthias, Timothy and Titus were commissioned (Acts 19:22; 2 Corinthians 12:18) by prophetic utterance (1 Timothy 1:18, 4:14) to be fellow workers with Paul (Romans 16:21; 2 Corinthians 8:23) through the laying on of hands.[46] They had teaching authority (1 Timothy 4:11-16; Titus 2:1,15) to guard the truth (1 Timothy 6:20), prohibit erroneous teaching (1 Timothy 1:1-7; Titus 1:10-16), and correct abuses (1 Timothy 5:19-20). Most importantly, they had the power to ordain other bishops (1 Timothy 3:1-7; Titus 1:7), presbyters (1 Timothy 5:17-18; Titus 1:5-6), and deacons (1 Timothy 3:8-13).

Paul too was chosen and commissioned through the laying on of hands for his apostolic authority (Acts 13:1-3).

Jim: Considering that the Scriptures never refer to Paul, Timothy, or Titus as the successors of the apostles nor give them the title of bishop, do not these verses prove the opposite of your position, namely, that apostolic succession is not required for the ministries you list?

John: Jim, obviously, Scripture doesn't give precise textbook definitions for *bishop* and *apostle*. If it did, then I failed to prove my point. Nevertheless, Peter didn't call Judas' successor an apostle but bishop, "his bishopric let another take" (Acts 1:20 KJV).

—

Can anyone interpret Scripture, or must Catholics depend on their bishops?

Jim: The Catholic Church seems to treat its members like children. It says that they can read the Bible, but they can't interpret it. Rome says "the task of interpreting the Word of God authentically has been entrusted solely to the Magisterium of the Church, that is, to the Pope and to the bishops in communion with him" [CCC 100]. Laymen are to receive Rome's teaching "with docility" [CCC 87]. The same is required of Catholic theologians. They must work "under the watchful eye of the sacred Magisterium."[47] They must always interpret the Bible "in that sense in which it has been defined by the Church."[48] Doesn't this leave Catholics spiritually dependent on the few men you call bishops? Paul told the Christians in Thessalonica to "test everything; hold fast what is good" (1 Thessalonians 5:21). Why doesn't the Church tell Catholics to do the same?

John: "Unless you…become like children, you will never enter the kingdom of heaven" (Matthew 18:3).

Jim, the Catechism you cite doesn't prohibit individual interpretation, but affirms the Magisterium's role to *authentically* "guard the truth" (2 Timothy 1:14)—Scripture—against misinterpretation and doctrinal controversies, as in Acts 15.[49] Hence "access to Sacred Scripture ought to be open wide to the Christian faithful" [CCC 131]. A few lines away from your quote, the *Catechism* encourages all readers to interpret the Bible [CCC 109].

The *Catechism*'s guideline for interpretation is titled, "The Holy Spirit, Interpreter of Scripture" [CCC 109-119]. It mentions the Magisterium only at the very end:

> For, of course, all that has been said about the manner of interpreting Scripture is ultimately subject to the judgment of the Church which exercises the divinely

conferred commission and ministry of watching over
and interpreting the Word of God.

[CCC 119]

Yes, Paul says we should test all prophesying, but nine
verses earlier he tells us to "respect those who labor
among you and are over you in the Lord and admonish
you" (1 Thessalonians 5:12), being "submissive to rulers
and authorities...[and] obedient" (Titus 3:1). If you lived
in the times of the apostles, would you have not obeyed
their Magisterial documents—rejoicing upon reading
them (Acts 15:31)—even without scriptural references?
Without obedience to their Magisterium, we'd still be circumcising converts.

Where is the bishop of Rome found in the Bible?

Jim: You write that "the Pope is Christ's vicar, as Moses was
God's." If this were true, it would be one of the ten most
important doctrines of the Christian faith. Surely the
apostles would have taught it everywhere they went. Yet
nowhere in their writings do we read that all Christians
are to submit to the bishop of Rome as Christ's personal
representative and substitute on earth. Further, I counted
over 800 references in the Bible to Moses. I couldn't find a
single reference to there even being a bishop of Rome.
Doesn't this tell us something?

John: Jim, does the number of biblical references decide the
truth? How many times is *trinity* found in Scripture? Yet is
this not a very important doctrine of faith?
        If you want numbers, then look at the New Testament,
where Moses is mentioned 80 times, and Peter (Simon or
Cephas) is mentioned 217 times. All the other apostles
together (including Judas) are mentioned only 171 times.
Peter definitely predominates.

The New Testament was predominantly written before Peter arrived in Rome. Even so, Peter mentions being in Babylon (1 Peter 5:13), which most interpreters apply to Rome. All the historical and archeological evidence confirms this fact.

What about all the Old Testament precedents and the New Testament evidence for Peter's vicariate given in my letter—are you not interested in discussing these?

Jim: My question regards your claim that "the Pope is Christ's vicar." The Bible doesn't state this or even mention there being a bishop of Rome in apostolic times. You respond by saying there are 217 references to Peter, more than any other apostle. What does this have to do with your bishop in Rome today being Christ's substitute on earth?

John: When Jesus gives Peter the keys (Matthew 16:13-20), He fulfills Isaiah 22:15-25. The holder of the key "shall be a father to the inhabitants of Jerusalem and to the house of Judah" (verse 21). The keys signify supreme power and succession (because keys are handed down from one generation to the next). Jesus refers to the keys as a special authority given to Peter.

Jim: At most, John, this would establish authority given to Peter. But what does this have to do with the present-day Pope, the bishop of Rome? I don't see any connection in your logic.

John: Obviously, the Old Testament model of authority must be fulfilled. Moses had successors and was God's vicar—he was as God to Pharaoh and Aaron. The early Christians saw this fulfilled in Peter.

Jim: But is there anywhere in the Scriptures that the apostles say these keys are going to be passed down from Peter to others?

John: One early Christian writer, Cyprian, wrote in A.D. 252:

> With a false bishop appointed for themselves by
> heretics, they dare even to set sail and carry letters
> from schismatics and blasphemers to the chair of
> Peter and to the principal Church, in which sacerdotal
> unity has its source; nor did they take thought that
> these are Romans, whose faith was praised by the
> preaching Apostle, and among whom it is not pos-
> sible for perfidy to have entrance.
>
> LETTER OF CYPRIAN TO CORNELIUS OF ROME, 59.14[50]

These early Christians were living out a tradition long established in Rome and throughout the Christian world.

Jim: In that you chose to answer my question by quoting Cyprian from the third century, am I correct in inferring that there is no Scripture to support this doctrine?

John: True, no scriptural passage that mentions *directly* Peter's successor in Rome with the keys. However, all the scriptural evidence points to this truth, including words of our Lord and the many passages I have cited.

Jim: You write, "We obey the Pope and bishops united to him, because our Lord says, 'He who hears you hears me, and he who rejects you rejects me, and he who rejects me rejects him who sent me' (Luke 10:16)." Here Jesus is speaking to 70 of His followers, whom He is sending out to preach (see Luke 10:1,17). He tells them that whoever listens to *them* is listening to Him. Whoever rejects *them*, rejects Him. How can you apply Luke 10:16 to the Pope and bishops of the Catholic Church when in context it refers to someone else?

John: The seventy disciples received authority as Christ's representatives, as did the apostles:

> He who receives you receives me, and he who receives
> me receives him who sent me. He who receives a
> prophet because he is a prophet shall receive a

prophet's reward, and he who receives a righteous man because he is a righteous man shall receive a righteous man's reward.

MATTHEW 10:41

Paul compliments the Thessalonians for listening to his Magisterial—prophetic—preaching, "not as the word of men but as what it really is, the word of God" (1 Thessalonians 2:13).

Jim: I must again take issue with your free application of these scriptures to your Pope and bishops. In Matthew 10:41, Jesus is speaking to the 12 apostles. First Thessalonians 2:13 refers to the teaching of Paul, an apostle and prophet of God. Can you give me a scripture that says that all Christians should obey the Roman Catholic Pope and bishops?

John: Paul says,

Remember your leaders, those who spoke to you the word of God; consider the outcome of their life, and imitate their faith....Do not be led away by diverse and strange teachings.

HEBREWS 13:7,9

We believe we submit to God by submitting to the authority He has established in our leaders. Effectively, every Protestant is a Pope because he must obey and submit to no one but himself.

Doesn't Scripture forbid calling spiritual leaders *father?*

Jim: I am aware that some called religious leaders *father* by the end of the second century. Nevertheless, Jesus' command still stands. He said, "Call no man your father on earth" (Matthew 23:9). If this does not forbid calling spiritual leaders *father* as a title of honor—such as is the practice in

Catholicism—then to what does the prohibition properly apply?

John: If you take our Lord's words categorically, then "no man" means absolutely no human being. Thus your daughters could not call you *father;* Christians could call nobody *teacher, doctor* ("teacher" in Latin), *professor, boss, mister* (master, lord), and so on.

Some interpret our Lord's words as hyperbole, emphasizing the Pharisees' pride and interest in titles rather than serving the people with their authority. Christ does something similar when He says, "If your right eye causes you to sin, pluck it out and throw it away; it is better that you lose one of your members than that your whole body be thrown into hell" (Matthew 5:29). Few Christians believe our Lord wants us to physically pluck out our eyes.

Another possible interpretation is that our Lord is confirming that all authority comes from the Father, and that we should obey all authority and believe all teachers only to the extent they have authority from our Father, God.

I've already cited John, Paul, and Peter speaking of their spiritual fatherhood.[51] Paul is very explicit with Philemon: "I appeal to you for my child, Onesimus, whose father I have become in my imprisonment" (verse 10). Paul also affectionately states, "Though you have countless guides in Christ, you do not have many fathers. For I became your father in Christ Jesus through the gospel" (1 Corinthians 4:15).

Did "infallible" Jewish leaders err?

Jim: You wrote that "Moses and Joshua's authority had to be infallible, since God required everyone to obey their leadership and Scripture interpretation." You extended this power to the ruling Jews of Jesus' day, saying "this Old Testament model of authority continued until our Lord's time." You go on to say, "Jesus recognized that scribes and

—

99

Pharisees legitimately sat on Moses' seat, requiring all to obey them." By your reasoning, then, they also were infallible—something I find impossible to accept. Along with the chief priests, the Pharisees formed the Sanhedrin, the highest council of the Jews. This is the council that tried Jesus. During the trial the high priest asked Jesus, "Are you the Christ, the Son of the Blessed?" (Mark 14:61). Jesus answered, "I am; and you will see the Son of man sitting at the right hand of Power, and coming with the clouds of heaven" (verse 62). Here Jesus quotes Psalm 110:1 and Daniel 7:13. The high priest responded by accusing Jesus of blasphemy. The council then condemned Jesus to death. Does this not prove that they were not only capable of error but also guilty of the greatest error?

John: What was their teaching error? They knew Jesus claimed to be divine as the *Son of God* and the *son of man,* making Himself equal to God (John 5:18). Although the high priest, Caiaphas, personally rejected Jesus, he did not teach anything erroneously, but even prophesied by the Holy Spirit that Jesus should die for the nation (John 11:45-53).

Let me repeat what I said in my letter: infallibility does not refer to sinlessness or perfection in thought and action. An infallible teacher could still reject Christ. Infallibility is a special grace of office ("bishopric" Acts 1:20 KJV). By this grace Peter and his successors, or all the bishops in communion with him, were and are protected from error when interpreting God's Word. This makes it possible to profess the true faith without error [CCC 890]. Infallible teaching can never contradict God's Word, but that doesn't mean that it's perfect—one may always express doctrine better or more completely.

Could God not make Moses and Joshua infallible in their teaching? Could God not make the evangelists and the other writers infallible in composing Scripture? If God protected these individuals from teaching error, why not the Pope, Peter's successor?

And if we Catholics believe that God protects the Pope as Peter's successor with the gift of infallibility in matters of doctrine and morals, then should we not obey and submit to that gift?

Jim: When the Sanhedrin formally met to try Jesus, the high priest solemnly ordered Him, "I adjure you by the living God, tell us if you are the Christ, the Son of God" (Matthew 26:63). Jesus responded that He was indeed the Son of God. The high priest proclaimed, "He has uttered blasphemy. Why do we still need witnesses? You have now heard his blasphemy" (verse 65). He then asked the highest council of the Jews, "What is your judgment?" (verse 66). They answered, "He deserves death" (verse 66). Was this not an authoritative rejection of Jesus as the Jewish Messiah, an error of the greatest magnitude?

John: The Sanhedrin sinned in rejecting their God and Messiah. The scribes blasphemed against the Holy Spirit by ignoring His inspiration to discern and teach Jesus' divinity, saying instead He was possessed (Mark 3:22,29-30). However, the Sanhedrin never "formally" taught that Jesus wasn't God or the Messiah. The scribes never proclaimed erroneous magisterial teaching; they just refused to exercise their teaching authority.

Jim: If the Pharisees and Sadducees of the ruling council of the Jews were infallible, why does Jesus in Matthew 16:12 tell His disciples to beware of their teaching?

John: Jesus once asked the chief priests and elders whether John's baptism was from heaven or not. They refused to use their authority to decide this matter (Matthew 21:23-27). By the same conniving politics they sought to kill Jesus (Mark 11:18). Perhaps Matthew 16:12 refers to this human calculation as improper exercise of authority.

Jim: If the Pharisees were infallible, then why did Jesus oppose their teaching concerning the picking of heads of grain on the Sabbath (Mark 2:23-24), healing on the Sabbath (Mark 3:1-6), ceremonial washing before eating (Mark 7:1-9), and the practice of Corban (Mark 7:8-13)? He called the Pharisees "blind guides" (Matthew 23:16).

John: Our Lord rejected practices that contradicted Scripture and God's will as "traditions of men." Our Lord Himself made mistakes—or so it appears—such as choosing Judas, who would betray Him. This doesn't mean our Lord's *teaching* was fallible.

Jim: I would like to discuss these matters at greater length, John, but we probably need to draw this to a conclusion. I'll send you a response in the next week or so. Thanks for clarifying your position.

John: Jim, thank you for bearing with me. Your questions were challenging. Please take your time to mull over the Scripture I have presented and please point out where my interpretation is clearly and undeniably incompatible with the whole of Scripture.

Jim: Steve Miller, senior editor at Harvest House Publishers, called me last week. He said that Carolyn McCready, head of editorial, and he have reviewed our book proposal and think it's a "fantastic idea." The next step is to bring it before the publication committee. I'll keep you up to date.

Letter 14

WEDNESDAY, JANUARY 2, 2001

Dear John,

I hope you had a blessed Christmas with ample time to reflect upon God's "inexpressible gift" (2 Corinthians 9:15), the Lord Jesus Christ. We spent Christmas Day with my brothers and sisters and their families in San Francisco. We returned there three days later to celebrate the birthdays of two of my sisters and my daughter Elizabeth's twenty-first. I have felt older ever since! Fortunately, Jean and I were able to get a couple days away in Monterey to recoup. I am now back in my office, refreshed, and getting ready for the start of classes. At the top of my list of priorities is this letter to you.

We have made progress in understanding one another. I don't believe, however, we are moving toward agreement. I find your case for Catholic teaching and ruling authority is lacking in crucial areas.

Where is the Council of Bishops?

First are the claims of your bishops. I asked you to explain why the Bible makes no mention of a council of bishops with the exclusive right to interpret the Word of God. To my way of thinking, such an omission is highly significant.

You referred me to Matthias, whom you identified as "the first successor of an apostle," implying there were others. When I pointed out that the Bible mentions only him, and that your bishops do not meet the qualifications the apostles required of Matthias, you answered, "Obviously, the specific criteria that Peter detailed can no longer be met." Is it not equally obvious, then, that your bishops cannot claim to be in his line of succession?

You said Paul used different requirements when commissioning bishops, citing Timothy and Titus. When I pointed out that Scripture does not identify Timothy or Titus as bishops or call them successors of Paul, you replied, "If we were to take Scripture as a textbook with precise definitions, then I failed to prove my point."

All I am asking for is something specific. I think that is reasonable. Furthermore, you never directly responded to my original question. Where is the biblical evidence for a *council of bishops* ruling and teaching the worldwide church?

Where is the Roman pontiff?

Second, I asked you to explain why the Bible makes no mention of a Roman pontiff functioning as Christ's representative on earth. You replied that Jesus promised to give Peter "the keys of the kingdom of heaven" (Matthew 16:19). You say these symbolize "supreme power and succession (because they will be handed down from one generation to the next)."

I think they better represent the privilege Peter had in opening the doors of salvation to the Jews (Acts 2:14-36), Samaritans (Acts 8:4-25), and Gentiles (Acts 9:32–10:48). With respect to the latter, Peter said, "Brethren, you know that in the early days God made choice among you, that by my mouth the Gentiles should hear the word of the gospel and believe" (Acts 15:7). Peter initially and Paul later were the human instruments by which God "opened a door of faith to the Gentiles" (Acts 14:27).

In any case, when I asked you for some evidence that Peter passed these keys on to others, you conceded that there is "no scriptural passage that mentions *directly* Peter's successor in Rome with the keys." You qualified this, saying, "However, all the scriptural evidence points to this truth."[52] What evidence? I know of nothing in the Bible, *direct* or *circumstantial,* of Peter having a successor in Rome, *with* or *without* keys. There's nothing! The Roman papacy is not in the Bible. It's a tradition of men that evolved well after the apostolic era. Some historians say the first Pope in the modern sense did not come on the scene until the end of the sixth century when Gregory the Great (A.D. 590-604) took control of the Western Church.

Where is papal infallibility?

Papal infallibility is another Catholic doctrine without a biblical basis. You reason that because the Scriptures tell us to "obey your leaders and submit to them" (Hebrews 13:17), the church must have "ultimate and infallible authority."[53] I disagree. Only God has ultimate authority. Delegated authority is always subordinate. Further, when those whom God has given authority misuse their position, God expects us to obey him, not them. When the high priest and ruling council of the Jews ordered Peter and the apostles to stop preaching the gospel, they answered, "We must obey God rather than men" (Acts 5:29).

Your argument that the Pharisees were God's appointed and infallible teachers and that He has now transferred their authority to your bishops is untenable. How can you call infallible the same men Jesus calls "blind guides," "hypocrites," and "a brood of vipers," warning His disciples to beware of their teaching (Matthew 16:12; 23:13,16,33)?

How can you even consider Peter infallible? I cited three examples of grave error on Peter's part. You answered that infallibility does not imply perfection or sinlessness. I understand that distinction, but did not Peter promote error when he tried to persuade Jesus not to die on the cross (Matthew 16:21-23)? Jesus apparently thought so, rebuking him: "Get behind me, Satan!" (Matthew 16:23). Later Peter denied the Lord three times (Matthew 26:69-75). At Antioch Paul rebuked Peter for not being "straightforward about the truth of the gospel" (Galatians 2:14).

If Peter could be wrong about things of this magnitude, could he not be wrong about others?

Where is exclusive teaching and ruling authority?

Finally, I must reject Rome's claims to exclusive teaching and ruling authority for a simple reason: There is no consistent way to accept them. Your Pope and bishops say that only *they* can authentically interpret the Word of God. As for the rest of us—including you as a Catholic priest—they say we lack the authority and competency to judge the meaning of revelation. But if we are incompetent to judge the Word of God, the basis of their claims, how are we to accept their claims? Are we to do so simply because they assert them?

Scripture tells us to "test everything; hold fast what is good" (1 Thessalonians 5:21). It warns us of "false apostles, deceitful workmen, disguising themselves as apostles of Christ" (2 Corinthians 11:13). Christ commends the Christians in Ephesus for having "tested those who call themselves apostles but are not, and found them to be false" (Revelation 2:2). Must we not do the same?

In Christ's love,

Jim

Letter 15

SUNDAY, JANUARY 7, 2001

Dear Jim,

It sounds like you had a wonderful Christmas, which is such a special opportunity to contemplate the Christ-child and become more intimately part of His family. After Christmas I helped with a Tijuana service project for high school boys. Lessons were had by all. We saw firsthand the kind of poverty the holy family must have experienced in Bethlehem. What a joy it was to serve Christ in these people.

We are confronting the tough issues. Your last letter raised some new challenges to my broad overview of church authority in Scripture and early Christianity. Yet, upon further reflection, you should find your answers in what has been said. For example, although I didn't identify the exact phrase *council of bishops* in Scripture, you could have drawn that connection from my references to the apostles' authoritative *council*[54] and *episcopal* succession.[55]

Legalistic Notions

You seem to treat *apostle* as a precise *legal* term used exclusively for Christ's 12 handpicked men. Jim, we Catholics view Scriptures as family letters and diaries, not as legal documents or textbooks. They lead us into *the* truth through types and metaphors, rather than through laws and legal descriptions.

Apostle broadly means "one who is sent," appearing 215 times (*apostello, apostole, apostolos*) in the Greek New Testament. It was applied to Jesus (as in John 20:21), angels, and Old and New Testament leaders. Matthias filled Judas' bishopric (Acts 1:20 KJV) as *apostle* (Acts 1:25-26). Paul and Barnabas became *apostles* (Acts 14:4,14), *sent,* commissioned, through the imposition of hands (Acts 13:1-3). Similarly, Paul commissioned Timothy and Titus, who would later commission other bishops.[56] Yet neither Paul nor Barnabas fulfilled your *legal* requirements for *apostolic* succession.[57]

Perhaps a legalistic vision of *bishop* keeps you from seeing what the early Church saw—that apostolic succession is necessary: "Joshua...was the successor of Moses in prophesying" (Sirach 46:1). Long before Gregory the Great in the seventh century, Clement wrote this in A.D. 80, just 14 years after Peter and Paul's deaths:

> Our Apostles also knew, through our Lord Jesus Christ, that there would be contention over the bishop's office. So, for this cause, having received complete foreknowledge, they appointed the above mentioned men [bishops and deacons[58]]...so that, as they died, other approved men should succeed to their ministry.
>
> *LETTER TO THE CORINTHIANS*[59]

God entrusted the chief bishopric and keys to Peter. Scripture points to Peter being in Rome,[60] where historical and archaeological records say he was martyred in A.D. 66, after most of the New Testament had been written.

Your theory about the keys as symbols of Peter's privilege of opening salvation to the Jews, Samaritans, and Gentiles wrenches Matthew 16:19 totally out of context, going against all rules of scriptural interpretation accepted by most Protestants. The context gives no indication that Jesus intended to say what you say, and no early Christian interpreted it that way.

Essential Signs of Infallibility

Infallibility is a difficult notion, perhaps needing more attention. The Pharisees' rigid perspective of God's oneness made the Trinity and Christ's divinity a stumbling block. The same could happen with infallibility. Since neither *trinity* nor *infallible* are found in Scripture, we look for essential signs of them instead.

Essentially, infallible teaching:

* *binds:* God requires all to submit and obey it, just as His people were to submit to Moses' and his successors' teachings[61] (after Christ's death, God transferred their teaching authority to the apostles);[62] Christ gave Peter binding and loosing power[63] by which he—with the apostles and presbyters—gave the early church binding teaching and loosed them from circumcision;[64]

* *excommunicates,* excluding some from God's people for failing to submit to or obey church authority.[65]

Conditions for Infallibility

There are very strict conditions for a teaching to be infallible. To be infallible, a teaching must be:

* an act of the Pope (Old Testament high priest) or of all bishops united to him;

* a public act of his office as successor to Peter (Moses);

* intended to be binding, requiring submission;

* regarding faith and moral (not appointments, politics…);

* consistent with Scripture and previous infallible teaching.

Notice that not everything the Pope does is infallible, nor may he freely teach whatever he pleases. Your examples opposing infallibility fail to fulfill these conditions, such as when Peter took

Jesus aside privately (not publicly) to dissuade Him from the Passion.

Errors and Scandals of Leaders

Infallibility does not mean that our leaders are impeccable or perfect.[66] Solomon infallibly wrote Proverbs, Song of Solomon, Wisdom and some psalms, yet later fell into idolatry and polygamous marriages with foreigners (1 Kings 11:1-8). Christ appointed Judas. Paul mistakenly commissioned Demas, who deserted his ministry for worldly gain (2 Timothy 4:10).

Yes, Paul corrected Peter; do we discard 1 and 2 Peter because Peter made mistakes? Mark failed Paul (Acts 15:37-40). Does his Gospel go, too? Obviously, committing sins and mistakes doesn't encroach on infallible teaching.

Christ predicted that His church would have weeds mixed in with the wheat (Matthew 13:24-30), with leaders causing scandals (Matthew 18:5-9), yet He still makes "his appeal through" His "ambassadors"; we hear and obey Christ in them (2 Corinthians 5:20). Succession of infallible teaching authority guarantees continuity in the truth necessary for salvation.

If we are fallible, how are we "competent" to judge our leaders? Would this be submitting to their God-given authority? Do you want your daughters to judge you and Jean, using Scripture to justify disobedience?

Jim, I'm sorry that there isn't space to answer all your objections. Hopefully we will clarify the rest as we go along. I look forward to seeing you Monday, God willing. Perhaps we can discuss the remaining objections then. In the meantime, may Christ's peace be with you and your family.

Yours in Christ, the Shepherd and Guardian of our souls,

John

Letter 16

SATURDAY, FEBRUARY 17, 2001

Dear John,

Thank you for visiting in January. I appreciate also the time you gave to answering the questions of the interns studying in our church. They valued the opportunity to hear the perspective of a Catholic priest.

Over the past months you have presented the Catholic position on teaching and ruling authority. I have been able to ask my questions. Now it's time to change places. Here is a brief summary of my beliefs on the topic.

> Christ expresses the close relationship between Him and His church by His direct leadership of His people. He is our chief shepherd and high priest (1 Peter 5:4; Hebrews 8:1). Over each local church, He appoints *elders* to care for the flock (1 Timothy 3:1-7). Assisting them are *deacons*, servants of the church (1 Timothy 3:8-13). Each Christian has direct access through Christ "in one Spirit to the Father" (Ephesians 2:18). As such, every Christian is a priest unto God (1 Peter 2:4-10). The Holy Spirit is the church's infallible teacher, guiding us in the truth (John 16:7-14). The Scriptures are our text, the inspired Word of God (2 Timothy 3:14-17).

111

Let me know your initial thoughts. In my next letter I will explain further and try to answer your questions.

In Christ's love,

Jim

Letter 17

MONDAY, MARCH 5, 2001

Dear Jim,

I enjoyed my January trip to the Bay Area and conversing with your interns, but especially the treat of your wife's hospitality. I hope this visit helped your interns understand and appreciate the Catholic approach to Scripture. By the way, besides your book, do you ever expose your interns to books or tapes from Catholic converts from evangelicalism, like Scott Hahn, David Currie, or Stephen Ray?

Now, regarding your statement on church authority, I found it surprisingly consistent with Catholicism; nothing you said directly contradicts anything the Church teaches. However, you leave out the elements that divide us. My primary concerns are:

Direct Access to God

With the Holy Spirit as your teacher and Scripture as your text, you have "direct access" to God. This *Sola Scriptura* theory seems to exclude any church leaders. Why would you need any intermediaries at all, such as deacons and presbyter-elders?

Bishops

First Timothy 3:1-7 authorizes Timothy to appoint *episkopos* "bishops" not *presbyter* "elders." Perhaps you meant to quote Titus 1:5-9, where Paul authorizes Titus to appoint bishops and elders.

Whatever happened to the bishops in Christ's church? Did they disappear with the 12 apostles?

Delegation of Authority

In letter 4, I asked where Scripture affirms that it "delegates authority to the church, to parents, to governments,"[67] as the *"source and standard of truth...alone."*[68] If true, then men would be "true and authoritative only to the extent that they accurately communicate the truths of God's Word."[69] Does that mean that Scripture delegates authority to deacons and presbyters, not the imposition of hands? Where does the Bible mention this teaching so essential to Protestantism?

Obedience

Obedience to authority is important to Catholics. In previous letters, you implied that obedience to authority is childish, that we should *only* listen to and submit to Scripture,[70] not church leaders (except those who knew Christ firsthand).[71] If church leaders have true authority, then what should our attitude be toward them?

Infallibility

Another of our concerns is infallible interpretation. As God, the Holy Spirit is unquestionably infallible; nevertheless, Bible interpreters are human, thus can err.[72] Can anyone infallibly interpret the Bible or judge between two contradictory interpretations? How do we know?

Excommunication

Paul commands the Corinthians "to deliver this man to Satan" (1 Corinthians 5:5). Excommunication exemplifies church authority: either you have authority to kick someone out or you do not. Who (if anyone) in your church has the authority to excommunicate?

That does it for now. You and your family are in my prayers.

Yours in the Lord,

John

Letter 18

Dear John,

The questions in your last letter caused me to realize that we have never discussed at any length my position on the church. I am thankful, therefore, for this opportunity. I believe this may also help you to understand my perspective on other topics as well. I will begin with the nature and origin of the church.

The Nature of the Church

The Scriptures call those people who have entered into a family relationship with God through Jesus Christ the church. "To all who received him," the apostle John writes, "who believed in his name, he gave power to become children of God" (John 1:12). They have the privilege of addressing God as "Abba! Father!" (Romans 8:15). This is a permanent relationship. Should one of His children go astray, the Father disciplines him in love (Hebrews 12:6), but He does not cast him out.

Elsewhere the Bible describes the intimate relationship between Christ and His church as that of a groom to his bride (2 Corinthians 11:2; Ephesians 5:25-33). Speaking of marriage, the Bible says: "Christ loved the church and gave himself up for her" (Ephesians 5:25).

Scripture also uses the human body as a picture of the church. Christ is "the head of the body, the church" (Colossians 1:18). The redeemed are "the members of the body" (1 Corinthians 12:12).

115

The church is "God's people" (1 Peter 2:10). The Bible calls them "saints" (Philemon 5), "believers" (1 Corinthians 14:22), and "Christians" (Acts 11:26). It describes them as "saved" (Ephesians 2:8), "ransomed" (1 Peter 1:18), "forgiven" (1 John 2:12), at "peace with God" (Romans 5:1), and "holy and blameless before him" (Ephesians 1:4).

Some mistakenly think of the church as a building with cross and steeple. The church of the New Testament, however, has no walls. More than an organization, it is an *organism*—a living entity of interdependent members. Consequently, Christians don't "go to church"; they *are* the church.

The Birth of the Church

The church did not exist in Old Testament times. Nor did God reveal its design and purpose to Moses or the other prophets of the Old Covenant. We learn of the church from Jesus, "the mediator of a new covenant" (Hebrews 9:15) and His apostles, the "ministers of a new covenant" (2 Corinthians 3:6). Scripture calls the church "the mystery of Christ" (Ephesians 3:4). He unveiled it. He is at the center of it and is the source of its life.

In the months before His crucifixion, Jesus said, "I will build my church" (Matthew 16:18). This is the first occurrence of the word *church* in the New Testament. Here Jesus speaks of it as something yet future. When did it begin? Before ascending into heaven, Christ promised His disciples, "Before many days you shall be baptized with the Holy Spirit" (Acts 1:5). We know from Paul's teaching that the baptism of the Holy Spirit is when a person becomes part of the church, the body of Christ (1 Corinthians 12:13).

The Church Is Not Israel

God's people of the Old Covenant are the nation of Israel, the Jews. God's people of the New Covenant are the church. We must not confuse the two.

116

Israel has its beginnings in the call of Abraham. To be a Jew, one must be a descendant of Jacob, also named Israel. Membership is by physical birth. The Jews formerly entered into the Old Covenant with God at Mount Sinai. Leviticus 26 summarizes this contract. God would bless them if they obeyed Him, and He would curse them if they forsook Him. Theirs was a conditional relationship based upon performance. Their promised blessings had an earthly focus—long life and prosperity in the land of Israel. Jerusalem was to be the center of their worship. Their priests were to be of the tribe of Levi. Their high priest was to be Aaron, Moses' brother, or one of his descendants.

The church differs from Israel in every respect. It began at Pentecost. Membership is by spiritual birth through faith in Christ Jesus (John 1:12). It is open to all people, both Jews and Gentiles (Galatians 3:28). In Christ they become "one new man in place of the two" (Ephesians 2:15). Theirs is an unconditional relationship based on grace. The blessings of the church have a heavenly focus—eternal life and an inheritance with Christ. Its worship also has a heavenly focus. Their high priest is Christ, "who is seated at the right hand of the throne of the Majesty in heaven" (Hebrews 8:1).

It won't do to take God's religious order for the Jews, christen it, and apply it to the church. The church is something new, something far more wonderful. Christ expressed this when He taught: "No one puts new wine into old wineskins; if he does, the wine will burst the skins, and the wine is lost, and so are the skins; but new wine is for fresh skins" (Mark 2:22).

God's Design for the Church

The Holy Spirit has preserved Christ's revelation of the church in the New Testament. He shows us the church in Acts, and tells us its foundational truths in the epistles.

The model God shows us for the church in the New Testament is marked by simplicity. The disciples preached the gospel. Some believed and were baptized (Acts 2:41). The apostles gathered these new believers into groups. These early Christians devoted themselves to the study of the apostles' teaching, sharing their lives with one another, remembering the Lord with bread and wine, and praying (Acts 2:42). Scripture refers to each group of Christians by the city or town in which it was located: "the church in Jerusalem" (Acts 8:1), "the church at Antioch" (Acts 13:1), "the church of God which is at Corinth" (1 Corinthians 1:2). We sometimes call these *local* churches to distinguish them from the church as a whole, or the *universal* church.

The epistles tell us that the universal church is one: "There is one body and one Spirit, just as you were called to the one hope that belongs to your call, one Lord, one faith, one baptism" (Ephesians 4:4-5). Regardless of a person's church affiliation, all born-again believers, having been baptized by the Holy Spirit, are one in Christ.

Ruling Authority in the Church

Ruling the worldwide church is Christ Himself. "He is the head of the body, the church" (Colossians 1:18), the "chief Shepherd" (1 Peter 5:4), and "high priest" (Hebrews 8:1). In all things He is to be "pre-eminent" (Colossians 1:18).

Christ has ordained elders, also known as bishops, to serve under Him over each local church (Acts 14:23). The Greek word translated "elders" is *presbuteroi*. It means "older men," indicating the spiritual maturity required for the position. The qualifications for the position are found in Titus 1:5-9 and 1 Timothy 3:1-7. "Bishops" is the translation of *episkopoi*, literally meaning "overseers." This word has their function in view. They supervise the people and ministries of the church. We can see the nature of their calling in Paul's exhortation to the elders of the church of Ephesus: "Take heed to yourselves and to all the flock, in which the Holy Spirit has made you guardians, to feed the church of the Lord which he obtained with his own blood" (Acts 20:28). Note that it is the Holy Spirit who makes an overseer, not the apostles or the church.

Assisting the elders are deacons. Paul lists the qualifications of a deacon in 1 Timothy 3:8-13. Deacons serve in various ministries, such as distributing food to the needy (Acts 6:1-6).

Serving Christ together with the elders and deacons are the other members of the church. The Holy Spirit, Scripture tells us, has given each Christian a spiritual gift for the common good (1 Corinthians 12:1-7). This is a supernatural ability for service. It involves ministries such as teaching, pastoring, evangelizing, exhorting, giving, leading, helping, and showing mercy (Romans 12:4-8; Ephesians 4:11). As each person does his or her part, they build up one another in the faith. The church matures and becomes more like Christ (Ephesians 4:11-16).

In the New Testament, there is no further governmental structure provided for the local or universal church (see Figure 18:1).

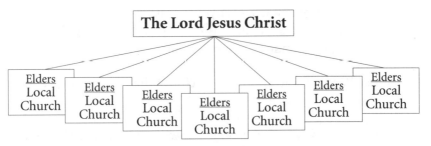

Figure 18:1
Organizational Diagram of the New Testament Church

I will pause here and answer the five questions from your last letter concerning church leadership.

➤ "Whatever happened to the bishops in Christ's church? Did they disappear with the 12 apostles?"

No, bishops, also known as elders, serve today in local churches in cities and towns throughout the world, even as in New Testament times. Following the biblical pattern, several bishops govern a local church.

- "Does Scripture delegate authority to deacons and presbyters, not the imposition of hands?"

We recognize the office and authority of the elders because God delegates authority to them through His Word. When we publicly recognize a new elder, we formally state before the congregation that we believe the Holy Spirit has called and ordained the man to serve as an elder. The current elders pray for him, laying hands on him. This is a symbol of their association with him as a fellow elder.

- "If church leaders have true authority, then what should our attitude be toward them?"

Scripture answers: "Obey your leaders and submit to them; for they are keeping watch over your souls, as men who will have to give account. Let them do this joyfully, and not sadly, for that would be of no advantage to you" (Hebrews 13:17).

- "Who (if anyone) in your church has the authority to excommunicate?"

The elders of the church, together with the congregation as a whole, have this authority (Matthew 18:15-20; 1 Corinthians 5:9-13). Such action is uncommon and reserved for cases of grave, unrepented sin.

Teaching Authority in the Church

As Jesus prepared to return to heaven, He promised His disciples that the Father would give them "another Counselor" (John 14:16) to be with them forever. Taking up residence within each believer, the Holy Spirit of God is the Christian's principal and infallible teacher of the church, "the Spirit of truth" (John 14:17). Jesus said the Spirit "will teach you all things" (John 14:26). He "will guide you into all the truth" (John 16:13).

The Spirit primarily teaches us in two ways. The first is directly through the Scriptures, opening our minds to understand them (1 Corinthians 2:10-16). Paul refers to having "the eyes of your hearts enlightened" (Ephesians 1:18). We call this *illumination.* The Spirit also instructs us through other Christians, especially those who have the gift of teaching (Ephesians 4:11). The two remaining questions from your last letter relate to this.

+ "Why, if we have the Holy Spirit and the Scriptures, would we 'need any intermediaries at all, such as deacons and presbyter-elders?'"

Ultimately speaking, Christians are not dependent on other people to grow in a knowledge of God, but can learn directly from His Word through the Spirit's teaching ministry. The apostle John wrote, "The anointing which you received from him abides in you, and you have no need that any one should teach you; as his anointing teaches you about everything, and is true, and is no lie, just as it has taught you, abide in him" (1 John 2:27). The Spirit often teaches us, however, through gifted teachers and the elders of the church. The latter "must hold firm to the sure word as taught, so that he may be able to give instruction in sound doctrine" (Titus 1:9). Deacons, on the other hand, serve primarily in support ministries, not as teachers.

We do not consider elders to be "intermediaries," serving as priests for the congregation. The New Testament knows nothing of a priestly class of Christians that went before God on behalf of the laity of the church. According to the New Testament, all Christians are priests and have direct access to God (1 Peter 2:5,9; Revelation 1:6).

+ "Can anyone infallibly interpret the Bible or judge between two contradictory interpretations?"

Only the Holy Spirit is infallible. The rest of us are capable of error. Therefore, we look to God's Word as our standard and source of truth, not the teachings of men. Should a doctrinal dispute arise within the church, it is the responsibility of the elders to resolve it. They must "be able both to exhort in sound doctrine and to refute those who contradict" (Titus 1:9 NASB).

I look forward, John, to our upcoming conversation on this topic. I'm sure you will have some interesting follow-up questions.

In Christ's love,

Jim

Conversation 4

Jim: I think we made a mistake scheduling this phone call for a Saturday afternoon. It's a beautiful spring day here in San Jose. It's a shame being inside here at the computer. What's it like down there in Southern California?

John: It's a little hazy, what *Angelinos* call "June Gloom," but it's very early this year. How are your Easter preparations? Do you use Lent to prepare for Holy Week and our Lord's passion and resurrection?

Jim: We emphasize the Lord's resurrection on Easter Sunday, but this isn't a season of special preparation for us. Knowing that Christ might return for us at any time, we seek to "be ready in season and out of season" (2 Timothy 4:2 NASB).

Does Israel find fulfillment in the church?

John: Well, let's get started.

Jim, your description of the Church mirrors the Second Vatican Council's *Lumen Gentium,* which describes the Church as God's people, family, Christ's body, the assembly of believers and saints, etc., based on spiritual bonds and not buildings. However, I have difficulty with your statement, "The church differs from Israel in every respect." This implies God had a very superficial relationship with Israel, whereas we see Israel as a prophetic image of Christ's

123

Church. Christ came not to destroy but to fulfill Israel in His Church (Matthew 5:17).

Like the church, Israel is called God's people (Deuteronomy 7:6), privileged to address Him, "Abba, Father!" (Jeremiah 3:18-22), as His children (Deuteronomy 32:6; Malachi 2:10) and firstborn son (Exodus 4:22). God disciplined Israel in love (Proverbs 3:11-12), promising not to forsake them (Deuteronomy 31:6-8; Joshua 1:5). Israel was also God's bride (Jeremiah 2:2; Isaiah 54:5-8) and sheepfold.[73]

The main difference between the Old and New Testament people of God seems to be that the Church fulfills the prophetic "pattern" that Israel represented (Hebrew 8:5). Would you concur?

Jim: No I wouldn't, John. God has a special place in His heart both for Israel and for the church, but they differ as to origin, membership, blessings, priesthood, and the nature of their relationship with God.

Does the priesthood of the faithful differ in Old and New Testaments?

John: You say "every Christian is a priest unto God," offering "spiritual sacrifices acceptable to God through Jesus Christ" (1 Peter 2:5). All Israelites were also priests, as God said: "Tell the people of Israel...you shall be to me a kingdom of priests" (Exodus 19:3,6; see also Isaiah 61:6) to offer pleasing sacrifices of broken and contrite hearts (Psalm 51:17), open ears (Psalm 40:6), thanksgiving (Psalm 50:14,23), and righteous deeds (Proverbs 21:3), similar to praising God and doing good (Hebrews 13:15-16) as suggested in the New Testament.

Does the New Testament priesthood of the faithful differ substantially from the Old?

Jim: Yes, substantially. Following the giving of the law at Mount Sinai, the Bible refers to Aaron and his sons alone as priests. Others of the tribe of Levi assisted them. The rest of Israel, members of the other 11 tribes, are simply called the "people." This threefold division of Israel—priests, Levites, people—is clear in the Old Testament (2 Chronicles 30:27; Ezra 9:1; Nehemiah 8:13).

Contrast this with New Testament priesthood. Peter wrote, "You are a chosen race, a royal priesthood, a holy nation, God's own people, that you may declare the wonderful deeds of him who called you out of darkness into his marvelous light" (1 Peter 2:9). The Christian's priesthood is stated as fact. Every Christian, whether Jew or Gentile, has direct access to the Father through the Lord Jesus Christ. Paul wrote, "For through him we both have access in one Spirit to the Father" (Ephesians 2:18). We don't need human intermediaries to approach God in prayer or worship.

Another important difference between the Jewish and Christian priesthoods is their sacrifice. God required the Aaronic priesthood of the Old Testament to continually offer blood sacrifices. For the Christian priesthood, "there is no longer any offering for sin" (Hebrews 10:18). Christ paid for sin in full at the cross (Mark 10:45). As He died, He proclaimed, "It is finished" (John 19:30). We, therefore, as New Testament priests, "continually offer up a sacrifice of praise to God, that is, the fruit of lips that acknowledge his name" (Hebrews 13:15).

John: I think I'm missing something. How does "sacrifice of praise" (Hebrews 13:15) differ *substantially* from a "sacrifice of deliverance and praise" (1 Maccabees 4:56), "thanksgiving" (Psalm 50:14), and "a broken spirit" (Psalm 51:17) offered by David—a non-Levitical Old Testament priest?

Jim: I wouldn't make a distinction between these. The distinction I made is that the New Testament priesthood does not make a blood sacrifice. We celebrate Christ's finished work of salvation. That's why I quoted Hebrews 10:18, "there is no longer any offering for sin."

John: Although Paul said, "I complete what is lacking in Christ's afflictions for the sake of his body, that is, the church" through his suffering (Colossian 1:24), the priestly sacrifices in 1 Peter 2:5 and Hebrews 13:15-16 do not detract from or add to the sacrifice of Christ, do they?

Jim: No. Christ's work on the cross was perfect.

Is fallible interpretation trustworthy?

John: If your scriptural interpretation is fallible, why should I or anyone else listen to it or to any other fallible intermediaries, especially when we all have direct access to God? Why would your fallible opinion be any more trustworthy than mine?

Jim: You seem to think that unless a person is infallible, he has nothing worth saying. Why then, might I ask, John, do you teach? You don't consider yourself infallible. Neither do the other priests and bishops of your church consider themselves infallible (with the exception of your Pope), yet they all teach. For that matter, why did anyone listen to the Pope before the bishops of your church declared him infallible in 1870?

As for trustworthiness, we require that a man be of high character and good reputation before we allow him to teach. Ultimately, however, it is not the man but the Scriptures that we trust. No matter who the speaker is, we turn to God's Word to carefully judge everything that is taught (1 Corinthians 14:29).

John: If we have direct access to the Holy Spirit, who is infallible and omnipotent, then wouldn't each Christian's interpretation illumined by the Holy Spirit also be infallible?

Jim: That's a good question, John. Apprehension of the Holy Spirit's leading is a spiritual exercise. It requires that a person be walking with God, have a good knowledge of

126

God's Word, and be willing to obey what God tells him to do. If these qualifications are lacking, the person's understanding will be imperfect.

John: Earlier you said we should turn to the Bible to resolve doctrinal controversies because God's written Word should have the final say.[74] Now you say it is "the responsibility of the elders to resolve it." We seem to be getting closer.

If elders from another "local church" (see Figure 18:1 on page 119) insisted that Scripture demands women be ordained pastors (since now, "there is neither male nor female; for you are all one in Christ Jesus" Galatians 3:28) yet the elders of your "local church" concluded that this contradicts Scripture, could your "local church" excommunicate another for a fallible interpretation of Scripture approved by its elders?

Jim: As for your first point, I don't see any contradiction. If a question arises in the church with regard to corporate worship or what will be publicly taught, it is the responsibility of the elders to resolve it. They are to turn to the Bible for the answer.

With regard to your question about excommunicating another church, we would not consider such action. Christ has not given us jurisdiction over other churches. He is the head of the church, not us. Scripture says, "Who are you to pass judgment on the servant of another? It is before his own master that he stands or falls" (Romans 14:4).

John: Catholics insist on infallibility, because as individuals, we err and make mistakes, and when we are left to our own devices, we tend to water down the truth for an easier lifestyle. I understand your concern that men in authority can err—like Peter, you, or I—but would you eliminate Peter's letters from the Bible simply because Paul rebuked him?[75]

Jim: I don't think anyone has suggested that we remove Peter's epistles from the Bible. Written under the inspiration of the Holy Spirit, they are in a class by themselves with the rest of Scripture. It is outside of his inspired writings that I have called into question Peter's alleged immunity to error. I should add that Peter himself never claimed to be infallible. It is the Roman Catholic Church that asserts this claim as part of its attempt to argue for the infallibility of its Pope.

John: You see the need and possibility of the Holy Spirit guiding Peter's words while he writes, despite his past misbehaviors, but not while he looses and binds. Can't the Holy Spirit accomplish this, too? Why place limits on the Holy Spirit's omnipotence?

Jim: We are not trying to limit the Holy Spirit. We are trying to keep people from asserting powers and prerogatives that God hasn't given them.

John: Jesus said to Peter, "Whatever you bind on earth shall be bound in heaven, and whatever you loose on earth shall be loosed in heaven" (Matthew 16:19). Does Jesus ever promise anything like, "Whatever Scripture binds will be bound in heaven, and whatever it looses will be loosed in heaven"?

Jim: Jesus said, "Truly, I say to you, till heaven and earth pass away, not an iota, not a dot, will pass from the law until all is accomplished" (Matthew 5:18).

Does submitting to leaders oppose Scripture?

John: Saying "Obey your leaders and submit to them" (Hebrews 13:17) doesn't contradict the need to submit to and obey Scripture, does it?

Jim: Not at all. As I said previously, all delegated authority is subordinate. Even elders must submit to the rule of Scripture. Should they go astray and ask us to do something contrary to God's Word, "We must obey God rather than men" (Acts 5:29).

John: But earlier, commenting on Hebrews 13:17, you said, "God expects us to obey Him, not them,"[76] "them" being Catholic Popes and bishops. How can you interpret the same passage to show it is all right for you to obey your leaders and wrong for us Catholics to obey ours?

Jim: I think the context of my comment is important here. I said, "When those whom God has given authority misuse their position, God expects us to obey Him, not them. When the high priest and the ruling council of the Jews ordered Peter and the apostles to stop preaching the gospel, they answered, 'We must obey God rather than men' (Acts 5:29)."[77] This applies to all leaders, whether they are in your church or my church—we must obey God first.

Where does the Bible teach that it delegates authority?

John: How God delegates authority is important, to identify who has authority and who doesn't, who we are obliged to obey and who not. Again, where does the Bible affirm that it "delegates authority to the church, to parents, to governments,"[78] as the *source and standard of truth...alone?"*[79] Would you admit there is no such scriptural reference?

Jim: No, I wouldn't. I will need to restate what I actually said, however, before explaining. I said that "Scripture is our chief authority, but we recognize that it delegates authority to the church, to parents, to governments." The Bible teaches the authority of the church in Matthew 18:15-20; Hebrews 13:17; 1 Thessalonians 5:12-13; 1 Peter 5:1-5; the authority of parents in Ephesians 6:1-4 and Colossians 3:20-21; the authority of government in Matthew 22:21 and Romans 13:1-7.

In another place I said, "God has preserved and transmitted to us the teachings of Christ in the Bible. When contrasting our position with that of Rome's, however, we express this belief with specific emphasis, saying: *the source*

129

and standard of truth is God's written Word alone." I provide extensive biblical support for this in Letters 3 and 5, as well as in Conversation 1.

Are your elders qualified?

John: Your interpretation that elders (*presbuteroi*) are the same as bishops (*episkopoi*) is interesting. Paul certainly distinguishes the two in Titus 1:5-6 and 7-9 and in 1 Timothy 3:1-7 and 5:17-20. If they are identical, then that makes Matthias the first replacement elder, since he is the first bishop (*episkope*, Acts 1:20).[80]

That being the case, then does your church require that elders be someone "who have accompanied us...beginning from the baptism of John until the day when he was taken up from us" (Acts 1:21-22)? These are qualifications you require for Catholic bishop-elders![81]

Jim: Your church has three degrees of ordination, namely: the "episcopate, presbyterate, and diaconate" [CCC 1536], the offices held by your "bishops, priests, and deacons" [CCC 1554]. I understand, therefore, why you would want to make bishops (*episkopoi*) and elders (*presbuteroi*) into two distinct groups. I think you are mistaken, however, in this effort. The New Testament identifies them as one and the same. We can see this in the way the Bible uses the words interchangeably in the same context. For example, Paul "sent to Ephesus and called to him the elders of the church" (Acts 20:17). When the "elders" arrived, Paul addressed them using the Greek term that translates to "bishops" or "overseers" (see Acts 20:28). In his letter to Titus, Paul tells him to "appoint elders in every town" (Titus 1:5). Two verses later, while giving the qualifications of an elder, he writes: "For a bishop, as God's steward, must be blameless" (Titus 1:7). Finally, compare the qualifications listed there, Titus 1:5-9, with those for the office of bishop in 1 Timothy 3:1-7. They are virtually the same.

This does not mean that every use of either word regardless of context refers to the leadership of the local church. As mentioned in my previous letter, the Greek word translated "elder" (*presbuteros*) means "older man." It can refer simply to an aged man (1 Timothy 5:1; Titus 2:2). Other places it refers to Jewish rabbis, the presiding body of the synagogue in Capernaum, and certain members of the Jewish high council (Mark 7:3-5; Luke 7:3; Luke 22:66).

The word translated "bishop" (*episkopos*) means an "overseer" or "superintendent." Greek literature uses it with reference to government officials, trustees, military strategists, and even the Greek gods. It occurs five times in the New Testament. Four times it refers to the leaders of the local church (Acts 20:28; Philippians 1:1; 1 Timothy 3:2; Titus 1:7). Once it is used of Christ, the "Guardian of your souls" (1 Peter 2:25).

The word you refer to in Acts 1:20, *episkope,* is related to the word for bishop, *episkopos,* but has a different meaning. It occurs four times in the New Testament. Twice it is translated "visitation" (Luke 19:44; 1 Peter 2:12); once it is translated "office of a bishop" (1 Timothy 3:1); once "office" (Acts 1:20). Context determines which meaning is correct.

Your question relates to the last occurrence of the word in Acts 1:20. Peter suggests that a replacement be sought for Judas, who had killed himself. He quotes David, who prophesied, "His office *[episkope]* let another man take" (Acts 1:20). Judas' office, of course, was that of apostle, not church bishop. Two candidates met the requirements set by the apostles, and the apostles "cast lots for them, and the lot fell on Matthias; and he was enrolled with the eleven apostles" (Acts 1:26).

We do not consider our bishops to be the successors of the apostles. If we did, we would require that they meet the biblical qualifications for apostolic succession that you list from Acts 1:21-22.

John: Your identification of bishops and elders is fallible interpretation, but would you trust it over Clement of Rome's—
the first-century Christian whom I cited earlier[82]—or over
Augustine's, bishop of Hippo, who believed bishops indeed
succeeded the apostles?[83]

Jim: I would like to see more of what Clement and Augustine
said about these things, whether or not they do indeed disagree with me on these matters.

I am not alone in my position that bishops and elders
are one and the same. The editors of the Catholic *New
American Bible* included this footnote on Titus 1:5-9: "This
instruction on the selection and appointment of presbyters, [is] substantially identical in 1 Timothy 3:1-7....In
Titus 1:6,7 and Acts 20:17; 20:28 the terms *episkopos* and
presbuteros ('bishops' and 'presbyter') refer to the same persons."[84]

John: First Corinthians 12:12-31 says that members of Christ's
body fulfill different roles or ministries, "first apostles,
second prophets, third teachers" (verse 28), but "the eye
cannot say to the hand...nor again the head to the feet, 'I
have no need of you'" (verse 21). Yet you boldly say Christ's
body no longer needs apostles—that is, it no longer needs
a mouth to proclaim His gospel in an authoritative way.

Jim: We hold that the Word of God should be proclaimed with
authority. It is not the authority of the speaker, however,
but of the source, God's Word.

John: In many ways we are not that far apart on some of these
issues.

Jim: You've asked some good questions, John.

Letter 19

Monday, April 9, 2001

Dear Jim,

Our last conversation was a pleasant surprise. I expected a more defensive response to my tough questions. You answered them well, addressing most of the issues (although I felt that you misunderstood or dodged me on one or two of them). We basically agree on many issues, differing in the extent of their application. May God grant us continued light along this path.

Please remember that as I point out our agreements and differences, I never intend to misrepresent your position. I am human and I may misread you at times.

Nature of the Church

We both see that the all-holy God (Leviticus 19:2) made Israel a holy people in His everlasting love (Isaiah 54:8). Holiness was their true identity (2 Maccabees 15:22-24), which found fulfillment in Christ's Church. Although we both see many parallels between Israel and the Church, you seem to avoid the ones linking Old and New Testament priesthood.

I tried to prove how every Jew was a priest, not just conditionally. You seemed to have missed my point: King David wasn't a ministerial priest; nevertheless, the Spirit inspired him to exercise his royal priesthood, which did not replace or eliminate the ministerial priesthood. Yet his royal priesthood found true fulfillment in the Christian.

The Old Testament ministerial priesthood included ministering the Word and reconciliation. Parallel ministries occur in the New Testament: the apostles (Acts 6:4), Paul (Colossians 1:25), and Luke (Luke 1:2) ministering the word; Paul ministering reconciliation, appealing to God on our behalf (2 Corinthians 5:18-20). Perhaps we need to study how the Old Testament ministerial priesthood could find fulfillment in the New,[85] and how the multitude of Old Testament sacrifices find fulfillment in Christ's one sacrifice on the cross and is applied to each Christian.

At least we fully agree that the sacrifice of the New Testament priesthood—whatever the form it takes—does not add to or detract from Christ's sacrifice on the cross.

Infallibility and Excommunication

We have tackled some real issues here. First, we both agree that bishop-elders have an important role in resolving doctrinal controversy without contradicting the essential role of Scripture.

Second, we both believe in the gift of infallibility, while differing in its application. You seem to limit infallibility to the Spirit protecting the prophets or evangelists as they write, and the Church as she selects the canon of Scripture. Catholics extend this infallibility to include the Holy Spirit protecting Popes (and bishops in communion with the Pope[86]) as they publicly exercise their office in binding Christians regarding something in faith and morals. Catholics believe that His protection continues to be at work.

We did much to dispel the stereotype that human sinfulness makes infallibility impossible, since Peter's sinfulness and errors didn't limit the Spirit's omnipotence as he guided Cephas in writing 1 and 2 Peter.[87]

It's hard to obey sinful leaders. Christ warned us that some in His Church would cause scandal (Matthew 18:5-10), since His Church has weeds mixed in with the wheat (Matthew 13:24-30). Yet this doesn't limit God's power, who commanded the Jews to obey even the woefully sinful scribes and Pharisees:

> The scribes and the Pharisees sit on Moses' seat; so practice and observe whatever they tell you, but not what they do; for they preach, but do not practice.
>
> MATTHEW 23:2-3

The Catholic Church agrees that we should not obey leaders who ask us to do something contrary to God's will, our conscience, Scripture, or some higher authority.[88]

You seem to acknowledge having no authority to condemn the errors of other Christian churches, yet do you condemn the Catholic Church?

Finally, we both agree that God's Word is binding in heaven; we differ on whether church authority is similarly binding.

Delegation of Authority

Of course Scripture "teaches the authority of the church...of parents...of government,"[89] but that's not the question. You must have misunderstood me.

Bishops

You showed that the terms *elder* (*presbuteros*) and *bishop* (*episkopos*) are *not* precisely defined legal terms in Scripture,[90] as I did with the term *apostle*.[91] Christ is "the apostle and high priest of our confession" (Hebrews 3:1), *bishop* of our souls (1 Peter 2:25), and our only *pastor* (Ezekiel 37:24). Ignatius of Antioch,[92] Clement of Rome,[93] etc., show us how early Christians understood these terms, which was later confirmed by Augustine.[94]

We both agree that the specific conditions for Judas' replacement in Acts 1:15-26 don't apply to our own bishops today. Moreover, we seem to be dispelling other stereotypes, like the problem issue of calling Popes and Catholic priests *father*, as we see spiritual paternity lived out in Scripture.[95]

Jim, I could go into more. Let's continue to ask the Holy Spirit's guidance in our journey.

135

This is somewhat delayed because I got snowed in last weekend giving a retreat to college men in the San Bernardino mountains. I hope your weather was better. Please give Jean and the girls my best.

In His Word,

John

Letter 20

Dear John,

Sorry to hear about the snow. We've had mild weather here. I haven't been able to enjoy it, however. I've had jury duty this week. It's made me more thankful for salvation in Christ, knowing I will not have to stand before God in judgment.

Priesthood

According to Scripture, all true Christians are members of the same priesthood. It is a "holy" and "royal priesthood" (1 Peter 2:5,9). There is no clergy/laity distinction in the New Testament. Your case for a separate "ministerial priesthood" lacks both definition and biblical support. Neither do I concur with your conclusion that we have overcome the problem with calling men by the title of *father*. When Jesus said, "Call no man your father on earth" (Matthew 23:9), He was prohibiting the use of the title to honor one man as spiritually superior to others. This is the very context in which it is used in Catholicism. I suggest we revisit these issues later when we take up the topic of worship. This is too important to leave unresolved.

Infallibility

Your case for papal infallibility rests heavily upon Jesus' statement concerning the Pharisees in Matthew 23. You quote this again in your last letter: "The scribes and the Pharisees sit on

Moses' seat; so practice and observe whatever they tell you" (Matthew 23:2). Note, however, that Jesus does not say that they "have been seated" (passive voice), implying God put them there. Rather, He said "the Pharisees sit on Moses' seat." The Greek verb is in the active voice. The *New American Standard Bible* translates the verse: "The scribes and the Pharisees have seated themselves in the chair of Moses" (Matthew 23:2). They came to power during the latter half of the Greek era (332-63 B.C.), gradually gaining influence over the people, and that without divine authorization. In Matthew 23:2, Jesus is simply stating a widely accepted fact among the Jews of that period. He is not validating the position which the Pharisees had assumed for themselves. To the contrary, Jesus said of them, "Every plant which my heavenly Father has not planted will be rooted up" (Matthew 15:13).

Why, then, did Jesus go on to say, "...therefore all that they tell you, do and observe..." (Matthew 23:3, NASB)? The logical connector between the two verses is "therefore," introducing a conclusion. The scribes and the Pharisees had taken *Moses' seat* as the teachers of the Law. "Therefore," Jesus tells His disciples, "all that they tell you, do and observe," meaning *all from the teaching of Moses*. The command does not apply to their false teachings based on the traditions of the rabbis. As explained earlier, Jesus refused to submit to these, and taught His disciples to do likewise (Mark 7:1-13).[96]

For these reasons, we should not consider Matthew 23:2-3 a blanket endorsement of the Pharisees' official teaching. Neither can we infer from these verses that Jesus considered the Pharisees to be infallible, or that their infallibility was transferred to your Popes. Contrary to your position, in the verses that follow, Jesus condemns the Pharisees in the strongest of terms. He pronounces woe upon them as "hypocrites" (Matthew 23:13), "blind guides" (Matthew 23:16), "blind fools" (Matthew 23:17), "sons of those who murdered the prophets" (Matthew 23:31), and "serpents" (Matthew 23:33). He concludes by warning them: "How are you to escape being sentenced to hell?" (Matthew 23:33).

I spoke with Steve Miller, senior editor at Harvest House. Their publication committee reviewed our book proposal last week. Steve said there was much discussion. It's not every day that an evangelical publisher considers a book coauthored by a Catholic priest. Nevertheless, the outcome was positive. The committee thought an open and honest discussion of the issues separating Catholics and evangelicals was an excellent concept for a book. They asked if you and I could join them in Eugene to talk further about the project and meet their staff. If you are open to this, John, please e-mail me some dates that would be convenient for you in May or June. I'll work out the details with Steve.

In Christ's love,

Jim

TOPIC 3
Initial Salvation

How does
one obtain it?

Letter 21

THURSDAY, APRIL 26, 2001

Dear John,

Thanks for the dates you sent for a visit to Eugene. They all work for me. I forwarded them to Steve Miller. I will let you know as soon as I hear something.

This letter begins our discussion of salvation. Along with authority, it is at the heart of the issues that divide Roman Catholics and evangelicals. I think I should point out that the order we settled on for the next four topics fits better into your way of thinking than mine. Evangelicals understand eternal salvation primarily in terms of a single life decision that settles the matter once and for all. Catholicism presents salvation as a process, spanning a person's life. I assume that is why you would like to first discuss the initial stages of salvation, then the Eucharist, Mary, and lastly, the final stages of salvation. I think I can make this order work for the sake of our discussion.

I'll begin with a summary of my position of the topics we have grouped under "initial salvation."

> The good news of Jesus Christ is that He "came to seek and to save the lost" (Luke 19:10). On the cross, Jesus gave "his life as a ransom for many" (Mark 10:45). On the third day He arose, never to die again. God now graciously offers us complete forgiveness and eternal life (Romans 6:23). We receive these through faith in

Christ: "By grace you have been saved through faith; and this is not your own doing, it is the gift of God— not because of works, lest any man should boast" (Ephesians 2:8). The moment we trust Christ, we are born again to the newness of life (John 3:7; Romans 6:4). Baptism is an outward expression of this inward decision. The Holy Spirit helps us grow in holiness by enabling us to understand our blessing in Christ and to walk accordingly.

In my next letter I will explain these concepts more fully. Send me your opening questions, and I will try to address them as well.

In Christ's love,

Jim

Letter 22

Dear Jim,

Thank you for pursuing publishing possibilities. Perhaps we should slow down, however. It is more important to ascertain Christ's true teaching and what the Holy Spirit is saying to us in Scripture than publishing books or winning arguments. Some comments in Letter 20 seemed rushed to me, almost as though you had missed some of our previous discussion. For example, I never used Matthew 23 in my case for infallibility.

If I try to highlight obvious areas of agreement, you return to accentuate our differences. This is a bit frustrating, but—I keep reminding myself—it is not my arguments but the Holy Spirit that must convict us of the truth. The desire to forge a greater unity in Christ's body moves me to continue this dialogue despite the differences.

I do appreciate your accepting the order of topics. It is true—Catholics don't look upon salvation as "a single life decision that settles the matter once and for all," but as an ongoing relationship with Christ, a relationship nourished by our response to grace and ruptured by grievous infidelity.

Your position statement is ironically similar to the *Catechism of the Catholic Church*:

> Justification has been merited for us by the Passion
> of Christ who offered himself on the cross as...

atonement for the sins of all men. Justification is conferred in Baptism, the sacrament of faith. It conforms us to the righteousness of God...[which] "has been manifested apart from law...through faith in Jesus Christ for all who believe....[All] are justified by his grace as a gift, through the redemption which is in Christ Jesus, whom God put forward as an expiation by his blood, to be received by faith...[God] himself is righteous and that he justifies him who has faith in Jesus (Romans 3:21-26)."

[CCC 1992]

However, one comment, "The moment we trust Christ, we are born again to the newness of life" needs further refinement to be acceptable to us Catholics. Hopefully we can refine its meaning.

Faith and Baptism

Catholics believe that faith and baptism...

* erases our past sins by rebirth [CCC 1262-3] (John 3:5-6; Acts 2:38),

* justifying us in the Holy Spirit [CCC 683, 1215, 1266, 1992, 2020] (Romans 3:21-26; Titus 3:5)

* as children of God [CCC 1243, 1265, 1997] (John 1:12-13; Galatians 4:3-7),

* members of Christ's body, the Church [CCC 790, 1267-70] (1 Corinthians 12:13; 1 Peter 2:5-9).

In describing how faith and baptism in Christ produce justification, how does your interpretation compare?

Justification a Single Event

Where does the Bible describe salvation as "a single life decision that settles the matter once and for all"?

Faith and Sin

If our relationship with Christ is *spousal*, it demands an ongoing *response*. One act of infidelity can destroy it. But Luther wrote:

> Be a sinner—and a big sinner—but have faith in Christ....No sin can separate us from Him, even if we were to kill or commit adultery thousands of times each day.[97]

How is this consistent with Scripture?

Sacraments

You don't answer your own question, "What is a sacrament?" Are they mere symbols?

Infant Baptism

Orthodox, Lutheran, Anglican, Methodist, Reformed, Presbyterian, and some evangelical churches allow infant baptism. From previous discussions, you've condemned this practice as contrary to Scripture. Baptists, Churches of Christ, Assemblies of God, Mormons, Jehovah's Witnesses concur with you. Other churches eliminate baptism altogether. Is this one of those topics where you just don't have "jurisdiction over other churches" and shouldn't "pass judgment"?[98]

This should start our discussion.

In Christ's peace,

John

Letter 23

Dear John,

Thanks for the questions you sent. I am concerned, however, that you felt Letter 20 was rushed and somewhat missed your point. My schedule does not always allow me adequate time for our correspondence. In addition to my regular responsibilities here in San Jose, I am preparing for several upcoming conferences. I leave in the morning for a retreat in Wisconsin, where I will be teaching students from Emmaus Bible College. Next week I'm in Southern California, speaking at a conference in Claremont. Later in August, I will be in Honduras. I am sorry if in the rush of things I misrepresented you.

Matthew 23 and Infallibility

You mentioned Matthew 23 as an example of how I had misunderstood you. You said you never used it in your case for infallibility. Here's what I thought I heard you saying:

- Moses and Joshua had to be infallible—since God required all to obey them (Deuteronomy 34:9).[99]

- The Pharisees had to be infallible—since Christ required all to obey them (Matthew 23:1-3).[100]

- Similarly the leaders of the church must be infallible—since God requires Christians to obey them (Hebrews 13:17).[101]

One thing I know for certain is that I am not infallible, so maybe I missed your point.

Agreements and Disagreements

You also said you were a bit frustrated at my approach to our dialogue. You wrote, "If I try to highlight obvious areas of agreement, you return to accentuate our differences."[102] Possibly we should consider for a moment the goal of our correspondence and the presumptions upon which it is based. Here I will speak only for myself.

We are divided by doctrine. We understand the Christian faith differently. Our differences are substantive; our positions mutually exclusive. You may consider such emphasis counterproductive to achieving unity. I do not. As I stated earlier, when Jesus prayed for the church "that they may all be one" (John 17:21), He also asked the Father to "sanctify them in the truth" (John 17:17). Truth precedes unity. We are divided because we disagree as to the truth. Nothing of lasting value can be achieved by minimizing our differences or claiming there is agreement where there is not. We must find common ground *in* the truth, not *despite* the truth. I believe this can only be accomplished by facing our differences head-on.

I'm interested in hearing your perspective on this matter. Until then, I shall proceed to present my understanding of initial salvation.

Our Problem

God created Adam and Eve to enjoy friendship with Him forever. He placed them in the Garden of Eden and gave them free rein, with one restriction. God commanded Adam, saying, "Of the tree of the knowledge of good and evil you shall not eat, for in the day that you eat of it you shall die" (Genesis 2:17). The penalty would be more than just physical death (the separation of their souls from their bodies); it would also be spiritual death (the separation of their spirits from God's). Tempted by Satan, Adam and

Eve chose to disobey God. The results were tragic and far-reaching. God cast them out of the Garden, banishing them from His presence. Sin, suffering, and death became part of their everyday lives. This spread like a plague to their descendants (Romans 5:12). For this reason we enter life alienated from God and sinners by nature. Should we die in this condition, we will experience eternal separation from God. This is the "the second death" (Revelation 20:14), what the Bible calls "hell" (Luke 12:5).

God's Solution

Moved by His mercy and love, God sent His beloved Son to rescue us. Jesus did this by becoming one of us. Born of Mary through the power of the Holy Spirit, He took on human nature, though without sin (Philippians 2:5-8; 1 John 3:9). He came, in His own words, "to give his life as a ransom for many" (Mark 10:45). On the cross, God placed the penalty of our sins upon Jesus, punishing Him in our place. There, Jesus gave His life for ours. Christ "died for sins once for all, the righteous for the unrighteous, that he might bring us to God, being put to death in the flesh but made alive in the spirit" (1 Peter 3:18). Prophesying 700 years earlier, Isaiah wrote of the Messiah, "All we like sheep have gone astray; we have turned every one to his own way; and the LORD has laid on him the iniquity of us all" (Isaiah 53:4).

God's Offer

God now makes a most gracious offer: complete forgiveness and eternal life, if we will repent and believe the gospel (Mark 1:15).

Repentance is a change of mind about God and self. It is admitting that I am a guilty sinner, helpless to save myself. It is not *reformation,* an attempt to somehow clean up my life and become acceptable to God. Neither is it *reparation,* an effort to make amends for my sins through pious acts, remorse, or good works. Rather, repentance is an inward response to the convicting ministry of the Holy Spirit (John 16:8-11). One might express repentance by saying, "Lord, I have sinned against You. I'm sorry. I want to live a life pleasing to You, if You will make me able. Help me!"

Believing is placing my faith in Jesus to save me. He is the object of faith. What I believe about Him is the gospel: "that Christ died for our sins in accordance with the scriptures, that he was buried, that he was raised on the third day" (1 Corinthians 15:3-4). This is not mere intellectual ascent or simple agreement, such as reciting a creed. Rather it is *heartfelt dependence,* praying, "God, thank You for sending Your Son to die for my sins. I place my trust in Jesus to save me."

The New Birth

The moment we trust Jesus for salvation, life-changing effects take place. God forgives our sins (Colossians 2:13). He breaks the power that sin had over us and sets us free to live in the "newness of life" (Romans 6:4-7). We are "born anew" (John 3:5) and become "a new creation" (2 Corinthians 5:17). Peace with God is restored (Romans 5:1-2). We are united with Christ (Romans 6:5). We become a child of God, and He welcomes us into His family (John 1:12; Galatians 3:26). The Holy Spirit gives us a spiritual gift that we might serve others (1 Corinthians 12:7-11). God grants us eternal life (John 10:28), making us citizens of heaven (Philippians 3:20). The Holy Spirit comes to dwell within us (Romans 8:9), guaranteeing us an inheritance in heaven (Ephesians 1:13-14). The list of blessings goes on. It may well be endless, as Ephesians 1:3 and 2:7 seem to indicate.

Justification

Concurrent with these effects is a change in our legal standing before God. The Bible calls this change *justification.* It is a judicial act of God. Prior to it, we stand guilty before God and condemned. After justification God considers us innocent, righteous, and blameless in His sight. Justification is a ruling that no one may challenge: "Who shall bring any charge against God's elect? It is God who justifies; who is to condemn?" (Romans 8:33-34).

More than the forgiveness of sins, justification includes a positive reckoning in which God declares the person righteous in His sight, crediting to his account "the righteousness of God" (Romans 3:22). Abraham serves as an example. He "believed God," the Bible tells us, "and it was reckoned to him as righteousness" (Romans 4:3).

God "justifies him who has faith in Jesus" (Romans 3:26). Thereafter God considers him perfectly righteous in His sight. This is not because the person has cleaned up his life and is living a perfectly righteous life, but because of his faith in Jesus. Paul wrote, "To the one who does not work, but believes in Him who justifies the ungodly, his faith is credited as righteousness" (Romans 4:5 NASB).

Living the New Life

Though the standing of the newly justified believer is perfect before God, his personal condition may be in need of a major overhaul. We call the process by which a Christian learns to live more holy and become like Christ *sanctification*. Sanctification has various aspects in evangelical theology. *Positional sanctification* refers to the believer's perfect standing before God in Christ. *Experiential sanctification*, the kind being discussed here, refers to the process by which the believer becomes more like Christ in his daily living. *Final sanctification* refers to the state of ultimate perfection the believer will enjoy in the next life.

Sanctification is a work of the Holy Spirit (Romans 8:1-17). The new Christian must learn to "put to death the deeds of the body" (Romans 8:13) and to "walk by the Spirit" (Galatians 5:16). Step by step, he learns to replace sinful practices with godly disciplines, such as prayer, participation in the Lord's Supper, Bible study, Christian fellowship, and service (Acts 2:42). He must learn to yield his life each day to God as "a living sacrifice, holy and acceptable to God" (Romans 12:1). The local church helps him in this process by providing teaching, pastoral care, and training for service (Ephesians 4:11-16).

Questions and Answers

Before concluding, I want to answer the questions from your last letter.

- In describing how faith and baptism in Christ produce justification, how does your interpretation compare with Catholicism?

Not very well. We agree as to some of the benefits of justification, but not as to the means by which a person receives them. Scripture teaches that we are justified by faith, not by baptism or by faith plus baptism. Paul wrote: "We maintain that a man is justified by faith" (Romans 3:28 NASB).

- Where does the Bible describe salvation as "a single life decision that settles the matter once and for all"?

Under the heading "The New Birth" on page 151, I listed 12 of the many blessings a person receives the moment he or she believes, each with a Scripture reference. These blessings are permanent and irreversible, thus settling a person's eternal destiny the moment he believes.

- Is Luther consistent with Scripture when he counsels, "Be a sinner—and a big sinner—but have faith in Christ....No sin can separate us from Him, even if we were to kill or commit adultery thousands of times each day"?[103]

This letter is from Luther to his colleague Philipp Melanchthon. Luther begins by explaining, "God does not save those who are only imaginary sinners." He wants Melanchthon to understand the full extent of his sinfulness that he might better appreciate the saving work of Christ. His reference to killing or committing adultery "thousands of times a day" is clearly hyperbole, an obvious exaggeration used for effect. His point is that

Christ paid an infinite price for our sins, not a meager one that can only cover a finite number of sins.

◆ What is a sacrament? Are they mere symbols?

We neither use the word *sacrament* nor find the Catholic concept of it in the Bible.

We have two practices that some call *ordinances,* for Christ formally ordained them. These are baptism (Matthew 28:19) and the Lord's Supper (1 Corinthians 11:20). Baptism is an outward symbol of the inward change that takes place the moment a person trusts Christ. We will be discussing the Lord's Supper later.

◆ Is infant baptism one of those topics where you just don't have "jurisdiction over other churches" and shouldn't "pass judgment"?

I wrote earlier that we do not have "jurisdiction over other churches"[104] with regard to a question you asked about excommunicating another church. This comment should not be applied to the context of examining whether a doctrine is correct or not. The Bible tells us to "test everything; hold fast what is good" (1 Thessalonians 5:21).

With regard to infant baptism, there is no mention of it in the Bible. Those who say that baptism justifies an infant are teaching contrary to Scripture. God justifies the one who has faith in Christ, not the one who is merely baptized.

Give me a call when you get a chance. I would like to discuss these issues. I'll be back in my office May 14. Harvest House would like us to visit Eugene to discuss the book the second week of June. They will be contacting you directly about the trip.

In Christ's love,

Jim

Conversation 5

TUESDAY, MAY 22, 2001

John: How was your trip to Southern California? I would have loved to have seen you and your family.

Jim: We thought about coming by but the weekend was over-scheduled as it was. We drove a 12-passenger van down after school on Thursday, arriving at about 10:30 P.M. Each of the girls brought along a friend. Michael Puopolo, whom you have met, also came. The nine of us spent Friday at Disneyland. Saturday and Sunday we were at the conference at which I was speaking. Immediately after lunch on Sunday, we headed for home. There wasn't a moment to spare. Hopefully we can talk during our visit to Eugene in three weeks.

Were Old Testament Jews saved without faith in Christ?

John: Your letter reassured me of your commitment to unity based on the truth. In this we are united.

Now, to our current issue. You jump from "Our Problem" to "God's Solution" without mentioning the Old Covenant, as though it has little importance to God's plan of salvation. If justification effects "a change in our legal standing before God," were Old Testament Jews saved or justified even though they had no opportunity to believe in Christ?

155

Jim: Who had more opportunity to believe in Christ than the Jews? Their prophets had been telling of the coming of the Messiah for centuries. Many believed and were saved. Abraham, the father of the Jews, was justified by faith (Galatians 3:6). The same was true of King David (Romans 4:5-8). Moses believed, looking to the coming of the Christ (Hebrews 11:24-26). So did Daniel (Daniel 9:26). By faith they looked *forward* to the Messiah's coming. By faith we look *back* to Christ's incarnation, crucifixion, and resurrection.

John: Jim, clearly baptized believers who are faithful to Christ shall be saved. But what about persons who die having lived a good life—perhaps Buddhists or Muslims—without any opportunity to hear and believe Christ's gospel? Would these persons be damned to hell for all eternity?

Jim: To some extent, God has revealed Himself to every person, giving each an opportunity for salvation. The Bible says, "Ever since the creation of the world his invisible nature, namely, his eternal power and deity, has been clearly perceived in the things that have been made. So they are without excuse" (Romans 1:20). He has also given us a conscience. It reminds us of our moral accountability to God (Romans 2:14-16). I believe that if a person responds to the light God has given him, God will give him greater light. We have examples of this in the lives of the Ethiopian eunuch (Acts 8:26-40), the Roman centurion Cornelius (Acts 10:1-48), and the Areopagite Dionysius (Acts 17:16-34).

We might also ask, Who, other than Jesus, ever died "having lived a good life"? The Bible answers, "None is righteous, no, not one" (Romans 3:10). "All have turned aside, together they have gone wrong; no one does good, not even one" (Romans 3:12). This applies to Buddhists, Muslims, Catholics, and evangelicals, regardless of how "good" others might think them to be.

Finally, divine forgiveness is not a matter of leniency toward better-than-average sinners. Rather, it is the just cancellation of the penalty of our sins based upon Christ having paid the penalty for us. What remedy for sin do Buddhism and Islam offer?

John: None, for Catholics believe that they too can only be saved in and through Christ Jesus.

Now, the *Catechism of the Catholic Church*, with its scriptural references, states that one cannot possibly please God (Hebrews 11:6), become a child of God, and be justified and attain eternal life without believing and being faithful to Christ [CCC 161]. Will a Catholic Christian trusting Jesus and trying to be faithful to Him make it to heaven?

Jim: Salvation isn't a matter of one's church affiliation. Any person who places his trust in Christ to save him—believing that Christ died, was buried, and rose again—will be saved. But when you throw in that extra little phrase, "trusting Jesus *and trying to be faithful to Him*," you mix faith with works. This was the error of the Galatians. They thought that in addition to faith in Christ they had to perform certain aspects of the Jewish law to be acceptable to God. Paul condemns this teaching in his letter to the Galatians.

Are not faith, baptism, and obedience essential?

John: You say, "Scripture teaches that we are justified by faith, not by baptism or by faith plus baptism." Didn't Christ tell the apostles: "Go...preach the gospel....He who believes *and is baptized will be saved;* but he who does not believe will be condemned (Mark 16:15-16), and "make disciples of all nations, *baptizing* them in the name of the Father and of the Son and of the Holy Spirit, teaching them *to observe all that I have commanded you*" (Matthew 28:19-20)? Are not faith, baptism, and observing Christ's commands essential elements of becoming His disciple?

Jim: No, they are not. We *become* a disciple of Christ by repenting and trusting Him as Lord and Savior. Baptism and obedience to Christ's commandments follow as responsibilities of *being* a disciple of Christ.

John: If baptism and obedience are *responsibilities* of a disciple, does that make them *optional?*

Jim: No, it doesn't. When the Lord Jesus Christ tells us to do something, we should do it, for He is Lord and Master. But that is not to say that our salvation is dependent upon it. For example, when I tell my daughters to do something, I expect obedience, and they know that. Their familial relationship to me, however, is not dependent upon their performance.

John: You say baptism is "an outward symbol of the inward change that takes place the moment a person trusts Christ." Suppose a woman in your congregation needed a symbol of God's love for her. If you were to show "an outward symbol" of the Father's love by giving her a strong hug and then show a symbol of Christ's spousal love by giving her a kiss; would your wife, Jean, be wrong in taking offense at this (since they were only symbols, what's important is the inward attitude)?

Jim: Maybe I should have you ask Jean how she would feel.

Do you believe in faith *alone?*

John: Jim, contrary to my reading of Mark 16 and Matthew 28, you seem to imply that we are saved by faith *alone,* without baptism or struggle against sin. But Paul tells us that faith without love gains us nothing (1 Corinthians 13:1-3). James adds, "Man is justified by works and not by faith alone....faith apart from works is dead" (James 2:24,26). Do you believe in faith *alone?*

Jim: Faith alone *for what?*

I believe that Abraham was justified by faith alone (Genesis 15:6; Romans 4:3; Galatians 3:6; James 2:23). The Bible teaches that the "one who *does not work* but *trusts* him who justified the ungodly, his faith is reckoned as righteousness" (Romans 4:5, emphasis added). So, if what you are asking is, What does God require of a sinner before He will justify him? I answer, faith alone. God "justifies him who has faith in Jesus" (Romans 3:26).

But if what you are asking is, Do I believe that true saving faith results in a new life that is devoid of good works? The answer is no. James writes, "Faith apart from works is dead" (James 2:26). The fruit of genuine living faith—the kind of faith that saves—is righteousness. James' statement "You see that a man is justified by works and not by faith alone" (James 2:24) must be understood as the conclusion to a discussion that begins ten verses earlier. James asked, "What does it profit, my brethren, if a man says he has faith but has not works? Can his faith save him?" (James 2:14). In other words, if someone *says* he has faith, but his life does not show it, does that person indeed have genuine faith? Is he truly saved?

In the verses that follow, James shows that true faith manifests itself by good deeds. A faith that is only talk is "dead" (James 2:17) and "barren" (James 2:20). Jesus uses Abraham as an example to illustrate that if a person has real faith, he will demonstrate his trust in God by living righteously.

James' goal is to help his readers evaluate their lives. He suspects that some of them, living lives of hypocrisy, are in fact unsaved. He wants them to understand that if they are going to claim to have faith, then their conduct should demonstrate it.

James 2:14-26 is not talking about how to get to heaven by doing good works. The subject is the *kind* of faith that saves (James 2:14). The passage is talking about living faith as opposed to dead faith (James 2:17). It is about a faith that is evidenced by good works. James' challenge is, "Show me your faith" (James 2:18), even as Abraham showed his.

John: Some Christians have been "saved"—"born-again"—three, four, even five times, having fallen into sin in between. Moreover, they were *certain* they were "saved" each time they took Jesus as their Lord and Savior. Can one really know his faith is "genuine" and thus truly be "saved"?

Jim: I also have met people who are confused about their status with God. Nevertheless, in Scripture we don't find the concept of one losing his salvation and then needing to be born again and again.

How can someone know if he is saved? I usually point people to the first epistle of John. There we find tests of life, the kinds of things that are true of a person who is saved. For instance, John wrote with reference to Christ, "If you know that he is righteous, you may be sure that every one who does right is born of him" (1 John 2:29).

John: Are you absolutely certain that you are "saved" and possess eternal life?

Jim: Yes, John, I have confidence based on the Scriptures that I have been born again and have received eternal life through faith in Christ.

John: Scripture says, "Work out your own salvation with fear and trembling" (Philippians 2:12) and, "He who does right is righteous, as he [Christ] is righteous" (1 John 3:7). They seem to imply that salvation and righteousness (justification) come from working at righteous or just deeds. Would you agree?

Jim: The biblical use of the word "salvation" encompasses the whole work of God by which He delivers us from sin— past, present, and future. The verses you quote talk about two different aspects of salvation. John taught that if a person has been born again, he will practice righteousness. John wrote, "No one who is born of God practices sin, because His seed abides in him" (1 John 3:9 NASB). In Philippians 2:12, Paul is talking about present deliverance from sin, what some call *experiential sanctification.* This is the work of the Holy Spirit delivering the believer from sin in his life. So, no, I wouldn't say that salvation from the penalty of sin is dependent upon one's performance. It is dependent upon whether one has faith in Christ.

Where does Scripture teach one is saved *the moment* he believes?

John: Jim, when I asked, "Where does the Bible describe salvation as 'a single life decision that settles the matter once and for all'?" you responded, "Under the heading 'The New Birth,' I listed 12 of the many blessings a person receives the moment he or she believes." Yet not one of those passages even alludes to "a single life decision."

First Corinthians 12 mentions a variety of gifts—one of which is faith (verse 9) but the more excellent one is love (verse 31)—from the one Spirit by whom we are all *baptized* into Christ's body, the Church (verse 13), being *sealed* (baptized?) by the Spirit (Ephesians 1:13-14). Thus Colossians 2:11-12 and Galatians 3:27 mention *baptism and faith* and John 3:22-30 speaks of being *born again of water and spirit* in the context of *baptism.* Romans 6:5 *doesn't even mention faith*—just that we are buried with Christ through *baptism* (which you mention later). Freed from the slavery of sin, we become reconciled to God *by repentance of sin* (2 Corinthians 5:18-21), *to live no longer according to the flesh but according to the Spirit* (Romans 8:1-17).

Indeed we are saved and justified by grace through faith, but in the context of *persevering in good works* (Ephesians 2:10), *suffering, and hope* (Romans 5:3), which leads to a heavenly reward (Philippians 3:20) *if we stand firm in the Lord* (Philippians 4:1). Believing and receiving the Word (John 1:12) includes *following Christ* (John 10:27) and *doing what Jesus did* (John 13:15-17).

Where is the reference to *the moment* a person believes?

Jim: Because of the broad theological meaning of *salvation,* a more useful term in discussions such as ours is *justification.* God "justifies him who has faith in Jesus" (Romans 3:26). One moment a person is under the condemnation of God. When in the next he trusts Christ as Savior, God declares him righteous in His sight. There is nothing more for Him to do: "For we hold that a man is justified by faith apart from works of the law" (Romans 3:28). And again: "For man believes with his heart and so is justified" (Romans 10:10).

Concurrent with justification are the many blessings I listed under "The New Birth." One moment we are "dead through our trespasses"; the next, God has "made us alive together with Christ" (Ephesians 2:5). One moment we are "enemies" (Romans 5:10) of God; the next, "we have been united" with Christ (Romans 6:5). One moment we are devoid of the Spirit; the next, we are "a temple of the Holy Spirit" (1 Corinthians 6:19). The Bible says, "By one Spirit we were all baptized into one body" (1 Corinthians 12:13). Either you have been baptized by the Spirit and are part of the body of Christ or you are not. There is no in-between state by which we can make this a process. Scripture says, "Any one who does not have the Spirit of Christ does not belong to him" (Romans 8:9).

John: Still, the Bible doesn't explicitly mention the *moment* of conversion. Why would God require us to read between the lines on such an important issue?

Jim: We may not find the expression "the moment you believe," but we certainly find the concept. For example, Paul wrote, "By grace you have been saved through faith" (Ephesians

162

2:8). Here Paul uses the Greek perfect tense. It presents salvation as a process having reached its completion and existing in that finished state. It is a "past act of rescue plus the resultant condition of safety."[105] When Paul wrote, "You have been saved through faith," he was referring to the salvation one receives the moment he believes.

Does accepting Jesus give us a *right* to eternal life?

John: John said, "He who believes in the Son has *eternal life*" (John 3:36). If we believe and "accept Jesus as our Lord and Savior" with our "life decision," does this gives us a *right* to eternal life?

Jim: Paul wrote, "The free gift of God is eternal life in Christ Jesus our Lord" (Romans 6:23). We receive this gift through faith. As the verse you quote in your question states, the one who believes *has* eternal life. It is his present possession. Other verses that say this include John 3:16; 5:24; 10:28; and 1 John 5:13.

John: Peter said, "As the outcome of your faith you obtain the salvation of your souls" (1 Peter 1:9). It sounds like our faith—our choice to take Jesus Christ as our Lord and Savior—*earns* salvation. Doesn't salvation remain a free gift from God?

Jim: Yes, eternal life is the free gift of God. We are told that in Romans 6:23.

Are we free and responsible to cooperate in sanctification?

John: I'm glad you clarified Luther's quote, which many Catholics *and* Protestants misunderstand. Nevertheless, in the section "Living the New Life," having given our life to Christ through faith, sanctification appears almost like a process that occurs automatically—without any free effort on our part.

Are we in any way free and responsible to cooperate in our sanctification?

Jim: The verbs I used with respect to *sanctification* speak of the responsibilities of the believer in cooperating with the work of the Holy Spirit in his life. The Christian must learn to live a holy life, walk by the Spirit, replace sinful practices with godly disciplines, and yield each day to God. Kenneth S. Wuest said it better than I can. He wrote that the Christian life "is not a *let go and let God* affair. It is a *take hold with God* business. It is a mutual co-operation with the Holy Spirit in an interest and an activity in the things of God. The saint must not merely rest in the Holy Spirit for victory over sin and the production of a holy life. He must in addition to this dependence upon the Spirit, say a positive NO to sin and exert himself to the doing of the right."[106] Wuest is referring here to the process of sanctification by which we become more like Christ. We should not confuse this with justification, which is instantaneous and by faith.

Did *Sola Scriptura* fail Calvin?

John: You say, "Those who say that baptism justifies an infant are teaching contrary to Scripture." Yet Calvin does an extensive *Sola Scriptura* defense of infant baptism in his principal work *Institutes of the Christian Religion*.[107] Has *Sola Scriptura* failed us in this matter?

Jim: God's Word hasn't failed us, only Calvin's use of it. Unable to find support for infant baptism in the plain teaching of Scripture (there is no mention of it), Calvin took an allegorical approach. He compared circumcision to baptism, citing mystical or spiritual parallels. He then inferred that since Jews were to circumcise their infants, Christians should baptize theirs. There is a French proverb that says "to compare is not to prove." It applies in this case. The allegorical method can be useful for illustrating truth. But it is an unreliable tool for establishing it.

John: Infant baptism declined in the fourth century. Consequently, Basil, Gregory of Nyssa, Ambrose, John Chrysostom, Jerome, and Augustine were baptized as adults. Nevertheless, each insisted on baptizing infants as a practice originating in apostolic times.[108] Arguing against the Gnostics, Irenaeus says infant baptism was common practice in the second century.[109] Does such reliance on apostolic tradition cause these early Christians to misread Scripture? How would you explain it?

Jim: It is difficult to know why they baptized infants. I would expect that if it was an apostolic tradition, we could read about it for ourselves in the teaching of the apostles found in the epistles of the New Testament or in the book of Acts, the history of the apostolic church. Since infant baptism is lacking in both places, we can only assume the men you cite received the doctrine from other sources. As Calvin does with infant baptism, many fourth-century teachers took an allegorical approach to Scripture. This led them to unusual interpretations, often disagreeing with one another.

John: Suppose a person who was baptized as a child became a believer and took Jesus as his Lord and Savior, yet felt pressured by his church to be baptized again. This person sincerely believes that he was "justified by faith" (Romans 5:1) when he came to believe, and that for him rebaptism would be an insult to God, putting more faith in a mere symbol rather than in Christ's saving love. Must he be rebaptized to be saved?

Jim: The Bible doesn't teach salvation by baptism under any circumstance. Salvation—deliverance from the penalty of sin and reception of the Holy Spirit—is through faith in Christ.

John: Thank you, Jim, for your insightful answers. I could easily go on with more. After I digest your answers, I'll let you know my reservations.

Letter 24

Friday, May 25, 2001

Dear Jim,

Tuesday's conversation was enjoyable and enlightening, with frank responses to challenging questions.

Your one position—baptism is *unnecessary*[110] yet not *optional*[111]—I find somewhat fickle. Beyond that, profound agreement seems to underlie our other differences and approaches. You insist *faith devoid of good works* is not genuine faith;[112] Catholics insist *works without faith* are not genuine works in the Spirit. We agree our relationship with God is dependent not on performance, but on God's grace working in our lives. Each backs his position in Scripture.

Knowing Eternal Life

You indicated that some reformed Christians—like some Catholics—are confused or insecure regarding their status with God. I appreciate this answer and respect you more for it. Some Protestants take incomplete gospel truth—that one may *know* that he has eternal life (1 John 5:13)—to undermine and damn Catholics who fail to express such confidence. But you didn't.

John uses *know* 37 times in his short letter! *Knowledge* of eternal life (1 John 5:13) seems to imply *knowing* God (4:6,8*), including:

---

* The following is an analysis of 1 John. This and the following citations are from 1 John, unless noted otherwise. Only the chapter number and verse number are cited for the sake of simplicity.

- the Father, who abides in us and we in Him; being of God, we love God's children (2:14,28; 3:24; 4:6,13,15-16; 5:2,19-20).

- Christ, who is from the beginning, the righteous one, who gives us understanding to know Him who is true, and His love; that He took away our sins, He who has no sin, by dying for us (2:3,13-14,29; 3:5,16; 4:16; 5:20);

- the Spirit of God, having been born of God, anointed (baptized?) by the Holy One, who teaches us truth (2:20,27,29; 4:2);

A Christian also *knows* where he is going (2:11) and that:

- it is the last hour (2:18);

- Christ hears us in whatever we ask (5:15);

- no lie is of the truth, knowing the spirit of truth and the spirit of error, being of the truth (2:21; 3:19; 4:6);

- anyone born of God does not sin…and the evil one does not touch him, although the world is in his power (5:18-19);

- no murderer has eternal life (3:15);

- when He appears we shall be like Him, for we shall see Him as He is, having passed out of death into life (3:2,14).

You acknowledge that we can be assured of *knowledge* of God and our status before Him if we do what is right (2:29; 3:7).[113] This implies genuine *faith* (3:23; 4:2,15; 5:1,4,5,10,13)[114] and that we have:

- loved God (5:2);

- fellowship with Christ, walking in the light in the same way Christ walked, keeping His commandments, abiding in His word and in John's (1:6-7; 2:3,5-6,24; 3:22,24; 4:6; 5:2-3);

+ received His Spirit (13);

+ confessed our sins, overcome evil, purified our hearts so they don't condemn us; abiding in love, loving one another, laying down our life for the brethren (1:8-9; 2:10,14; 3:3,11,14,16,18,20-21,23; 4:7,11,16,19-21; 5:1).

Knowledge of God is incompatible with:

+ walking in the darkness (1:6);

+ hating our brother or ignoring those in need (2:9,11; 3:10,14-15,17; 4:8,20);

+ disobeying God's commandments, committing sin, or failing to do right (2:4; 3:4-6,8-10; 5:18);

+ being of the world, loving it, or things in it (2:15; 4:4-5);

+ denying Jesus Christ (2:22-23; 4:3).

If we live all this, Catholics and evangelicals should have no fear or shame at His coming (2:28) because we:

+ know Him, are in Him, and in the truth (2:3,5; 3:19);

+ are born of Him as children of God, perfected in love (2:5,29; 3:1; 4:18);

+ will receive from Him whatever we ask (3:22; 5:14).

Doing God's Will

The Sermon on the Mount is clear: Not everyone who accepts Jesus as Savior and Lord "shall enter the kingdom of heaven, but he who does the will of my Father" (Matthew 7:21,24). Assurance doesn't mean presumption of salvation. Genuine faith implies our correspondence to the Father's will. The Father's will includes the beatitudes; fulfilling the Old Testament moral law; trusting God and not riches by almsgiving, prayer, fasting; doing good; not judging others, and so on (Matthew 5:1–7:48).

Everyone will be judged according to his works (Matthew 7:15-20; Romans 2:5-10). Faith is indispensable for salvation, but faith doesn't replace works, just as good works do *not* replace faith. Works do not *earn* eternal life any more than faith does.

Necessary Works

Nowhere does Scripture say we are saved without baptism, gratitude, repentance, obedience to God and His moral law, mercy, prayer, and personal sacrifice, such as taking up our cross.

Faith itself is a work (John 6:28-29). Only Old Covenant ordinances (circumcision, Passover, and so on) are works contrary to faith because they are fulfilled in the New Covenant ordinances (Baptism, Eucharist, and so on). Jewish converts shouldn't trust Old Covenant ordinances by saying, "Unless you are circumcised according to the custom of Moses, you cannot be saved" (Acts 15:1). At great length Paul combats those who did (Romans 2:17–5:1; 1 Corinthians 7:18-19; Galatians 2:1-21; 5:1-14; 6:12-15; Philippians 3:2-11; Colossians 2:11–3:11), because such acts repudiate faith in Christ's gospel.

Jim, I have principally critiqued just aspects of your position antagonistic to Catholicism because they do not hold up under scriptural scrutiny.

I hope everything is well with Jean and the girls (is one of your girls graduating this year?). Please assure each one of them that they are in my prayers along with you.

In Christ's truth,

John

Letter 25

WEDNESDAY, MAY 30, 2001

Dear John,

Thanks for your prayers for my family. They are all doing well. With regard to your question, none of my daughters will be graduating this year. The next in line is Faith (17). She will be a senior in high school next year. She plans then to go to college and get a credential in elementary education. She wants to teach first graders and has already designed how her classroom will look.

Good Works Are the Result, Not the Cause

Your recent letter was helpful. Some have caricaturized the evangelical position as *everyone who claims to believe in Jesus can be confident of heaven even if he lives like the devil.* Some misguided souls may actually believe that. As you point out, however, the Scriptures teach that if a person is born again his life will show it. They also teach, however, that "God reckons righteousness apart from works" (Romans 4:6). Justification is by faith alone. Good works play no part in getting right with God, maintaining our relationship to God as His children, or determining whether we will get into heaven. Scripture says, "Now to the one who works, his wage is not credited as a favor, but as what is due. But to the one who does not work, but believes in Him who justifies the ungodly, his faith is credited as righteousness" (Romans 4:4-5 NASB).

True faith in Christ results in justification and the life-changing effects of the new birth. Good works follow after. They

---

171

are the *fruit*, not the *root*, of justification. We might picture it this way.

faith ➤ justification, new and eternal life ➤ good works

Paul expressed this relationship well in his letter to the Ephesians. Speaking of salvation from the penalty of sin, he wrote: "By grace you have been saved through faith; and that not of yourselves, it is the gift of God; not as a result of works, so that no one may boast" (Ephesians 2:8-9 NASB). Salvation is by faith apart from works. Where do good works fit in? They are the *result* of new life in Christ. Paul explains this in the next verse: "We are His workmanship, created in Christ Jesus for good works, which God prepared beforehand so that we would walk in them" (Ephesians 2:10 NASB). We are born again to a life of good works.

The Galatian Heresy

Contrary to these truths is the belief that in addition to faith you must work for your salvation, that justification and eternal life are earned rewards. We might present this as:

faith + good works ➤ justification ➤ eternal life

False teachers spread this heresy among the churches of Galatia in the first century. They taught that in addition to faith in Christ, one needed to obey certain aspects of the Jewish law (Galatians 4:21), receive circumcision (Galatians 5:2-4), and observe the Sabbath and feast days (Galatians 4:9-10). Paul condemned these teachers in the strongest of terms (Galatians 1:8-9). He warned anyone who followed their teaching that Christ would be of no benefit to them (Galatians 5:2-4). Rather, they would be under the curse of God (Galatians 3:10).

I cannot agree with you that baptism is necessary for salvation, or, as Rome puts it, that baptism is the "instrumental cause"[115] of justification. Scripture teaches that justification is by faith

(Romans 3:26; 3:28; 3:30; 4:5; 5:1; 10:4; Galatians 2:16; 3:8; 3:11; 3:24). None of these many verses even mention baptism. Baptism follows after justification as an act of obedience. It is a public testimony of faith in Jesus. One can readily see this in the conversion of Cornelius (Acts 10:1-11:18). An angel told Cornelius that Peter would "declare to you a message by which you will be saved, you and all your household" (Acts 11:14). The message that saves is the gospel of Jesus Christ. It is "the power of God for salvation to every one who has faith" (Romans 1:16). After Cornelius had believed the gospel and received the Holy Spirit, Peter baptized him in water.

Please send me a summary of your position on the initial stages of Catholic salvation. I am also interested in learning more about your ministry to the students at UCLA and other Catholics in Southern California. What is a typical week for you, John?

In Christ's love,

Jim

Letter 26

Dear Jim,

Last Sunday I had the joyous opportunity of receiving an 85-year-old gentleman into the Church. I regularly attend to the spiritual care of his wife, a member of Opus Dei. Although completely bedridden, he is quite alert and uses his inactivity to pray and think about the important things of life...of Life. What joy filled the house as his six children—and grandchildren galore—witnessed his profession of faith and reception of the sacraments. Since he is unable to witness to his faith outside his home, I suggested he does so by praying for us, that you and I reach the fullness of Christ's gospel.

Now let me explain Catholic teaching regarding faith, works, and salvation. This is a big topic, so my statement will be fairly broad:

> Grace is God's unconditional and unsolicited gift of Himself to us. As a gift, salvation is from God alone. Yet God doesn't force Himself on us, but invites us into a threefold relationship with Him, i.e. salvation.
>
> As our Father, God provides us life, sustenance, discipline, forgiveness of sin, and truth. We ought to respond to His grace with gratitude, obedience, repentance, and faith, establishing a father-child relationship between Him and us.

Christ's self-gift is total, immolating Himself on the cross for us; we ought to embrace our cross in total, reciprocal, spousal self-giving.

The Spirit empowers us with authority to pray for, teach, and pasture those under our care.

Sacraments are sacred signs of love-grace between Christ and us, just as a kiss, hug, or marital union expresses and increases love-grace between spouses. Baptism expresses our faith response in accepting God's love, establishing us as His children.

Jim, I hope this gives you an idea of our belief. I'm certain the Bible will confirm this teaching. I look forward to your questions.

In Christ Jesus,

John

Letter 27

MONDAY, JUNE 4, 2001

Dear John,

Thank you for your letters and this opportunity to discuss our faiths. I appreciate the time you have been giving to this correspondence. As you present the initial stages of Catholic salvation in your next letter, I would be grateful if you could address the following questions.

Justification

We need to get to the heart of the doctrine of salvation and discuss it accurately. A precise definition of Roman Catholic justification would be helpful.

Sacraments

Rome says that the seven sacraments of the Church confer saving grace through the proper performance of the ritual. This occurs "by the very fact of the action's being performed" [CCC 1128]. This seems rather mechanistic, unlike something that Christ would institute. Can you help me to understand this from a Catholic perspective?

Infant Baptism

My parents had me baptized at St. Monica's Church in San Francisco when I was just a few days old. Later, I learned that the sacrament of baptism had supposedly freed me from original sin, made me innocent before God, regenerated my soul, and made me part of Christ's body, a temple of the Holy Spirit, and a member of the Roman Catholic Church. Not only did I not have faith in Christ at the time of my baptism, I was incapable of even understanding what was happening. Is there any biblical basis for attributing these effects to the baptism of an uncomprehending infant?

Adult Baptism

In recent years the Catholic Church has established the *Rite of Christian Initiation of Adults* (R.C.I.A.). This program prepares adults for baptism through extensive instruction, acts of purification, the performance of good works, and a series of rites. I understand it typically takes from six to 12 months to complete. For some it takes years. In the New Testament, by contrast, the apostles immediately baptized those who, upon hearing the gospel, believed. The Ethiopian eunuch and Cornelius are examples (Acts 8:36-39; 10:47-48). Why must adults seeking baptism in the Roman Catholic Church undergo such an extensive time of preparation?

Working for Salvation

Scripture says, "whoever enters God's rest also ceases from his labors as God did from his" (Hebrews 4:10). Have you as a Catholic priest entered God's rest for salvation, or are you still striving to achieve it?

I look forward to being with you next week in Eugene to discuss the book with Harvest House. Hopefully we will also have some time just to chat.

In Christ's love,

Jim

Letter 28

SUNDAY, JUNE 10, 2001

Dear Jim,

Sundays are busy for me, usually preaching a day of recollection, but to a different small group each week. This morning I gave one to college women. A day of recollection is like a mini-retreat, a half-day each month dedicated exclusively to our relationship with our Lord. I give two or three half-hour reflections on Scripture, celebrate Holy Mass, and so on; I also give spiritual counseling and sacramental confession during the quiet time. The idea is to work on some resolution in the coming month. I too benefit from each recollection.

I tell our Lord that you and I strive for a common foundation upon which to build...a foundation in Christ (1 Corinthians 3:6-14), the apostles (Ephesians 2:19-22; Revelation 21:9-14), and the Church (1 Timothy 3:15)...a foundation that Christ lays (Hebrews 11:8-10) through the preaching of older brothers in the faith (Romans 15:15-22; Hebrews 6:1-6), making us "ready for any good work" (2 Timothy 2:21). We cooperate in laying the foundation of our eternal life (1 Timothy 6:18-19) by believing and doing His Word (Matthew 7:24-27; Luke 6:46-49) and taking up our daily cross (Luke 14:26-29).

Justification (initial salvation) is an important part of this foundation. I hope to show that your teaching on *salvation through genuine faith shown by works* needs completion by the Catholic teaching of salvation through grace, faith, and works.

What is justification?

If salvation is a loving relationship with each person of the blessed Trinity, then justification is the process of establishing this relationship—of "falling in love." God's *grace* initiates this process.

Theologians tend to define *grace* quite narrowly. But grace is simply God's unconditional and unsolicited gift to us (Romans 11:5-6; James 1:17; 1 John 4:16,19). As a gift, salvation is from God alone (Romans 3:24). Yet God treats us not as slaves, but as children and friends (Romans 8:14-17; John 15:15), with the dignity of free human beings. Without forcing Himself on us, God calls each (2 Timothy 1:9) to freely answer His invitation to enter into a threefold relationship with Him, to freely choose life or death (Deuteronomy 30:6-20; Sirach 15:15-18).

We see no dichotomy between justification and sanctification. We see both as an ongoing pilgrimage—dialogue with God— leading to our definitive homeland, heaven. In baptism, we cross the sea out of Egypt (1 Corinthians 10:1-6) with Christ, our Good Shepherd (John 10:11-15), leading us through the desert into the promised land. If we do go astray, Christ finds us and brings us back (Luke 15:4-7).

Good Works: *Icons* of Love

Every day your wife, Jean, shows her love by preparing your meals, laundering your clothes, and more. These works—these *icons* of love—move you to love her more, do they not? Your self-giving love for Jean—your grace—is not conditioned on her service (you'd still love her if she were incapacitated), but that doesn't mean it is indifferent to her service. Communal life is a dialogue of self-giving works. The same is true with your daughters, who listen and obey you, showing you many details of love.

As our Father, God provides life (1 Corinthians 8:6), sustenance (2 Corinthians 9:8), and discipline (Hebrews 12:5-11), especially by teaching us the Law (Romans 7:12-14). He mercifully forgives our sins (Titus 3:5-7), sacrificing His only son for us (Romans 3:23-25). The Lord's prayer (Matthew 6:9-15) summarizes God's fatherly graces.

We accept God as Father by...

* repentance (2 Corinthians 7:9-10);

* trusting divine providence (Matthew 6:19-34), not material wealth (Hebrews 13:5-6);

* gratitude (Luke 17:12-19; 1 Thessalonians 5:16-18);

* obeying His commandments (Matthew 19:16-19; Romans 3:31);

* believing in Christ (John 12:44-50) and His emissaries (1 John 4:6);

* forgiving others (Matthew 18:21-35; Luke 6:35-36).

None of these works are *optional,* just as obedience is not *optional* for your daughters.[116]

Faith and love are indispensable responses to grace; works—*icons* of love—are not enough. If a daughter obeyed reluctantly (or even resentfully)—fearing punishment or to exact something from you—this wouldn't please you. God too desires more than obedience, He desires love, which the prodigal son's older brother lacked (Luke 15:11-32). As Paul says, *faith* and *works* are worth nothing without love (1 Corinthians 13:1-3).

Perhaps Adam's lack of faith initiated the original sin, but God convicted him of disobedience (Genesis 2:16-17; 3:1-24), whereas Abraham pleased God with faith manifested by loving obedience and was justified (James 2:21-24). We "strive to enter [God's] rest" (Hebrews 4:11) with "active" works of faith and love.

Throughout the Old Testament, God taught the Israelites to have trusting faith as an obedient child. This prepared them for a more intimate nuptial relationship with Christ: To respond to Christ's total, immolating gift of Himself on the cross for us, we must embrace our own cross in total self-giving. Also, we respond to the Holy Spirit's gift of power and authority to pray for, teach, and pasture those under our care. But let's stick to the topic of initial salvation and our filial response.

Sacraments

Besides *icons* of faith and love, God constantly shows His love *sacramentally*. The Greek word for *symbol* is foreign to Scripture. Sacraments are not symbols, but sacred signs of love-grace in our relations with God. In human relationships, a kiss, hug, or marital union expresses and increases the love-grace between spouses. True, these human "sacraments" are signs of love and trust. Yet every time a husband kisses his wife—though it appears mechanical—they express and increase their love and trust with this sign, renewing their covenant of love. This is what we mean by saying *sacraments cause and increase grace.*

Giving your wife flowers is a wonderful *symbol* of your mutual love, but a "ritual" kiss has greater significance.

The Old Testament is filled with sacraments. The rainbow was God's "covenant sign" with Noah (Genesis 9:8-17). A sacrifice was God's sacramental guarantee of His promise to Abraham (Genesis 15:1-21). God established circumcision as a covenant sacrament initiating men into His people (Genesis 17:9-14); the Passover sacrament sustained Israel on their pilgrimage (Exodus 12:1-32); and sin-offerings provided sacramental forgiveness (Leviticus 4–19).

Circumcision was the purification *required* before partaking of the Passover sacrifice (Exodus 12:43,48) and entering into the promised land (Joshua 5:2-7), an image of heaven.

Sacraments were not *optional*. Although in Genesis 15 Abraham was reckoned righteous for believing (Romans 4:3), without circumcision he would have been "cut off from his people; [for having] broken my covenant" (Genesis 17:14, comment added). Firstborn Jews who didn't eat the Passover died in Egypt (Exodus 12).

New Testament sacraments are sacred signs of Christ's love-grace towards us, fulfilling and perfecting the Old. Baptism fulfills circumcision (Colossians 2:11-15), incorporating the Christian into God's covenant people by accepting God's love as His child. Thus being "born of water and the Spirit" is necessary for salvation (John 3:5).

181

For Jesus, sacraments weren't mechanistic rituals! He insisted John baptize Him (Matthew 3:13-17), not as a symbol of faith or repentance from sin—He had no sin! (1 John 3:4-6)—but to manifest the Holy Spirit dwelling in Him (Matthew 3:13-17; John 1:29-34).

Infant Baptism

Much scriptural evidence exists for infant baptism. First, Scripture describes how Peter and Paul baptized whole families (Acts 10:1-11:14; 16:13-15; 16:27-34; 18:8; 1 Corinthians 1:14-16). *Nowhere* does Scripture exclude small children from baptism.

Scripture mandated circumcising eight-day-old children (Genesis 17:12; Leviticus 12:3). The first Christians—all Jews—naturally fulfilled, not abolished (Matthew 5:17-20) the Law and the prophets by baptizing their newborns instead.

Other Old Testament precedents for baptizing children include:

* Samuel: dedicated to the Lord at age two (1 Samuel 1:17-28);

* Isaiah (49:1-6) and Jeremiah (1:4-10): chosen and consecrated to God (Sirach 49:4-7) in their mothers' wombs.

Ezekiel 36:25-28 prophesied a baptism that purges sin and infuses God's Spirit (Matthew 3:11; Mark 1:4-8; Luke 3:16; John 1:28-34; Acts 1:5; 11:16-17), whereas John's baptism was of repentance and faith in Christ only (Acts 18:24–19:7). Christians are baptized into one Spirit (1 Corinthians 12:13) who is:

* promised to believers (Galatians 3:1-5, 11-14);

* a gift to the obedient (Acts 5:27-32) through baptism and the imposition of hands (Acts 2:38-39; 8:14-19);

* the pledge of our salvation (2 Corinthians 1:22; 5:1-10; Ephesians 1:13-14).

John was "filled with the Holy Spirit, even from his mother's womb" (Luke 1:15). Infants can receive the Spirit! So, let's baptize them, "for all who are led by the Spirit of God are sons of God" (Romans 8:14). Peter's words challenge us: "Can any one forbid water for baptizing these people who have received the Holy Spirit just as we have?" (Acts 10:47). Would you forbid little children—who can "know the Father" (1 John 2:13)—from receiving His Spirit in baptism?

Isaiah also prophesied, "I will pour my Spirit upon your descendants, and my blessing on your offspring" (Isaiah 44:3). "If you then, who are evil, know how to give good gifts to your children, how much more will the heavenly Father give the Holy Spirit to those who ask him!" (Luke 11:13).

Refusing to baptize infants—because they cannot make *explicit* acts of faith in Christ—would be like refusing to kiss or hold a child until he was old enough to express faith and love in his mother or father. Did you do this with your daughters? You wouldn't have dreamt of it! So can we refuse to let our heavenly Father *kiss* and receive that child into His household (Ephesians 2:19) through baptism? Our Lord says, "Let the children come to me, do not hinder them" (Mark 10:14).

Christian parents baptize newborns as an act of faith, humbly recognizing that all are sinners in Adam (Romans 6:6-14; 1 Corinthians 15:20-50), including "innocent" children. These parents trust Christ's atoning work to save and liberate their child from slavery to sin. During the ceremony, they beseech God to give their child...

+ new life in the Spirit;

+ fidelity to Christ and His covenant;

+ the call to be a gospel witness as he matures.

At their child's baptism, parents also pray for grace to be good parents and that their example, discipline, and words may cultivate the child's Christian life.

By baptizing their child, parents recognize through faith that their child is not their property but belongs to God alone—that they are just *overseers* of God's gift. At baptism, they give their child back to God, much like what Mary and Joseph did with Jesus in Luke 2:21-38. Jewish parents understood this as part of their covenant commitment to God. Do you think that Joseph ("a just man," Matthew 1:19), Mary ("blessed is she who believed," Luke 1:45), and Simeon (inspired by the Holy Spirit, 2:25) were fulfilling a mechanical, ritualistic practice?

Adult Baptism

Christ took some three years to prepare the apostles before they fully believed. Likewise, adults ought to be baptized and received into the Church when they believe fully. As it is imprudent for couples to marry the moment they experience "love at first sight," so too the Catholic Church wants each individual to understand Christian beliefs and his commitments as Christ's disciple.

In this regard, I mentioned Bill's conversion in my last letter. He decided to become Catholic just two weeks earlier. Since I knew him well—that his decision was mature—I didn't wait. Each person's situation is unique.

That's enough for now. I look forward to seeing you tomorrow evening. This time around I'll even be able to give you this letter by hand.

Yours in Christ, the Foundation of Truth,

John

Conversation 6

THURSDAY, JUNE 21, 2001

Jim: John, it was great being with you last week in Eugene. I returned home refreshed and with a deepened desire to see our discussion go forward. The enthusiasm of the Harvest House staff for the project was remarkable.

John: What warmth and openness! Their interest in us and our ongoing dialogue—with no antipathy toward me as a Catholic priest—was surprising and their enthusiasm, contagious. Their "healthy" ignorance and interest in Catholic belief and worship made me at ease sharing my faith with them.

Is not your proof for infant baptism merely an assumption?

Jim: I have a number of questions about your last letter.

You say that much scriptural evidence exists for infant baptism, yet give no specific example of an infant being baptized. In citing the occasions that whole households were baptized as proof for infant baptism, you are assuming that they contained infants. Is not your proof then merely an assumption also?

John: Jim, many things in Scripture are not explicit, like the Trinity. We also found no explicit mention of Scripture as "the final court of appeals" or as the *sole* source for truth

185

and certainty of revelation. Nor is salvation explicitly described as "a single life decision."

True, baptizing whole families doesn't "prove" infant baptism, only that infants were not excluded. It is just one piece of the abundant evidence showing infant baptism consistent with Scripture: infants (including Jesus) were offered to God, became members of God's people, were called to serve the Lord, and received the Holy Spirit; all this is associated with baptism.

Jim, you don't show Scripture explicitly forbidding infant baptism nor do you indicate how circumcision is fulfilled—as it must be (Matthew 5:17-20)—in the New Covenant.

Jim: You say extensive time for preparation is needed before adults can be baptized so they can understand what they are being asked to believe and the commitments they must make. Why then do you baptize infants soon after birth, who can do none of these things?

John: With baptism, one becomes a member of God's family. It is different for a child to join the family than for an adult. For example, when Elizabeth was conceived and born, you didn't expect much from her. She trusted you and Jean to give her what she needed and you made room for her in your lives. However, if Elizabeth now invited a young man to become part of your family—to become your son-in-law—you'd expect the two to take some time to seriously think over their proposed commitment, their compatibility, and their ability to raise a family. Once that was assured, you'd feel more comfortable making room for the new member in your lives and family. Does this make any sense?

Jim: Your comparison does a good job of highlighting why your practice necessitates two sets of requirements for baptismal justification. Do you have any authority from the teaching of Christ and the apostles for saying that there are two ways of being born again, one for adults and another for newborns?

John: We really don't see this as two distinct ways, but as a single way with distinct conditions to accommodate each person's particular situation and abilities.

Does the New Testament teach there are seven sacraments?

Jim: The *Catechism of the Catholic Church* states, "The Church affirms that for believers the sacraments of the New Covenant are *necessary for salvation*" [CCC 1129]. It lists seven such sacraments. Where do Christ and the apostles teach in the New Testament that there are seven sacraments necessary for salvation?

John: Although Scripture doesn't say explicitly why, *seven* [Hebrew *sheba'*] is a number intimately tied to God's covenant with man. To *seventh oneself* [Hebrew *shaba'*] means "to swear a covenant oath," as God does with Abraham after offering Isaac (Genesis 22:16). The *seventh day* was called the Sabbath [Hebrew *shabbath*], the day of rest [Hebrew *shabath*] commemorating the Covenant.

Thus, having seven sacraments makes some sense. Let's enumerate them:

* *Baptism,* new birth of water and Spirit necessary to be saved (Mark 16:16) and enter God's kingdom (John 3:5);

* *Confirmation,* receiving the Holy Spirit through the imposition of hands (Acts 8:14-17) after baptism (Acts 8:12-13);

* *Eucharist,* partaking of Christ's body and blood brings eternal life (John 6:48-58), fulfilling Christ's command (1 Corinthians 11:23-26);

* *Reconciliation,* God's power to forgive sin given to His ministers (John 20:22,23);

187

- *Ordination,* the imposition of hands (Acts 13:1-3) whereby Paul and Barnabas were made apostles (Acts 14:4,14), Christ's ministers;

- *Anointing the Sick,* presbyters praying over, anointing and saving the sick (James 5:13-15);

- *Marriage,* the *great sacrament* (Ephesians 5:32; Greek *to mysterion touto mega*), the sign of mutual love between Christ and His Church (Ephesians 5:21-33).

Jim: I am surprised that the translation of Ephesians 5:32 you quoted rendered the Greek word *mysterion* as "sacrament." Perhaps you could identify the version in which you found it. I have checked many modern Bible translations for the word *sacrament.* None of them, including the Roman Catholic *New American Bible* (1995), translate any word, Greek or Hebrew, as "sacrament." Why is the word *sacrament* absent from virtually every Bible translation? If there are seven sacraments necessary for salvation, one would think Christ and the apostles would have referred to sacraments regularly.

John: Let me remind you, Jim, that the word *Trinity* is found nowhere in the Bible but is a technical term developed to express in a non-technical way what the Bible taught.

Regarding Ephesians 5:32, Jerome—who knew Greek and Latin very well—translates this passage, *"Sacramentum hoc magnum est."* The Douay-Rheims Version—an English translation of Jerome's Vulgate—renders *mysterion* "sacrament."[117]

Is initial Catholic justification an event or a process?

Jim: You describe the Catholic concept of initial justification as the process of establishing a relationship *with* God, of "falling in love." I was raised under the tutelage of the Sisters of the Holy Names and the *Baltimore Catechism.* They taught me that because of Adam's *original sin* I was born spiritually dead and under the condemnation of God. Through baptism, I received *sanctifying grace* and came into a *state of grace.* Later I learned that the church calls this initial justification. Rome defines it as "…a transition from that state in which a person is born as a child of the first Adam to the state of grace and of adoption as children of God…."[118] This seems more like an event achieved by a rite than the process of falling in love, as you describe it.

John: One can oversimplify what the *Catechism* teaches, just as one can the Bible. Yet we want a complete picture.

Remember your wedding day, that singular and defining moment in your life. Was it not more than rite or ceremony? Yet that defining moment would've never occurred had you not met Jean, gotten to know her, and showed her abundant signs of love. Likewise, you'd never have remained married had you remained selfish, insisted she satisfy your every whim, and failed to show her how special she was with details of service and "sacraments" of your love (kisses, hugs, and other intimacies).

Just as marriage is more than the wedding ceremony, justification is more than a momentary reception of grace.

Look at the long development of Abraham's relationship with God:

- By leaving Haran for Canaan, Abraham believed and obeyed God, who swore to give him the promised land (Genesis 12:1-9);

- God rescued Sarah from Pharaoh and renewed the promise (Genesis 13:14-18);

- Having rescued Lot, God blessed Abraham through Melchizedek's sacrifice (Genesis 14:1-20);

- God promised Abraham descendents, ratifying His promise with a sacrifice (Genesis 15:1-20);

- Although Abraham disbelieved the promise by bearing Ishmael through Hagar (Genesis 16:1-15), God doubly renewed the promise, established a covenant, and changed Abraham's name (Genesis 17:1-22; 18:1-15);

- Abraham joined God's people by circumcision (Genesis 17:22-27);

- Finally, after Isaac was offered in holocaust, God promised to bless all nations in Abraham's descendents (Genesis 22:1-19).

What is the Roman Catholic formula for salvation?

Jim: If I understand you correctly, we agree that salvation is a gift from God. In Letter 25, I provided a simple formula expressing the evangelical understanding of the relationship between faith, good works, justification, and eternal life.

faith ➤ justification, new and eternal life ➤ good works

Can you give me a similar formula expressing how Roman Catholicism understands these relationships?

John: No simple formula can describe salvation or love. Letter 28 attempted to show how the myriad of Scripture passages fit together, interwoven to form a wonderful tapestry of God's salvation plan. But you seem more interested in legal formulas than in Scripture references.

Nevertheless, I'll try to summarize it for you. As we saw, salvation is a relationship that God establishes without any initiative from us. This is *grace*. God calls us to *respond* to His *grace* with faith and obedience; with our total gift of self to Christ; with our exercise of the Holy Spirit's gifts, and so on. This interchange between God's *grace* and our *response* leads to our communion with God, making us...

- children of the Father;

- one body—the Church—Christ's bride;

- temples of the Holy Spirit—the personification of the mutual love between the Father and the Son—which we maternally accept and nourish.

God's Grace (1ˢᵗ)   **Man's Response (2ⁿᵈ)**

Relationship with God = Salvation (3ʳᵈ)
(filial love, spousal love, maternal love)

As you can see, justification is no linear formula or process.

Jim: I don't understand why the Catholic plan of salvation is so complex that it takes a "myriad of Scripture passages" to explain it or why you can't give me a simple explanation of the relationship between faith, good works, justification, and eternal life. Am I correct in saying that Roman Catholicism teaches that eternal life is an earned reward?

John: No relationship—neither yours with Jean, nor mine with God—can be summarized in a formula.

Merit—earned reward—is part of salvation. As Paul said before he died, "I have fought the good fight, I have finished the race, I have kept the faith. Henceforth there is laid up for me the *crown of righteousness,* which the Lord, the righteous judge, *will award* to me on that Day" (2 Timothy 4:8).

Jim: How does one earn eternal life?

John: Scripture sometimes appears to say that we earn eternal life, such as by faith:[119] "To all...who believed in his name, he gave power to become children of God" (John 1:12). Yet it is still a gift from God. Again our Lord tells us:

> The kingdom of heaven is like treasure hidden in a field, which a man found and...he goes...and *buys that field*. Again, the kingdom of heaven is like a merchant...who, on finding one pearl of great value, went...and *bought it*.
>
> MATTHEW 13:44-46

Although eternal life (the kingdom of heaven) is bought, it remains a gift.

Jim: Rome recently said, "...eternal life is, at one and the same time, grace and the reward given by God for good works and merits."[120] How can eternal life be both by grace and yet a reward for good works and merits?

John: Faith also seems to earn salvation, since you must believe to be awarded salvation. Many passages express righteousness as a reward for good deeds. For example:

> The LORD rewarded me according to my righteousness; according to the cleanness of my hands he recompensed me. For I have kept the ways of the LORD.... I was blameless before him, and I kept myself from guilt. Therefore the LORD has recompensed me according to my righteousness.
>
> PSALM 18:20-24

Salvation is simultaneously a grace God freely offers to us, and a reward in response to His call, a dialogue through faith and good works.

Jim: Would it be wrong, misleading, or inadequate to simply tell people that if they trust in Jesus as their Savior, God will save them from hell and give them eternal life?

John: It would not be wrong, but incomplete. Our response of trust has other repercussions. If you committed adultery then came back to your wife and said that you trusted her and wanted her to trust you, would that be enough?

What does it mean to be "further justified"?

Jim: Evangelical Christians believe justification is perfect and complete. It is the declaration of God whereby He credits His divine righteousness to the sinner's account. Roman Catholicism, by contrast, teaches that justification is incomplete. It is a lifelong process. Catholics are "further justified"[121] through regular reception of the sacraments and the practice of good works. Can you explain what it actually means to be "further justified" as a Catholic?

John: Again, justification is entering into and deepening a relationship by dialoguing with God. We answer His call of grace with an engaging dialogue of love, deepening our love for him as He *further* pours His grace into our hearts.

   If you can grow and *further* deepen your relationship with Jean by an engaging dialogue, by "sacraments" of love and deeds of service, why not with God?

Do you consider yourself to be good?

Jim: The *Catechism of the Catholic Church* says in a passage that you quoted earlier, "Justification is conferred in Baptism, the sacrament of faith. It conforms us to the righteousness of God, who makes us inwardly just by the power of his mercy" [CCC 1992]. As you are probably aware, that last sentence expresses a Catholic doctrine that was at the center of the controversy of the sixteenth-century Reformation. Catholicism holds that through baptism the souls of Catholics are made beautiful and pleasing to God. Luther and other Catholic priests and theologians objected, saying that the Bible teaches that justification is a declaration of God whereby He credits His righteousness to the sinner. The sinner is holy and blameless before God in Christ, not in himself. I am interested in how you understand this. Do you see yourself as personally good, holy, and righteous, or as an unworthy sinner who can stand before God only because of Christ and His righteousness?

John: Nobody—not even a sinless person—is worthy of a relationship with God.

Imagine yourself back in grade school, Jim. A neighborhood girl approaches you, saying, "You must marry me, Jim, because I've kept myself sinless and perfect." Would this give her the *right* to marry you? No. Nothing gives her a *right* or makes her *worthy* of your spousal love...*unless* you chose her and she accepted you in marriage.

When you conferred your "grace" and favor upon Jean in marriage, she became *personally* lovable—despite any past sins—and you gave her a *right* to your love.

So too with God. *His unsolicited choice* makes us holy. Nothing unholy can be joined to God. By accepting God's grace by faith and baptism, we enter a relationship (become grafted onto Christ[122]), making us grace-filled, personally lovable, good, holy and righteous...but with a righteousness and holiness that God confers on us.

Can you enter God's rest through working?

Jim: Earlier I asked you about the scripture that says "whoever enters God's rest also ceases from his labors as God did from his" (Hebrews 4:10). You responded, saying Catholics "'strive to enter [God's] rest" (Hebrews 4:11) with "active" works of faith and love.[123] However, Hebrews 4 says that we enter God's rest by faith: "We who have believed enter that rest" (Hebrews 4:3). What is the basis of entering God's rest through good works?

John: Look at the context. Hebrews 4 continues Paul's analysis of Psalm 95, exhorting Jewish converts to persevere, i.e., in "our confession" (Hebrews 3:6,14; 4:14). Who can enter God's rest? Nobody with evil or unbelieving hearts (Hebrews 3:12,19), no sinful (Hebrews 3:13,17), rebellious

(Hebrews 3:16), or disobedient (Hebrews 3:18; 4:6,11) person; but those who strive to enter (Hebrews 4:11), persevering in the confession (Hebrews 3:14) with faith (Hebrews 4:2-3).

Christ was persecuted for teaching that good works were compatible with Sabbath rest (John 5:15-18). Your insistence that justification is based on faith apart from works relies heavily—exclusively—on two passages from Paul, Romans 3:1–5:1 and Galatians 2:15–3:29—"man is justified by faith apart from works."[124]

Although James 2:1-26 teaches that "faith apart from works is barren...is dead," you attempt to reconcile this with Paul by proposing two distinct uses of the word *faith*. You contrast James (*faith devoid of good works*) with Paul (*genuine living faith—the kind of faith that saves— manifested by good deeds*).[125]

There is an alternative solution to this dilemma. Perhaps James and Paul are using two distinct meanings of *works* instead of *faith*.

In the Romans and Galatians passages, *works* is closely tied to adherence to the law, works of the law, circumcision, and paying ministers. The *works* of Paul could be summarized by *adherence to the law and circumcision.*

The *works* that James refers to, however, are *attending to the poor, loving one's neighbor,* the Ten Commandments, forgiving, Abraham's sacrifice, and Rahab's hospitality... similar to the *works* of Matthew 5:1–7:29 and 25:31-46: *Whatever you did for the least of My brethren, you did for Me.*

Try substituting these meanings into the passages of Paul:

+ **Paul's original statement:** man is justified by faith apart from works.

+ **With your *faith* substitution:** man is justified by *genuine living faith—the kind of faith that saves—manifested by good deeds,* apart from works.

+ **With my *works* substitution:** man is justified by faith apart from *adherence to the law and circumcision.*

The same could be done with James:

+ **James' original statement:** faith apart from works is barren... is dead.

+ **With your *faith* substitution:** *faith devoid of good works* apart from works is barren...is dead.

+ **With my *works* substitution:** faith apart from *attending to the poor, loving one's neighbor,* and so on, is barren...is dead.

The *works* substitutions sound intelligible, whereas the *faith* substitutions appear self-contradictory. These substitutions work with Romans 9:30–10:13, too! Besides, in the passages cited there is no evidence for distinct meanings of *faith,* whereas there is for *works.*

Moreover, the proposed *works* substitution resolves those difficult passages in 1 John:

> Every one who does right [*attending to the poor, loving one's neighbor*] is born of him...He who does right [*attending to the poor, loving one's neighbor*] is righteous.
>
> 1 JOHN 2:29; 3:7

This particularly fits 1 John since John criticizes the same lack of concern for the poor (1 John 3:16-18) as James does in James 2.

As you see, "testing everything; holding fast what is good" (1 Thessalonians 5:21) can reaffirm Catholic teaching. Perhaps you'd like to propose a different substitution to resolve this dilemma.

Jim: I don't believe there is a dilemma. Let me see if I can clarify the issue with this question: When Paul wrote, "We hold that a man is justified by faith apart from works" (Romans 3:28), was he excluding works as a *cause* of justification or as a *result* of justification?

John: Using your *faith* substitution, Paul would be saying, "Man is justified by *genuine living faith—the kind of faith that saves—manifested by good deeds* apart from works."

With my *works* substitution, "man is justified by faith apart from *adherence to the law and circumcision*"—that is, justification is *not* the result of *adherence to the law and circumcision.*

Jim: You say that Paul and James have two distinct meanings of works in view. Paul, as you see it, speaks of works of the law. James, you say, is talking about works such as caring for the poor, loving one's neighbor, and keeping the Ten Commandments. Yet in the law of Moses, of which Paul is speaking, we find caring for the poor (Exodus 23:11), loving one's neighbor (Leviticus 19:18), and, of course, the Ten Commandments (Exodus 20:1-17). In what sense, then, are Paul and James talking about distinct forms of work?

John: Earlier in Romans, Paul wrote, "It is not the *hearers of the law* who are righteous before God, but the doers of the law who will be justified" (Romans 2:13). In Romans 1:16–2:24, *works (doers of the law)* refers precisely to the Ten Commandments. *Hearers of the law* are ones who "love in word or speech," not "in deed and in truth" (1 John 3:18). James says the same (James 1:22-25). In Romans 3:1–5:1, Paul focuses on the ceremonial law and circumcision—not the Ten Commandments.

Jim: If when Paul wrote "a man is justified by faith apart from works" (Romans 3:28) he meant apart from the works of the law, of which the Ten Commandments are clearly a part, then isn't the Catholic Church teaching the opposite when it says that keeping the Ten Commandments is necessary for salvation?[126]

John: Romans 3:1–5:1 doesn't mention the Ten Commandments, yet it does mention *circumcision, uncircumcision,* and *law* (27 times), contrasting them with *faith* and *believing* (26 times). Obviously, Paul is condemning the Judaizers, who trusted in circumcision and demanded that non-Jewish converts be circumcised to be saved (Acts 15:1).

Jim: When Saint Bernadette was on her deathbed, she spoke with regret concerning those who did not understand the need to work to get to heaven: "As for me," she said, "that will not be my case. Let us determine to go to Heaven. Let us work for it, suffer for it. Nothing else matters."[127] Do her words here accurately reflect Catholic theology concerning salvation?

John: Her words reflect an aspect of Catholic theology, as do some Scripture passages, such as when Paul says, "My beloved, as you have always obeyed, so now...*work out your own salvation with fear and trembling*...holding fast the word of life" (Philippians 2:12,16), and, "In Christ Jesus neither circumcision nor uncircumcision is of any avail, but faith working through love" (Galatians 5:6).

Jim: Thanks for your answers, John. I have some concerns about the complexity of the Catholic plan of salvation and the relationship of human works to eternal life. I'll put my thoughts on paper and send you a letter sometime next week.

John: Very good, Jim. I have to prepare for a retreat this weekend held at Thomas Aquinas College. In the summer the college dorms become available for retreats and workshops.

I'll be busy most of the weekend preaching and giving spiritual guidance. Please pray that I be a good channel of the Holy Spirit for these men—that each of them takes home a few good resolutions and improves in their personal relationship with God and in their witness to their family, friends, colleagues, and acquaintances.

Letter 29

SATURDAY, JULY 7, 2001

Dear John,

I trust your weekend retreat went well. I know you are praying, as I am, for God's guidance in our correspondence. Reading the transcript of our last conversation, however, I was struck afresh by how far we have to go. Only with God's help will we be able to understand one another and make progress toward resolution of the doctrines that divide us.

With regard to our present topic, my primary concerns are three.

Baptism of Infants

I do not doubt the sincerity of priests in baptizing newborns. Nevertheless, I believe in doing so they do both parents and infants a terrible disservice. Consider the Catholic teaching that baptism is the "instrumental cause"[128] of justification, the "sacrament of regeneration" [CCC 1213] by which the child is born again. The baptismal rite symbolically portrays these doctrines. Following the pouring of water upon the child, the priest instructs the parents to clothe the child in a white baptismal gown. It represents the supposedly new state of the child's soul—cleansed of original sin, made holy and innocent. As I have shown earlier, however, one receives salvation not through baptism, but through personal faith in Christ. The priest, therefore, pronounces a cure over the infant where there is none. He thus misleads parents and child as to the true condition of the soul and the need of salvation.

Sacraments for Salvation

Rome makes the problem worse by claiming that the seven sacraments of the Church, and thereby the Church itself, are necessary for salvation [CCC 846, 1129]. It makes Catholics dependent upon the Church and an endless cycle of rites and rituals, rather than directly dependent upon Christ.

Again, there is no biblical authority for such claims. Your appeal to the Catholic Douay-Rheims Bible translation of Ephesians 5:32 as an example of the word "sacrament" in the Scriptures is unconvincing. Greek lexicons provide no support for translating *mysterion*, meaning "secret" or "mystery" as "sacrament." As you know, the Douay-Rheims, a translation made in the sixteenth and seventeenth centuries, was not made from the original languages of the Bible but from the Latin Vulgate. As the translation of a translation, it is hardly the best place to look for the proper rendering of a Greek word. Significantly, no modern Bible, Catholic or Protestant, follows the Douay-Rheims' lead in translating *mysterion* as "sacrament." The *Jerome Biblical Commentary*, a leading Catholic work with which I am sure you are familiar, gives the reason. It notes that though "*mysterion* is translated in the Vulgate by 'sacramentum,'" this Latin word "does not mean 'sacrament' in our modern sense."[129]

It will not do to excuse the absence of teaching in the Scriptures on sacraments by comparing it with the Trinity. Though the Bible doesn't use the word *Trinity*, it plainly teaches the doctrine that God is one and exists as three distinct persons—Father, Son, and Holy Spirit. With regard to sacraments, the Bible neither uses the word nor teaches the doctrine. Citing seven events in Scripture, as you do, and calling them sacraments, does not make them so. One could easily list many other similar events. Where in the Bible is the theology of justification, sanctification, and salvation *through sacraments?*

Good Works

The Bible states that "a man is justified by faith apart from works" (Romans 3:28). You say this does not apply to Catholic works for salvation. You say Paul is "focusing on the ceremonial law, such as circumcision—not the Ten Commandments, and so on—which is evident from the context."[130]

I believe the opposite is evident from the context. Paul specifically mentions the Ten Commandments in the verses preceding Romans 3:28. Beginning in Romans 2:17, he confronts his Jewish kinsmen with their guilt before God. The Jews have the law, Paul explains, but they are unable to keep it to God's standard. They fail with regard to the eighth commandment: "While you preach against stealing, do you steal?" (Romans 2:21). Similarly the seventh commandment: "You who say that one must not commit adultery, do you commit adultery?" (Romans 2:22). Finally, the first and second commandments: "You who abhor idols, do you rob temples?" (Romans 2:22). Paul then shows that Jews, even as Gentiles, are guilty before God, having failed to keep the law of which they are so proud. He concludes, "All men, both Jews and Greeks, are under the power of sin" (Romans 3:9), and "no human being will be justified in his sight by works of the law" (Romans 3:20).

How, then, can anyone be saved? What is God's solution?

Scripture answers:

> Now the righteousness of God has been manifested apart from law...the righteousness of God through faith in Jesus Christ for all who believe. For there is no distinction; since all have sinned and fall short of the glory of God, they are justified by his grace as a gift, through the redemption which is in Christ Jesus.
>
> ROMANS 3:21-24

You cannot separate the Ten Commandments from circumcision. They are integral parts of one, unified covenant (Exodus 20:1-17; Leviticus 12:3). Paul stressed this, writing, "I testify again to every man who receives circumcision that he is bound to keep the whole law" (Galatians 5:3).

Accept the good news, John. God "justifies the ungodly" (Romans 4:5). He justifies the "one who does not work but trusts him" (Romans 4:5). Salvation is not in a church, rituals, sacraments, good works, or us. It's not in Jesus plus these things. It's in Jesus alone. Whoever believes in Him will be saved.

Please prayerfully consider these three points, John. We leave on Monday for our annual trek to Yosemite. Maybe we can talk when I get back.

In Christ's love,

Jim

Letter 30

FRIDAY, JULY 13, 2001

Dear Jim,

I hope you and the family enjoy your outing to beautiful Yosemite. As you relax and have fun, I'll reflect on your last letter to address your concerns.

Following Scripture

Neither of us wants the other to lose "his share in the tree of life" by adding to or subtracting from God's Word (Revelation 22:19). You condemn infant baptism as added without scriptural authorization; the Pharisees condemned plucking grain on the Sabbath (Matthew 12:1-8). Christ rebuked them with Old Testament analogies, not explicit formulas. God never meant Scripture to be a list of short, explicit, legal formulas, but a record of His dialogue with man, with insights only "lovers" can discern.

One can inadvertently subtract from Scripture by oversimplifying and disregarding practices actually taught therein. As Jesus warns:

> Think not that I have come to abolish the law and the prophets...but to fulfil them....not an iota, not a dot, will pass from the law until all is accomplished. Whoever then relaxes one of the least of these commandments and teaches men so, shall be called least in the kingdom of heaven.
>
> MATTHEW 5:17-19

Somehow the New Covenant fulfills Old Covenant circumcision, but how? Infant baptism? What concerns me is that you could totally erase circumcision from the Bible without affecting your doctrinal position.

The Spirit infallibly guides us into *all* truth by bringing to remembrance *all* that Jesus said (John 14:26; 16:13). With practices such as infant baptism, we should analyze *all* Bible passages. I try to do this; I expect the same from you.

The Spirit Justifies

Does faith *alone,* or faith and baptism, *cause* salvation? God's grace is salvation's *principal cause,* but He expects our cooperation. But even that free cooperation is driven by the Holy Spirit—thus a grace—moving us to believe:

> This knowledge of faith is possible only in the Holy Spirit...He comes to meet us and kindles faith in us....Through his grace, the Holy Spirit is the first to awaken faith in us and to communicate to us the new life.
> [CCC 683-684]

After we first believe, the Spirit also moves us to dialogue with God in prayer and good works: "No one can say 'Jesus is Lord' except by the Holy Spirit" (1 Corinthians 12:3). Thus God's Spirit is the *primary* cause of both justification and sanctification. But faith, repentance, and baptismal regeneration are indispensable *secondary* or *instrumental* causes (see Acts 2:38):

> We ourselves were once foolish, disobedient, led astray...[but] he saved us, not because of deeds done by us in righteousness, but in virtue of *his own mercy, by the washing of regeneration* and renewal in the Holy Spirit...so that we might be justified *by his grace* and become heirs in hope of eternal life.
> TITUS 3:3,5-7

It's not just grace, nor faith, but baptism, too. Some Old Testament analogies illustrate baptism's causal necessity:

> Christ also died for sins…[to] bring us to God…[as] in the days of Noah…in which a few, that is, eight persons, were saved through water. Baptism, which corresponds to this, now saves you.
>
> 1 PETER 3:18-21

> Our fathers were all under the cloud, and all passed through the sea, and all were baptized into Moses in the cloud and in the sea.
>
> 1 CORINTHIANS 10:1-2

Had Noah not entered the ark, had Moses not lead Israel through the parted waters, all would've died, despite their incredible faith. Along with faith, entering the ark and crossing the sea were necessary secondary causes. So is baptism.

Infant Baptism

Although Scripture isn't explicit, had Noah's daughters any infants, the ark would've saved them, too. And surely the Israelites would've saved their infants, taking them across the parted sea.

Jim, you seem stuck in the logic that without externalized faith, infants cannot be saved. Yet how does John the Baptist receive the Holy Spirit as an infant without externalized faith? Other infants were possessed by demons, such as the boy in Mark 9:14-29 (the Greek, *paidiothen,* indicates he was possessed *from infancy*). Without consciously inviting in demons, infants were possessed. Christ rebuked the demons and raised the boy with His touch. Moreover, Jesus insisted on touching infants (Mark 10:13). So, wouldn't He want His baptismal waters to touch infants, too?

Again, the Old Testament prophetically refers to the Church as the New Jerusalem, a mother nursing her infants (Isaiah 66:10-13). Yet, your church refuses to mother infants.

Sacramental *Mysterion*

Jerome—a Scripture genius recognized by Catholics and Protestants alike—considered s*acrament* a covenant oath or sign with *secret* or *hidden meaning*. This fits the Greek text, *mysterion,* in Ephesians 5:32.[131]

Perhaps between a prostitute and her solicitor, sex means nothing more than monetary and sensual gratification. In Christian marriage, however, it not only signifies the covenant oath between spouses, but also Christ's relationship to the Church—a *meaning hidden* from non-Christians. We'll develop this more later.

Works in *Romans*

Romans begins by describing pagan sinfulness (Romans 1:18-32) then Jewish sinfulness (Romans 2:1-24); both are justified as "doers" of God's law (Romans 2:13) written on their hearts (Romans 2:15); but you skip this conclusion.

As only a figure of New Testament baptism, circumcision is useless to save anyone (Romans 2:25–5:1). This is where Paul says that "faith apart from works"—apart from *adherence to the law and circumcision*—justifies (Romans 3:22-31; 4:13-14,24–5:1); Paul presumes the believer continues *"doing" God's law* (Romans 2:13).

You continue to insist on salvation apart from the Ten Commandments. When someone asked, "What shall I do to inherit eternal life?" Jesus commanded him to love God and neighbor (Luke 10:25-28) and do the Ten Commandments (Luke 18:18-23). He concluded, *"Do* this, and you will *live"* (Luke 10:28). As became clear in our conversation, your reading of Romans and Galatians makes Paul contradict himself. Now your letter makes him contradict our Lord. Isn't there a better solution?

———

Although we still remain divided on some issues (mostly logic and semantics), the Scriptures are bringing us closer. We have seen many Scripture passages and how they relate to each other's position. Let's continue to reflect on these Scriptures, and with them the Holy Spirit will resolve our concerns and bring us together.

In Christ,

John

TOPIC 4
Worship

What is the meaning of the Last Supper?

Letter 31

Dear Jim,

You are probably still digesting my last letter. I hope it helped.

We move on to Christian worship, especially the Eucharist, a treasure very dear to me. May we deal with this respectfully. Here is a summary of what Catholics believe:

> Melchizedek's sacrifice, the Passover sacrifice and manna prefigured the Eucharist, which Christ instituted at the Last Supper, wherein He actually changes bread and wine into His own body and blood, which we worship as divine. Christ invites us to believe His words, "to eat His body and drink His blood," to be saved.
>
> The Eucharist is a "trinitarian" sacrament of love, expressing and deepening our relationship to God.
>
> The Father provides Christ's body and blood as spiritual food for His children. Faith in His real presence expresses and deepens our trust and gratitude in His providence.
>
> In the Mass we personally experience the saving power of Christ's one, true sacrifice on the cross as a memorial re-presentation...no mere symbol.
>
> In Holy Communion, the Holy Spirit—the personification of divine love—produces a life-giving nuptial union between Christ and us.

I am certain the Bible will confirm this teaching, one that early Christians died defending.

I leave tomorrow to give a three-week course on Philosophy of Nature, as I did last year. I hope to find time to respond to your questions and concerns.

In Christ Jesus,

John

Letter 32

SATURDAY, JULY 21, 2001

Dear John,

How is the course you are teaching on philosophy going?

Our vacation in Yosemite was beautiful. We arrived in the middle of a thunderstorm, but it quickly cleared up. For the rest of the week the weather was mild and breezy. Our last day we hiked up the mist trail to the top of Vernal Falls. Panoramas in every direction proclaimed the majesty of God. What will heaven be like!

Your brief explanations of the Eucharist and the sacrifice of the Mass were helpful. This is an exceptionally complicated topic. I am grateful to be able to discuss it with someone of your expertise. The issues on which I would appreciate a fuller explanation are as follows.

Transubstantiation

You say the bread and wine change into Christ's body and blood. The bread and wine, however, look suspiciously similar—identical, in fact—before and after the consecration. Your church favors the theory of transubstantiation to explain the alleged change. Given your training as an engineer, I would like to know how you understand this theory and whether you think it makes good sense.

Spiritual Food

You say that Christ taught one must eat His body and drink His blood to be saved. How does taking Christ orally benefit one spiritually?

Adoration of the Eucharist

In your last letter you said that Catholics worship the conse-crated bread and wine as divine. Doesn't this contradict the Ten Commandments? There God ordered Israel, "You shall not make for yourself a graven image, or any likeness of anything that is in heaven above, or that is in the earth beneath, or that is in the water under the earth; you shall not bow down to them or serve them" (Exodus 20:4-5).

Sacrifice of the Mass

You describe the sacrifice of the Mass both as Christ's "one, true sacrifice" and as a "re-presentation." Are you saying the Mass is not a *representation* of the cross, but a *re-presentation* of it? Would you explain this and how can you say there is one sacrifice if every Mass is a true sacrifice?

In Christ's love,

Jim

Letter 33

FRIDAY, JULY 27, 2001

Dear Jim,

It sounds like you and your family enjoyed Yosemite yet again.

I'm teaching Christian philosophy to about 15 college and graduate students and young professionals. It's part of the doctrinal formation Opus Dei imparts to its members, helping them better communicate the gospel in their place of work, study, and society.

Our present topic, the Eucharist, is not complicated, but requires childlike faith (Matthew 18:3) in God's love: "For God so loved the world that he gave his only Son, that whoever believes in him should not perish but have eternal life" (John 3:16). God's love is personal, more intimate than between husband and wife or mother and child: although she "forget her sucking child…yet I will not forget you" (Isaiah 49:15).

The Greek *eucharistein* means "thanksgiving." Christ fulfills the Old Testament Passover and thanksgiving sacrifice (Psalm 50) at the Last Supper by instituting the Eucharist, a trinitarian sacrament of love (three sacraments in one): "Having loved his own who were in the world, he loved them to the end" (John 13:1). The Eucharist allows each Christian to personally experience love from each divine person: Father, Son, and Holy Spirit.

The Father: A Spiritual Provider

The Father loves His children. Good fathers not only engender new life, but as breadwinners, also provide and feed their children (men who engender without providing aren't true fathers). God prefiguring the true bread from heaven by feeding Elijah, strengthening him to travel 40 days and nights (1 Kings 19:1-8) and His people in the wilderness with manna (see Psalm 78:24; 105:40; Exodus 16):

> "It was not Moses who gave you the bread from heaven; my Father [a good father!] gives you the true bread from heaven. For the bread of God is that which comes down from heaven, and gives life to the world." [The Jews] said to him, "Lord, give us this bread always." Jesus said to them, "I am the bread of life…"
>
> JOHN 6:32-35, comment added

The Father gives us Christ's flesh as "food indeed" and His blood as "drink indeed" (John 6:55). Jesus concludes:

> "Unless you eat the flesh of the Son of man and drink his blood, you have no life in you; he who eats my flesh and drinks my blood has eternal life…so he who eats me will live because of me…he who eats this bread will live for ever."
>
> JOHN 6:53-54,57-58

Sacrament of Faith

Science cannot explain matters of faith, as it cannot explain your wife's love for you. If Christ walked into your church one Sunday saying, "I am God," how would you prove it? Would you dissect His body in search of some divine organ, perhaps a divine kidney? No! Only by faith in His Word could one accept such a claim. With the Eucharist, "he who believes has eternal life" (John 6:47), not the person who explains it scientifically. Miracles, not science, helped Jews believe Christ's teaching. Eucharistic miracles may help us believe, but we still need faith. "Blessed are those who have not seen and yet believe" (John 20:29).

Transubstantiation

Exactly how bread and wine becomes Christ's body and blood without changing its appearance is a mystery. Yet what happens when we eat? When you consume an apple, its flesh becomes yours. The atoms don't change, yet somehow your body assumes dominion over those atoms and molecules, making them its own. Somehow Christ's body takes dominion over bread and wine, making them its own. Is change in appearance essential?

When God said, "Let there be light," the power of His word created light (Genesis 1:3). At the Last Supper, Christ said over bread and wine, "This is my body...this is my blood" (Mark 14:22-25). Catholics believe His words have power to transform these elements into His body and blood. So, at His word, Christ's flesh assumes bread and wine to itself, making "himself wholly and entirely present" [CCC 1374].

Eucharistic Adoration

Most Jews didn't worship Jesus because they didn't discern His divinity. For those who did, adoring Christ's body was not sacrilege but true worship, because His body is no graven image.

Catholics do discern Christ's body and divinity in consecrated bread and wine. This allows us to actively believe His words and adore His body as divine.

The Holy Spirit's Communion of Love

Let's move on. The Holy Spirit personifies the love between the Father and Son as the fruit and bond of that love. Similarly, He loves us.

What is love but the union of two spirits? Love makes two people become spiritually one. Lovers stop seeking their individual good to begin one life project pursuing a common good. Yet everything spiritual about us must be expressed physically; for example, physical sounds, inked letters, and digital email physically express our spiritual thoughts and desires. Love's spiritual union is expressed by a bodily union, be it holding hands, kisses, hugs, or marital intimacy.

When Catholics receive communion, we become one body with Christ, receiving His body and blood. His whole body enters ours and ours enters His, expressing an intimate spiritual bond with Christ and, consequently, with all Christians: "The bread which we break, is it not a participation in the body of Christ? Because there is one bread, we who are many are one body" (1 Corinthians 10:16-17).

The Mass: The Word's Sacrifice

Finally, the Word shows spousal love for us: "Greater love has no man than...[to] lay down his life for his friends" (John 15:13). Love becomes spousal by a total gift of self. Christ died for each person individually. He wants each person to directly experience His great love—His total self-gift, dying on the cross—thus He gave us the Mass.

The Passover prefigured this, allowing Old Testament Jews to participate in Christ's future sacrifice on the cross. Christ is the true Passover Lamb of God (John 1:29,36; 1 Corinthians 5:7). This yearly sacrifice commemorated their exodus from Egypt (Exodus 11–14), prefiguring the great exodus in Christ from slavery to sin.

Many Protestants feel strange attending Catholic Mass. They shouldn't. Holy Mass is a "remembrance" (Luke 22:19; 1 Corinthians 11:24) that re-presents Christ's life leading up to His crucifixion and death [CCC 1366] so we can participate in it. Just as one peers into the night sky at light from stars and galaxies emitted millions of years ago, when we attend Mass we experience Christ who walked the earth two thousand years ago.

The Mass begins with the *Penitential Rite;* as John prepared Jews for Christ with a baptism of repentance, repenting of our sins prepares us to hear Christ's gospel and participate in His sacrifice.

In the *Liturgy of the Word,* Scripture is read and preached. Here we actually enter into our Lord's own preaching. It is as though He were speaking directly to us, because sacramentally He is.

The *Offertory* brings us into the Last Supper. The *Eucharistic Prayer* consecrates the bread and wine with Christ's words, "This is my body….This is by blood," with His blood present on the altar separately from His body. Just as death occurs when blood is drained from a body, so this makes us actually—sacramentally—present at the sacred moment when Christ expired and died (John 19:30). Then the consecrated host is then laid in the priest's mouth, as Christ's body was in the tomb. Finally—to be saved (Exodus 12:8)—the faithful partake of the Passover Lamb, fulfilling Christ's command, "Take, eat; this is my body" (Matthew 26:26).

Melchizedek's sacrifice of bread and wine (Genesis 14:18-20) prefigured Christ's priesthood (Hebrews 6:19–7:17)—especially His sacrifice on the cross (Hebrews 5:5-10). "The sacrifice Christ offered once for all on the cross remains ever present" in the Mass [CCC 1364; Hebrews 7:25-27].

The *Great Sacrament*

Doesn't the marital union also re-present a couple's commitment to love and cherish each other until death? When couples reserve sexual intimacy for marriage, that intimacy re-presents their love and commitment. Although their wedding occurred years earlier, every marital act recalls, re-presents, renews, and reaffirms their commitment of love. As couples find this profitable, we find physical communion with Christ profitable. This reemphasizes the importance of marriage as a sacrament:

> Husbands should love their wives….as Christ does the church, because we are members of his body. "For this reason a man shall leave his father and mother and be joined to his wife, and the two shall become one." This is a great mystery, and I take it to mean Christ and the church.
>
> EPHESIANS 5:28-32

219

In communion, we become more intimately united to Christ than husband and wife: "He who is united to the Lord becomes one spirit with him" (1 Corinthians 6:17). God gave us bodies principally for this purpose, to receive the Eucharist: "The body is not meant for immorality, but for the Lord, and the Lord for the body" (1 Corinthians 6:13).

Paul warned, "Do you not know that your bodies are members of Christ? Shall I therefore take the members of Christ and make them members of a prostitute? Never!...For, as it is written, 'The two shall become one flesh'" (1 Corinthians 6:15-16). No wonder Paul said that whoever eats the bread or drinks the cup of the Lord unworthily is "guilty of profaning the body and blood of the Lord....For any one who eats and drinks without discerning the body eats and drinks judgment [KJV: damnation] upon himself" (1 Corinthians 11:27-29).

The hidden *meaning* is that the Eucharist makes us one flesh with Christ and members of His body: "He who eats my flesh and drinks my blood abides in me, and I in him" (John 6:56)—a great benefit!

Cannibalism?

What an incredible gift and manifestation of love Christ has established! No human could've invented this! God's logic of love totally surpasses our feeble imagination. Yet the early Christians understood it. Less than 70 years after Jesus' death Peter's disciple, Ignatius of Antioch, exclaimed, "The Eucharist is the flesh of our Savior, Jesus Christ."[132]

Because of this teaching, Christians were accused of cannibalism. So, in A.D. 150, Justin Martyr had to explain the Mass to troubled Roman authorities:

> We do not consume the eucharistic bread and wine
> as if it were ordinary food and drink, for we have been
> taught that as Jesus Christ our Savior became a man
> of flesh and blood...so also the food that our flesh

and blood assimilate…becomes the flesh and blood
of the incarnate Jesus by the power of his own
words….

FIRST APOLOGY, 66-67

I pray that you too may someday receive the grace of recognizing Christ "in the breaking of the bread" (see Luke 24:30-35). Until then, please continue to pray for my work with these idealistic young men here just outside of Boston. I continue to pray for you and your family.

In Christ's body,

John

Conversation 7

Jim: Thanks for praying for my family, John. God has blessed us in innumerable ways. Tonight my two younger daughters and I will be traveling to Honduras. I will be teaching there for two weeks. This will be my sixth trip to that country. I always return home encouraged by the zeal of the Honduran Christians. Though financially they have much less than us in North America, spiritually they are way ahead. I think there's a connection.

John: Please have those Christians pray for you and I, that we be completely open to Christ's truth and ultimately united in that truth. Let's you and I pray that they may be united to their fellow Catholic Christians of that country as well.

What is transubstantiation?

Jim: You gave no explanation of transubstantiation, except to say that it is a mystery. Since official Roman Catholic documents regularly use the term [CCC 1413], I think my request for a definition of transubstantiation was reasonable. I understand it is based on an archaic and unscientific concept taught by Aristotle. Do you think it is still valid?

John: The *Catechism* uses *transubstantiation* only twice, perhaps because our modern culture lost the philosophical notion of *substance*. Protestant culture lost it in the 1800s and

Catholic culture in the 1960s. *Substance* can still be used here as well as the doctrine of the Trinity.

> ...by the consecration of the bread and wine there takes place a change of the whole substance of the bread into the substance of the body of Christ our Lord and of the whole substance of the wine into the substance of his blood. This change the holy Catholic Church has fittingly and properly called transubstantiation...therefore, the whole Christ is truly, really, and substantially contained.
>
> [CCC 1376, 1374]

In our apple example, we can say that when one eats an apple its whole *substance* becomes integrated into the substance of one's being. If this makes better sense to you, then I'll use that language. I have no problem with it.

Jim: The theory of transubstantiation says that at Mass the substance, the inner essence, of the bread and wine change, while their accidents, their outward appearances, remain the same. Yet when Jesus turned water into wine, the disciples *tasted* it for themselves (John 2:1-11). When He raised Lazarus from the dead, they *saw* it with their eyes (John 11:1-44). When God the Father spoke to Jesus from heaven, they *heard* it with their ears (John 12:28-32). When Jesus appeared to Thomas after the resurrection, He invited Thomas to *touch* the wounds left by the spikes and spear (John 20:26-28). What precedence is there for a "miracle," such as the Catholic Eucharist, that cannot be perceived by any of the senses?

John: Our Lord chastised Thomas for demanding to put his fingers and hand in our Lord's nail-prints and wounded side: "Blessed are those who have not seen and yet believe" (John 20:29).

There have also been many accounts of miraculous changes of the consecrated bread and wine into flesh and blood.[133] One such miracle is over 1200 years old. The scientists studying the specimen under a microscope described its outward appearance as a slice of *living* heart tissue. So, sometimes God does change outward appearances to manifest what occurs substantially.

Jim: Why, after Jesus supposedly changed the wine into His blood, does He refer to it still as wine, saying, "I tell you I shall not drink again of this fruit of the vine until that day when I drink it new with you in my Father's kingdom" (Matthew 26:29)?

John: Our Lord was anticipating His crucifixion and death. After eating the Passover lamb and singing the Hallel Psalms (Psalm 119; Matthew 26:30), Christ and the apostles should have drank another cup. Instead of finishing the Passover, they leave immediately for Gethsemane.

At the very end of His crucifixion, our Lord is offered some wine or vinegar. He then sips the "fruit of the vine" and says, "It is finished" (John 19:30). This final cup ends the Passover liturgy, uniting it to the cross as one sacrifice.

Jim: Jesus' statement in Matthew 26:29 was made in the Upper Room. Moments earlier He took the cup and said, "Drink of it, all of you; for this is my blood of the covenant, which is poured out for many for the forgiveness of sins" (Matthew 26:27-28). And so, Jesus is referring to the wine before Him as "this fruit of the vine" (Matthew 26:29), which you say He has turned into His blood.

John: Perhaps our Lord was referring to the last cup of the Passover liturgy, which would've been just a cup of wine.

Is Jesus speaking in plain or figurative language in John 6?

Jim: What I consider to be clearly figurative language in John 6, you take as plain or nonfigurative language. From this comes your concept of the Eucharist. I would like you to comment on two verses from John 6, giving special attention to their parallel structure.

> This is the will of my Father, that every one who sees the Son and believes in him should have eternal life; and I will raise him up at the last day.
>
> JOHN 6:40

> He who eats my flesh and drinks my blood has eternal life, and I will raise him up at the last day.
>
> JOHN 6:54

How many requirements would you say Jesus is placing on the reception of eternal life here: one, two, three, or four? In other words, is Jesus here talking about multiple things, or just one thing in different ways?

John: Let's put John 6 in context. It was the time of the Passover and unleavened bread (John 6:4). With five loaves and two fish, Christ fed 5000 (John 6:10), not counting women and children (Matthew 14:21). Consequently, the people took our Lord to be a prophet (John 6:14), perhaps *the* great prophet of Deuteronomy (John 18:15-19).

After pursuing Jesus to the other side of the lake, the Jews asked, "What must we do, to be doing the works of God?" (John 6:28). Jesus replied, "This is the work of God, that you believe in him whom he has sent" (John 6:29). But the Jews asked for a sign. The great prophet was to be greater than Moses, who fed the whole Jewish nation for 40 years on manna (Exodus 16:35), including more than 600,000 men, not counting women and children (Exodus 12:37). The Jews expected more from *the great prophet*.

So our Lord promised them a greater sign. He will feed not just 600,000, but all nations; not just for 40 years, but until his Second Coming; and not with manna, but with

---

His own body and blood. Those who do believe (John 6:40) that He is the bread of life (John 6:35) by eating His body and drinking His blood will have eternal life (John 6:54). This is just one requirement.

Does the figurative interpretation of John 6 have any merit?

Jim: Jesus often used figurative language, even when speaking of Himself. For example, He said, "I am the door" (John 10:9). Clearly He is not a door, but like a door. One enters God's fold through Him. A study of Christ's teaching at the Last Supper reveals several figures of speech. For example, Jesus said, "I am the true vine" (John 15:1). He referred to the New Covenant figuratively, saying, "This cup is the new covenant in my blood" (1 Corinthians 11:25). The cup was not the covenant, but symbolic of it. Have you considered the possibility that when Jesus said of the bread, "This is my body" (Luke 22:19), He may also have been speaking figuratively? Or, do you think the figurative interpretation is completely without merit?

John: Jim, 1 Corinthians is not figurative. Christ was not saying, "This cup is the symbol of the New Covenant," but, "This cup establishes the New Covenant ratified in My blood."

Our Lord corrected those who misinterpret or misunderstand Him. He corrected Peter's rebuke of His crucifixion prophecy (Matthew 16:21-28). He also corrected Thomas and Philip at the Last Supper (John 14:1-11). In John 6, however, instead of correcting the literal interpretation of His words, our Lord reinforced it, leaving no doubt that He was *not* using figurative language.

When the Jews doubted Jesus' literal words, "I am the bread which came down from heaven" (John 6:41), He reiterated them with stronger and clearer language: "If any one eats of this bread, he will live for ever; and the bread which I shall give for the life of the world is my flesh" (John 6:51). Jesus used a generic Greek word, *phago,* meaning "to eat."

When the Jews doubted Him more, "How can this man give us his flesh to eat?" (John 6:52), Jesus used a stronger word, *trogos,* meaning "to gnaw or chew" (which is never used figuratively in the Bible). To emphasize the literal, Jesus used *trogos* four times: "he who [chews] my flesh and drinks my blood has eternal life, and I will raise him up at the last day" (John 6:54, comment added).

Finally, because the Jews refused to believe Jesus' literal words, Jesus allowed them to abandon Him (John 6:66). They were thinking according to the "flesh" (John 6:63).

Does the Eucharist save?

Jim: You say that Catholics partake in the Eucharist in order to be saved. Yet when Jesus spoke about eating His flesh and drinking His blood, He concluded, "It is the spirit that gives life, the flesh is of no avail; the words that I have spoken to you are spirit and life" (John 6:63). Wouldn't this indicate that faith in Him is what He intended, rather than the eating of His actual body?

John: Christ said to Peter: "Flesh and blood has not revealed this to you, but my Father who is in heaven" (Matthew 16:17). By this, Jesus indicated that Peter's knowledge hadn't come from human reason or public opinion (Matthew 16:13-14), but from the Spirit of God, who revealed it to him.

Often, *flesh* is contrasted with *spirit.* Flesh indicates human reason or desire, whereas the person who lives by the Spirit allows God to move him to love, faith, joy, and so on (see Galatians 5:16-25 and Romans 8:1-27). "No one can say 'Jesus is Lord' except by the Holy Spirit" (1 Corinthians 12:3), so we shouldn't be surprised that some disciples would reject this hard saying (John 6:60)—which is "spirit and life"—by not believing (John 6:64) and relying on the flesh, which is "of no avail" (John 6:63).

Is the worship of the host idolatry?

Jim: God says through the prophet Isaiah, "I am the LORD, that is my name; my glory I give to no other, nor my praise to graven images" (Isaiah 42:8). How do you reconcile this with the Catholic belief that every consecrated wafer has become the glory of God and is to be worshiped as divine?

John: That's simple, Jim; we worship only what is divine, not symbols or images. Paul said,

> Have this mind among yourselves, which you have in Christ Jesus, who, though he was in the form of God…but emptied himself…being born in the likeness of men….Therefore God has highly exalted him and bestowed on him the name which is above every name, that…every tongue confess that Jesus Christ is Lord, to the glory of God the Father.
>
> PHILIPPIANS 2:5-7,9-11

If the Father exalts and glorifies Christ's humanity, then we should too. We do this by worshiping Christ's body and blood present in the consecrated host and wine.

Jim: Your Church, however, is claiming each week to consecrate millions of hosts, typically embossed with a symbol, each a divine object of worship. Jesus taught, "God is spirit, and those who worship him must worship in spirit and truth" (John 4:24). Since spiritual communion is the goal, why must Christ be bodily present in the Eucharist in order for Catholics to have an opportunity to worship Him?

John: Consider what Paul said:

> The cup of blessing which we bless, is it not a participation in the blood of Christ? The bread which we break, is it not a participation in the body of Christ?

Because there is one bread, we who are many are one
body, for we all partake of the one bread.

1 CORINTHIANS 10:16-18

If billions of people scattered all around the world can
become one body by "participation in the blood of
Christ....in the body of Christ," then it is not so prepos-
terous that Christ's body and blood would become present
in more than one place at the same time.

We are creatures with body and spirit. Through the
incarnation, God—pure spirit—takes on and divinizes our
flesh.

Is Christ victim or victor?

Jim: Scripture presents Christ as having been sacrificed once
and only once. Presently He is enthroned in majestic
splendor in heaven (Hebrews 1:1-13). From there we await
His glorious return. Roman Catholicism, on the other
hand, teaches that priests are constantly re-presenting
Christ in "a state of victimhood"[134] on Catholic altars
around the world. At each Mass, under the appearances of
bread and wine, Christ experiences an "unbloody immolation"[135] as the "most holy victim."[136] How can Christ be a
victorious Savior if He is still being sacrificed as the victim
of the cross?

John: There is no repeat sacrifice, but only one. The *Catechism*
makes this clear over and over again:[137]

> The Eucharist is thus a sacrifice because it re-presents
> (makes present) the sacrifice of the cross...: "[Christ],
> our Lord and God, was once and for all to offer himself
> to God the Father by his death on the altar of the cross,
> to accomplish there an everlasting redemption. But
> because his priesthood was not to end with his death,

at the Last Supper 'on the night when he was betrayed,'
[he wanted] to leave to his beloved spouse the Church
a visible sacrifice (as the nature of man demands) by
which the bloody sacrifice which he was to accomplish
once for all on the cross would be re-presented, its
memory perpetuated until the end of the world, and its
salutary power be applied to the forgiveness of the sins
we daily commit."

[CCC 1366]

The sacrifice of Christ and the sacrifice of the
Eucharist are *one single sacrifice:* "The victim is one
and the same: the same now offers through the ministry of priests, who then offered himself on the cross;
only the manner of offering is different.

[CCC 1367]

Christ is *not* re-sacrificed nor re-offered. The Mass
brings us anew into His one sacrifice on the cross.

Jim: I'll address the re-sacrifice issue in a moment. Here I am
asking about the Catholic concept that Christ is continually re-presented in His victimhood at the Mass. We see
this also in your crucifixes, on which Christ still hangs in
agony on the cross. If Christ is the risen victor, why are you
continually portraying Him in the Mass as victim?

John: Paul said,

Jews demand signs and Greeks seek wisdom, but we
preach Christ crucified, a stumbling block to Jews and
folly to Gentiles, but...the power of God and the
wisdom of God.

1 CORINTHIANS 2:22-24

We too preach Christ (the Lion of Judah) crucified (as
a slain Lamb) (see Revelation 5:5-6). Christ, the Lamb of

God in heaven, continually offers the marks of His victim-hood to the Father on our behalf.

Jim: I understand the fact that the priest consecrates the bread and wine separately is meant to portray Christ in His victimhood. The priest asks the Father to "Look with favor on Your Church's offering, and see the Victim whose death has reconciled us to Yourself."[138] It was Christ's enemies, however, who crucified Him, not those who loved Him. Mary and Christ's disciples watched in horror as those who hated Jesus cruelly nailed Him to a cross. Why would Catholics want to continue this savagely brutal act?

John: We don't re-crucify Christ. We don't continue the cruel act of the crucifixion, but give thanks for God's goodness and Christ's generosity in His most horrific sacrifice. Christ established the Mass, not the Catholic Church, so we can participate in Christ's sacrificial suffering.

Is the Sacrifice of the Mass effective?

Jim: Scripture contrasts the continuous and ineffectual sacrifices made by the Jewish priests with the single offering of Christ: "Every priest stands daily at his service, offering repeatedly the same sacrifices, which can never take away sins. But when Christ had offered for all time a single sacrifice for sins, he sat down at the right hand of God" (Hebrews 10:11-12). The fact that Christ sat down indicates His offering was perfect and accepted by God.

Today some 400,000 Catholic priests continually offer the sacrifice of the Mass, many on a daily basis. I estimate the number of Masses at more than 120 million a year. That's almost six billion Masses just during my lifetime. The total down through the centuries must be over 100 billion! Doesn't this say something about the inability of the sacrifice of the Mass to deal with sin?

John: Jim, Christ offers the Mass, not the priest. At the consecration—the sacrificial moment—the priest does not say, "This is Christ's body...this is Christ's blood." No. The priest pronounces the words, "This is my body...this is my blood." Christ speaks through the priest. As a priest, I loan my voice to Christ, and He offers His one sacrifice to the Father through me [CCC 1566]. I can say with Paul, "I have been crucified with Christ; it is no longer I who live, but Christ who lives in me" (Galatians 2:20). As John Chrysostom wrote:

> It is not man that causes the things offered to become the Body and Blood of Christ, but he who was crucified for us, Christ himself. The priest, in the role of Christ, pronounces these words, but their power and grace are God's.
>
> [QUOTED IN CCC 1375]

Like the Passover, the Mass points to the cross, allowing each person to enter into Christ's one sacrifice on the cross. So there is no conflict.

Jim: My question is not about *who* offers the Mass but *what,* if anything, this offering accomplishes. After more than 100 billion offerings, should it not rightly be compared to the Jewish sacrifices which "can never take away sins" (Hebrews 10:11)?

John: Our Lord taught us to say in the *Our Father,* "Give us this day our daily bread" (Matthew 6:11). God feeds His children. It pleases Him when we thank Him and remember, re-present, what Christ did for us 2000 years ago. We do this at Mass, partaking in the great benefits of that sacrifice. It also calls us to get out of ourselves, sacrificing our own well-being for the good of others.

Jim: Rome says that each Mass, even as the cross itself, is a propitiatory or appeasing sacrifice: "The Lord is appeased by this offering, he gives the gracious gift of repentance, he absolves even enormous offenses and sins."[139] How can you claim there is only one sacrifice and at the same time claim multiple and distinct effects each time a priest offers the sacrifice of the Mass?

John: The Mass unites us to Christ's one Passover Supper 2000 years ago. In the Mass, the graces Christ won for us on the cross are applied to us.

Similarly, when we are baptized, Christ's blood is applied to us. Like baptism, the Mass is repeated to allow Christ's merits to be applied to us.

Jim: Immediately before giving up His spirit on the cross, Jesus proclaimed, "It is finished" (John 19:30). Evangelical Christians celebrate the finished work of salvation. "Christ died for our sins...he was buried...he was raised on the third day" (1 Corinthians 15:3-4). Why does the Catholic Church choose to focus on continuing the sacrifice of the cross? Why not leave it finished?

John: For the same reason Paul insisted on preaching Christ crucified (Galatians 6:14). Although it is finished, we want to continually enter into it, first by believing that Christ actually died for our sins, and then by following Christ's example in offering our whole life for Him.

We also preach Christ's resurrection from the dead and His glorious ascension into heaven to be seated at the Father's right hand. The Mass re-presents our Lord's resurrection, too. Mass ends when the priest says, "Go in peace," sending us out as Christ did with the apostles, "Go...make disciples of all nations" (Matthew 28:19). In the Mass, our Lord sends us forth.

What must I do to be saved?

Jim: In our earlier discussion of salvation, you said that faith, baptism, good works, and obedience to the Ten Commandments are necessary for salvation. Here you have stated that reception of the Eucharist is also necessary for Catholics to be saved. Is this a complete list, or are there other things Catholics must also do in order to be saved?

John: Jim, all you have to do is do God's will (Matthew 7:21). If God's will is for you to be baptized, will you not be baptized? If His will is for you to obey the Scriptures, will you not read and obey them? If God wants you to believe Christ's word to eat His flesh and drink His blood, will you not have the humility and faith to follow His will?

Jim: You say all one has to do to be saved is to do the will of God. Are you able to do His will well enough for your salvation?

John: No one can fulfill God's will perfectly. We stumble and fall like children, and our Lord lifts us up again before we attempt a few more steps. The main thing is that we are striving to fulfill God's will perfectly.

Jim, to understand the Eucharist requires faith. I would encourage you to pray for the faith to believe in this sacrament of faith, if that is His will.

Jim: Thank you, John, for answering these questions. It is not common to find someone of your qualifications who is willing to address such difficult issues.

I'll ask the Christians in Honduras to pray for us. Hopefully we can continue our correspondence via email while I am there, but conditions are oftentimes unpredictable.

Letter 34

WEDNESDAY, AUGUST 15, 2001

Dear John,

I hope you are well. I am writing from Tela, a town of about 100,000 on the north coast of Honduras. Evangelical churches here conduct a two-year course in Christian discipleship for young adults. Along with two other teachers from California, I have come to help with the instruction. We have brought with us six young people, including my daughters Faith and Grace. They are participating as students, taking classes, serving in various ministries, and living in dormitories with the Honduran students.

Yesterday I visited Pedro, the Catholic parish priest in Tela. Originally from Salamanca, Spain, he has been here for the past 18 years. I met him four years ago during a previous trip, and gave him a copy of *The Gospel According to Rome*. We had a chance to discuss the book briefly. I also told him about our correspondence, and promised him a copy of our book when it is printed in Spanish. He is a very gracious man and was appreciative of the offer.

Thank you again for answering my questions about the Mass. I know this is an especially sacred topic for you. I respect your loyalty as a priest to the position of your church. Nevertheless, I want you to understand why I cannot accept the Catholic doctrine of the Eucharist.

Context of John 6

We disagree as to the meaning of John 6. It is clear that the Jews made a demand of Jesus: "What sign do you do, that we may

235

see, and believe you?"(John 6:30). We differ as to how the Lord responded. You say, "Our Lord promised them a sign, that they may see and believe. He will feed...all nations...with His own body and blood."[140] Nowhere do I find Jesus making such a promise. Indeed, earlier Jesus told unbelieving Jews, "An evil and adulterous generation seeks for a sign; but no sign shall be given to it except the sign of the prophet Jonah" (Matthew 12:39). This promised sign, of course, is His resurrection, not the Eucharist (John 2:18-22).

What kind of sign is the Eucharist? The Jews asked, "What sign do you do, *that we may see,* and believe you?" (John 6:30). Is not a sign something that can be perceived? The Catholic Eucharist, however, is the "miracle" that no one can see. Indeed, earlier when I asked what precedence is there for a "miracle" that cannot be perceived by any of the senses, you reminded me of Jesus' chastisement of Thomas: "Blessed are those who have not seen and yet believe" (John 20:29). Now you say Christ gave the Eucharist as a sign that we may believe. You even claim there is scientific evidence of living heart tissue in a 1200-year-old Eucharistic host. This, if it were true, would indeed be astounding. Have you examined this alleged evidence? Is it published in any journal? As you are aware, in the field of science, research becomes credible only after it has been published and subjected to peer review. The fact that the Catholic author of *Eucharistic Miracles* says that such scientific evidence exists is not in itself a compelling argument. The book is filled with claims of similar questionable miracles.

Rather than promising the sign of the Eucharist in John 6, I believe Jesus was speaking figuratively of Himself. The chapter began with the miraculous feeding of the 5000. The next day, Jesus told the crowd following Him that if they wanted to do the work of God, they should "believe in him whom he has sent" (John 6:29). The Jews, in their unbelief, demanded more proof from Jesus, yet another sign, before they would receive Him as their Messiah. They even went so far as to suggest that Jesus bring manna down from heaven as Moses had done (John 6:31). Jesus responded not with the promise of a sign, but by telling them of the importance of faith in Him. He did this by means of an analogy linked to their request. During Israel's 40 years in the wilderness, manna was the food essential to their physical survival. Jesus wanted the Jews to understand that He was essential to their spiritual survival. He answered, "I am the bread of life; he who comes to me shall not hunger, and he who believes in me shall never thirst" (John 6:35). In other words, those who put their trust in Him would be spiritually satisfied forever.

As the discussion intensified, Jesus restated His claim and pressed His analogy harder: "I am the living bread which came down from heaven; if any one eats of this bread, he will live for ever; and the bread which I shall give for the life of the world is my flesh" (John 6:51). Here Jesus foretold of His death on the cross, not the sacrament of the Eucharist. He was not speaking of literal bread, but of Himself as the source of eternal life for all those who believe. He stated this truth in plain language: "Truly, truly, I say to you, he who believes has eternal life" (John 6:47). He then stated this in figurative language: "I am the living bread which came down out of heaven; if any one eats of this bread, he will live forever" (John 6:51). The plain and figurative expression of this truth can also be seen in the parallel construction of John 6:40 and John 6:54.

The Sacrifice of the Mass

I found our discussion of the sacrifice of the Mass difficult. In this matter, Catholic theology is mystical rather than rational. You say the priest who offers the sacrifice of the Mass ceases to exist as an individual and becomes Christ—"another Christ,"[141] in the words of your church. The bread and wine also cease to exist, at least with regard to their substance. They transubstantiate into a form of matter that is "altogether unique"[142] and for which there is no parallel in nature. The time domain also enters an altered state. The _Catechism of the Catholic Church_ says the Mass "transcends all times while being made present in them all" [CCC

1085]. And although each offering of the Mass supposedly has a corresponding appeasing effect upon God, you say there is only one sacrifice. It is impossible to discuss these doctrines rationally, for the Roman Catholic Church has redefined reality at every point of criticism.

I am going to stick to a nonmystical reading of Scripture. At the Last Supper the bread and wine remained bread and wine. Jesus referred to them as symbolic reminders of His body and blood. The next day the Romans crucified Him. "There is no longer any offering for sin" (Hebrews 10:18). The Lord proclaimed, "It is finished" (John 19:30). That's good enough for me.

In Christ's love,

Jim

Letter 35

MONDAY, AUGUST 20, 2001

Dear Jim,

While you were in Central America, I was at a camp for girls near Pala, California. I celebrated Mass, heard confessions, and offered spiritual advice to those who wanted it. I also taught the counselors a class on the Pope's Apostolic Exhortation, *Novo Millennio Ineunte* (At the Beginning of the New Millennium). It is an exciting vision of evangelization for the new millennium.

This past week I taught Catholic social doctrine to married women of Opus Dei, to help them find ways to have a positive Christian influence on the world through their lives and witness. I'm sure you saw the need to assist the people in Honduras to overcome their poverty so they can live in conditions proper to their dignity as children of God.

Is John 6 figurative?

Jim, I found your "nonmystical" interpretation of John 6 in your last letter novel. Is it your own? Is it sound, or is it doctrine suited to your beliefs (2 Timothy 4:3)? Early Christians read John 6 literally, as do Catholics today. Read the apostolic fathers. If you do, I doubt you will persist in this novelty. Also, review the context of this passage, as we discussed in our last conversation.

Your interpretation is inconsistent with Scripture. Scripture uses *drinking blood* figuratively to mean martyring (Revelation 17:6,16) or risking innocent life (2 Samuel 23:15-17). Figuratively, *eating flesh* means destroying God's people by war (Isaiah 9:19-21; 49:25-26) or sinfulness (Psalm 14:4; Micah 3:1-3). But these figures don't fit John 6. Even if they did, you leave many questions unanswered: For example, why didn't John clarify Jesus' use of figurative language in this discourse, perhaps by saying, "My flesh is *not* food indeed" (see John 6:55)? Why didn't Paul and the other evangelists clarify the figurative nature of the Last Supper Passover? Jesus verified this teaching in John 6 with miracles (John 6:1-14,16-21). Did Jesus confirm any other parable or figure with miracles? Would our Lord risk losing disciples at Capernaum (and 1500 years of Christianity!) over semantics? Why do Christians only turn away after the Reformation? I'll stick with Peter.

The Eucharist and the Incarnation

In many ways, Jim, you have remarkable faith, living by biblical principles and believing in Christ's redeeming crucifixion. Yet you struggle with 1 Corinthians 10 and 11, John 6, and our Lord's Last Supper words. You seek precedents for the "Eucharist, that cannot be perceived by any of the senses." What about the incarnation? Nothing perceivable can convince the senses that Jesus is God!

In the Eucharist, bread and wine becomes Christ's body and blood while retaining their appearance as food; in the incarnation, God retains the appearance of man! The Jews doubted Jesus' ability to assume bread and wine to Himself, murmuring—correctly—"How can this man give us his flesh to eat?" (John 6:52); they also doubted Christ's divinity.

Jesus never explicitly said He was God! When Jesus told the paralytic, "Your sins are forgiven," the Jews murmured—correctly—"Who can forgive sins but God alone?" (Mark 2:7). Jesus confirmed their interpretation, but without saying it explicitly:

> "Why do you question thus in your hearts?...But that you may know that the Son of man has authority on earth to forgive sins"—he said to the paralytic—"I say to you, rise, take up your pallet and go home."
>
> MARK 2:8,10-11

They also murmured because Jesus "called God his Father, making himself equal with God" (John 5:18). So He reiterates it, calling God *His Father* throughout the next two chapters (John 5:19–6:65).

The Jews tried another tactic, putting themselves on Jesus' level by calling God *their* Father (John 8:41). But Jesus rebuked them: "'If God were your Father, you would love me, for I proceeded and came forth from God....before Abraham was, I am [Yahweh].' So they took up stones to throw at him" (John 8:42,58-59, comment added). They searched the Scriptures (John 5:39) and found none explicitly stating the Messiah would be God. Yes, the Messiah would be called the *Emmanuel*, "God-with-us" (Isaiah 7:14) and "Mighty God" (Isaiah 9:6). Jesus applies the Son of Man prophecy of Daniel 7:13-14 to Himself (Matthew 24:30). But they murmured and misunderstood Christ's word because they couldn't bear it (John 8:43-45).

The Eucharist Prefigured

Faith in the Eucharist is similar. Melchizedek's sacrifice, the thanksgiving and Passover sacrifices, manna...these prefigure the Eucharist, fulfilling God promise, "I will bless your bread" (Exodus 23:25), the bread of Presence (Exodus 25:30; 40:20-23), which was part of the priest's ordination (Exodus 29:1-34), and which only they could eat (Leviticus 24:8-9) or offer to God (21:6-17).

David's men had to be holy to eat blessed bread (1 Samuel 21:1-6); Paul reminds Christians they must be holy to receive the Eucharist (1 Corinthians 11:27-29). Moreover, the Messiah was to be born in the "house of bread"—*Bethlehem* in Hebrew (Micah 5:2; Matthew 2:1-6)—because He would be the bread of life!

"Believe the Works"

The Jews rejected Christ's divinity because they lacked faith in Him, relying on their "flesh" instead. So, Jesus confirmed His divinity with miracles:

> I and the Father are one....If I am not doing the works of my Father, then do not believe me; but if I do... believe the works...know and understand that the Father is in me and I am in the Father.
>
> JOHN 10:30,37-38

If you won't believe Christ's word, believe His works...investigate the Eucharistic miracles. Scientific documentation is available.[143] The Catholic Church approaches such miracles with skepticism, demanding rigorous scientific investigation before giving its *nihil obstat* certification that nothing present opposes the faith.

After the resurrection, our Lord's friends—Mary Magdalene (John 20:11-16) and the disciples going to Emmaus (Luke 24:13-35)—needed miraculous graces to recognize Him. My faith recognizes Him in the Eucharist: "That...which we have seen with our eyes...looked upon and touched with our hands...the word of life" (1 John 1:1), "the bread of life." And I will die for the Eucharist.

So did a young man, Tarsicius, around A.D. 275. He was carrying a pouch of consecrated hosts to the sick when a small gang of boys surrounded him, demanding that he reveal his hidden treasure. He refused. So they beat Tarsicius, trying to pry the pouch from his hands and chest. Although dead, he would not release the pouch containing his Lord until the priest arrived and touched his body. Then Tarsicius released his treasure. He died witnessing to this truth.

I look forward to hearing your version of the Lord's Supper and Christian worship. I hope it is something you would die for. Although you cannot believe what Catholics do, I thank you for treating this topic with great respect. I will try to do the same for you. Let's ask God for complete trusting faith in Christ's words and works.

You are in my prayers,

John

Letter 36

FRIDAY, AUGUST 24, 2001

Dear John,

We arrived in San Francisco late last Saturday, physically tired but spiritually inspired by the zeal of the Honduran Christians. Though it's great to be back home, my daughters are already talking about a return trip.

It doesn't sound like you are getting much of a break this summer. Your teaching load appears to be as heavy in the summer months as during the school year. Any hope of a vacation?

I found your explanation of the Roman Catholic doctrines of the Mass of great interest. Here's a summary of how I understand the form of worship that the Lord instituted at the Last Supper:

> Christ asked His disciples to take bread and wine "in remembrance of me" (1 Corinthians 11:24). The bread and wine were to serve as symbolic reminders of His body and blood given for us on the cross. This memorial feast is a bittersweet time: bitter, for the bread and wine remind us how much the Lord suffered that we might be redeemed; sweet, for we rejoice that we have a Savior, who is coming again to receive us to Himself (John 14:3). We take bread and wine to "proclaim the Lord's death until he comes" (1 Corinthians 11:26). As the first Christians, we call this the

"Lord's supper" (1 Corinthians 11:20) or the "breaking
of bread" (Acts 2:42).

Compared to the complexities of the Roman Catholic
Eucharist and sacrifice of the Mass, this must seem rather simple
to you, John. Yet we believe it accurately fulfills our Lord's instructions and is profoundly meaningful.

I welcome your inquiries.

In Christ's love,

Jim

Letter 37

Dear Jim,

I'm glad your trip was inspiring. Hondurans are good people, perhaps influenced, I hope, by their Catholic culture. God willing, I'd love to visit Honduras and the other Central American countries. As for vacation, just getting away from the phone and other interruptions to be with people with an evangelizing vision is restful and reinvigorating.

Intimate Love

Evangelicals often help lapsed Catholics to establish or re-establish a personal relationship with Christ. Nevertheless, many return to the church to re-experience Eucharistic intimacy with God. For evangelicals, the most intimate experience of God seems to be Scripture, God's "love letters" to man. Yet rereading "love letters" pales in comparison to the total self-giving of marital intimacy. What is the most intimate expression of love between you and God?

Heavenly Worship

Jewish worship was "patterned" after heavenly worship (Exodus 25:8-9,40; 26:30; Acts 7:44). "Now…we have such a high priest…a minister in the sanctuary and the true tent [tabernacle] which is set up not by man but by the Lord….[The Jews] serve a copy and shadow of the heavenly sanctuary…[God instructed Moses], saying, 'See that you make everything according to the

245

pattern which was shown you on the mountain'" (Hebrews 8:1-3,5, comments added).

Is your worship patterned after heavenly worship?

Passover Sacrifice

The Eucharist was instituted during Passover (Luke 22:7-20). Was the Last Supper a Passover liturgy, and is that significant in your worship?

Discern the Body

Interpreting John 6 and our Lord's Last Supper words, you say Christ's "flesh," "body," and "blood" are mere "symbolic reminders" of His crucifixion. This seems to imply that Christ's physical body and blood are not food and drink *indeed*. Can you discern Christ's physical body and blood in the bread and wine blessed by our Lord and in your own communion service?

Figurative Interpretation

Although your worship is simple, it depends on a complex figurative interpretation of John 6. The Catholic Eucharist is more elaborate, but depends on a simple literal interpretation.

Some scholars apply the same figurative techniques you used on John 6 to John 1, insisting that John—a figurative and mystical writer—cannot be taken literally. They say "the Word" is a figure of God's idea of the Messiah. Since "God is spirit" (John 4:24), He cannot become man. So, according to these scholars, John 1:14 ("And the Word became flesh...") means God's idea of the Messiah became a man, Jesus Christ. Jesus is not really God, just the fulfillment of God's idea of the Messiah. How would you handle such figurative *Sola Scriptura* interpretations?

I am eager to learn more about how you worship and how it fulfills the figures of Old Testament worship.

Your brother in Christ,

John

Letter 38

Sunday, September 9, 2001

Dear John,

I am writing from the Koinonia Christian Conference Center nestled on the western slopes of the Santa Cruz Mountains. We are about eight miles from the California coast, just south of the city of Santa Cruz. The two churches with which I am associated in the Santa Clara Valley are here for our annual end-of-summer retreat. It's a time of teaching, praise, and recreation. I am using one of the scheduled free times to complete this letter.

As we continue our discussion, I want to begin by responding to the issues you raised in your last letter. I will start with your request for more details as to the form of our worship and your question as to whether it corresponds to heavenly worship.

Observance of the Lord's Supper

In the book of Revelation, chapters 4 and 5, there is a description of worship in heaven. Twenty-four elders, representative of the church, and myriads of angels are gathered before the throne of Christ. There they proclaim with a loud voice, "Worthy is the Lamb who was slain, to receive power and wealth and wisdom and might and honor and glory and blessing!" (Revelation 5:12). Our goal in worship is to likewise glorify the name of the Lord Jesus. We, His church, the bride of Christ, focus our attention on Him. A line from a hymn we often sing at the Lord's Supper expresses this well:

The bride eyes not her garment,

But her dear bridegroom's face;

I will not gaze at glory,

But on my King of Grace:

Not at the crown He giveth,

But on His pierce'd hand:

The Lamb is all the glory

Of Immanuel's land.[144]

In our observance of the Lord's Supper—or Breaking of Bread, as it is also called in Scripture—we place the bread and wine on a table, as was done at the Last Supper (Matthew 26:20). That night the Lord Jesus enjoyed the company of His disciples. Similarly, we enjoy fellowship with God at the Lord's Supper, having found peace with Him through His Son. We do not use an altar, an object associated with sacrifice, for we come to worship Christ, not to sacrifice Him. We praise the risen Christ, remembering Him in the Breaking of Bread each Sunday, the "Lord's day" (Revelation 1:10), the day of His resurrection.

We do this, as He has asked, "in remembrance of me" (Luke 22:19). A *remembrance* is something that helps us to call something to mind. The Breaking of Bread, as we understand it, is a memorial feast, a remembrance of Christ and His saving work on the cross. The bread and wine serve as fitting symbols of His body and blood. We also refer to them as *emblems,* for they visually suggest that which they represent. The bread calls to our minds Christ's body broken for us on the cross. Additionally, the one loaf symbolizes our unity in Christ. Paul wrote, "Because there is one bread, we who are many are one body, for we all partake of the one bread" (1 Corinthians 10:17). The wine reminds us of Christ's blood poured out at Calvary "for the forgiveness of sins" (Matthew 26:28). In partaking of the bread and wine, each person is expressing that he or she personally shares in the benefits of Christ's saving work on the cross (1 Corinthians 10:16).

Unlike Old Testament law, which regulated every aspect of Jewish religious observance, the New Testament allows Christians living under grace considerable latitude in their worship. For this reason, observance of the Lord's Supper varies in evangelical churches. There are biblical principles, however, that guide us. Jesus taught, "The hour is coming, and now is, when the true worshipers will worship the Father in spirit and truth, for such the Father seeks to worship him" (John 4:23). Our goal is to enter into spiritual communion with God. We want our worship to be Spirit-led (Romans 8:26; Ephesians 2:18). Consequently, we don't use prewritten liturgies and prayers. Our aspiration is that worship be spontaneous and from the heart, expressing our love for God in our own words.

Another principle that guides us in our worship is that every believer is a priest unto God (1 Peter 2:5-9; Revelation 1:5-6; 5:10; 20:6). Scripture instructs, "When you come together, each one has a hymn, a lesson, a revelation, a tongue, or an interpretation" (1 Corinthians 14:26). Any of the men are welcome to lead the congregation in a hymn, a reading from Scripture, or a prayer of praise.

After a time of worship, we give thanks for the bread, break it, and distribute it among the believers. This is generally followed by a short time of silence for personal worship. In like manner, we give thanks for the wine and partake of it. The meeting concludes after about an hour.

Intimate Love

Your comment that evangelical worship seems to lack intimacy with God surprises me. Certainly we are guilty at times of carnality and our worship suffers. But I don't believe this characterizes us. Attendance at our worship service, though voluntary, is high. Singing is hearty. It is not uncommon for someone expressing his appreciation for Christ to become overcome by emotion and shed tears of love. I can't recall that happening during my 25 years of attending Mass.

We consider the Lord's Supper the primary meeting of the church, but it is not our only time of worship or intimacy with God. Abraham worshiped on a mountain top (Genesis 22:5); Eliezer at a well (Genesis 24:6); Jacob at the head of his bed (Genesis 47:31). David wrote, "I will bless the LORD at all times; his praise shall continually be in my mouth" (Psalm 34:1).

The Figurative Interpretation

I don't believe your comment that our understanding of the Lord's Supper depends on a complex figurative interpretation of John 6 is accurate. We don't use John 6 to interpret Christ's words at the Last Supper. As we understand it, John 6 and the passages describing the institution of the Lord's Supper (Matthew 26:26-29; Mark 14:22-25; Luke 22:17-20) are distinct and should not be confused. True, both John 6 and the accounts of the Last Supper refer to bread. Both occur during the season of Passover. These similarities, however, do not negate the fact that the contexts are significantly different. In John 6, the Lord is speaking to skeptical Jews who have followed Him to Capernaum on the Sea of Galilee. It is the day following Passover. Jesus is teaching the necessity of absolute faith in Him. He makes no mention of taking bread and wine in remembrance of Him. Indeed, there is no reference to wine at all.

The institution passages, on the other hand, record events that occurred one year later on the night of the Lord's betrayal. Jesus is speaking to His faithful disciples, Judas having departed. They are enjoying the Passover feast together. It is here that Jesus, taking bread and wine, instructs His disciples, "Do this in remembrance of me" (Luke 22:19). In that the contexts are completely different, treating these passages as referring to the same thing can only lead to error.

You asked whether we consider the Last Supper to be a Passover liturgy and whether that is important in our worship.

Certainly the Last Supper was part of the Jewish observance of Passover. God instituted the Passover through Moses as a feast for the Jews. Rich in symbolism, it helped the Jews recall their exodus from Egypt. It also looked forward to the time when Jesus, the Lamb of God, would be sacrificed for the sins of the world. The Lord's Supper is something new and different. Christ instituted it to be observed by His church. Also rich in symbolism, it helps us to look back to the cross, calling to mind that great event and our victorious Savior.

Discerning Christ's Presence

You asked whether we can discern Christ's physical body and blood in our communion service as food and drink for us, since we consider the bread and wine to be, in your words, "mere symbolic reminders." No, we do not discern Christ to be physically present. We experience His spiritual presence. I don't know whether you have ever attended the Lord's Supper in an evangelical church. Perhaps you would like to join us sometime and observe. It may be that only then will you begin to understand how profound these symbols can truly be and that there is nothing "mere" about them.

In Christ's love,

Conversation 8

FRIDAY, SEPTEMBER 14, 2001

Jim: It has been a tragic week, John, with the destruction of the World Trade Center and part of the Pentagon. It's hard to make sense of it.

John: Yes, it is. Events like these challenge our faith, that everything "works for good with those who love" God (Romans 8:28). Yet, they bring out much generosity and heroism. Among the many courageous, I heard that there were two Catholic priests who died: one in the airliner that went down in Pennsylvania and one in New York administering to the sick before the first tower collapsed.

Do you know anyone affected by the terrorists attack?

Jim: A young woman who died on one of the planes was a coworker of a friend of mine. I am sure also that Christians with whom I am associated in New York are more directly affected, though I don't have any specific information at the moment. President Bush, in his address at the National Day of Prayer and Remembrance yesterday in Washington, spoke about the priest you mentioned.

John: May God bless all who have died or lost loved ones.

Why is it okay for you to commemorate Christ's "victimhood"?

John: Jim, I found much of what you said in your letters on evangelical worship applicable to Catholic worship. The Holy Mass is also called the Lord's Supper and the Breaking of

Bread, fulfilling the Scriptures you cite. I was especially surprised that your bread and wine "serve as symbolic reminders of [Christ's] body and blood given for us on the cross…[reminding] us how much the Lord suffered that we might be redeemed." Being remembrances of "His saving work on the cross," your services recall "Christ's body broken for us on the cross" and "Christ's blood poured out at Calvary" that Christians may share "in the benefits of Christ's saving work on the cross." This sounds Catholic!

Yet you accused Catholics of continually re-presenting Christ—the risen victor—in His victimhood.[145] Why is it okay for you to commemorate Christ's "victimhood" and not so for Catholics?

Jim: If the Roman Catholic Church simply taught that Catholics should commemorate Christ's death on the cross, we would be in agreement. The Mass, however, goes far beyond commemoration. The Catholic Church claims the Mass *is* the sacrifice of the cross. The Mass and the cross are "one and the same sacrifice."[146] The primary purpose of the Mass is to "perpetuate the sacrifice of the Cross"[147] [CCC 1323, 1382]. At each Mass, Christ supposedly undergoes an "unbloody immolation"[148] as He offers Himself to the Father through the hands of the priest [CCC 1354, 1357]. This re-presentation occurs as the priest prays: "Father…we offer to you, God of glory and majesty, this holy and perfect sacrifice…."[149] According to Roman Catholic belief, every time a priest offers the Mass, the wrath of God against sin is soothed [CCC 1371, 1414]. The Mass, even as the cross itself, is an appeasing sacrifice: "this is a truly propitiatory sacrifice,"[150] says Rome.

John: Yet we agree in the essentials: there is only one high priest and one victim—Jesus Christ on the cross—and only one sacrifice that appeases God's wrath. You partake "in the benefits of Christ's saving work on the cross," we enter into our Lord's life, death, and resurrection re-presented in the Mass for our benefit, *without* re-crucifying or re-sacrificing Him who is our one sacrifice. The real difference—as I see it—is that we believe that our high priest, victim and sacrifice—the glorified Christ—is really present under the appearance of bread and wine whereas you do not. Would you agree?

Jim: That is an important part of it, but your description is incomplete. We do not agree there is one sacrifice that appeases God's wrath. The Second Vatican Council said, "As often as the sacrifice of the cross by which 'Christ our Pasch is sacrificed' (1 Corinthians 5:7) is celebrated on the altar, the work of our redemption is carried out."[151] So with every offering of the Mass, the work of redemption continues in Roman Catholicism. We, on the other hand, believe the work of redemption is finished.

Does becoming emotional signify intimacy?

John: Jim, you connect intimacy with emotion. If an emotional movie made you and Jean shed tears of sorrow and joy, would that make it an intimate experience? Or if you found Mormon services more emotional than your own, would you conclude they achieved greater intimacy with God?

Do you really think that having some people "becoming overcome by emotion" signifies greater depths of intimacy in worship?

Jim: When the Lord came to the tomb of Lazarus, Scripture tells us, "Jesus wept" (John 11:35). When those standing by saw this, they remarked, "See how he loved him!" (John 11:36). Might not we say the same of those whose eyes fill with tears as they call to mind the cross of Christ?

Does your communion service include the Passover lamb?

John: You mentioned that you observe what "was done at the Last Supper," which occurred as Jesus and His apostles enjoyed "the Passover feast together." If you fulfill Passover liturgy, then you'd eat the flesh of the lamb, as God commanded (Exodus 12:8); those who didn't were lost. Do you share a Passover lamb at your communion service?

Jim: No. I did not say that we observe the Passover as "was done at the Last Supper." What I said was that "in our observance of the Lord's Supper...we place the bread and wine on a table, as was done at the Last Supper (Matthew 26:20)."[152] God's command in Exodus 12 to observe Passover by sacrificing a lamb is directed to Israel, not to the church. Passover is a distinctly Jewish feast marking Israel's exodus from Egypt. As Christians we are under the New Testament, not the Law of Moses. This was affirmed at the Council of Jerusalem (Acts 15:1-29).

John: Jim, is it possible that Jesus said, "This is my body....this is my blood" (Matthew 26:26,28) to indicate that He is the "lamb of God" (John 1:29,36) for the Last Supper and the New Testament Passover?

Jim: Jesus is the fulfillment of the Passover lamb. If He had taken some of the roasted *lamb* that night and had said, "This is My body," He would have been emphasizing that fact. Instead, He took the bread and said, "This is My body," thus instituting a new feast for the church. It is different and distinct from the Jewish Passover.

How do you avoid judgment for not discerning the body?

John: When I asked whether you discern Christ's physical body and blood in your communion service, you replied, "No, we do not." Yet Paul described how early Christians ought to celebrate the Lord's Supper, saying:

> Whoever, therefore, eats the bread or drinks the cup of
> the Lord in an unworthy manner will be guilty of pro-
> faning the body and blood of the Lord....For any one
> who eats and drinks without discerning the body eats
> and drinks judgment upon himself.
>
> 1 CORINTHIANS 11:27,29

How do you avoid judgment for not discerning the body?

Jim: We seek to remember Christ with solemnity and reverence, discerning the bread and wine to be representative of Christ's body and blood. In 1 Corinthians 11:17-34, Paul is warning the Corinthians about the careless manner in which they were remembering the Lord. There was discord among them (1 Corinthians 11:18). Some, having brought food with them, were eating their meal, while others went hungry (1 Corinthians 11:21,33-34). Still others were getting drunk (1 Corinthians 11:21). In this way, the Corinthians were partaking of the bread and wine "in an unworthy manner" (1 Corinthians 11:27). God was judging them for this (1 Corinthians 11:30).

John: You seem to say that Catholics incur judgment for profaning a *representation* of Christ's body by not "discerning the bread and wine to be representative of Christ's body and blood." Whereas Catholics understand Paul as saying Christians incur judgment for profaning Christ's actual body by not discerning Christ's flesh and blood in the Lord's Supper. Is that distinction accurate?

Jim: I don't believe it is. The emphasis of 1 Corinthians 11:17-34 is elsewhere. It's not on *what* the Corinthians were discerning the body to be. Rather, Paul is addressing *the way* the Corinthians were behaving at the Lord's Supper. Some, with disregard for the sacred ground on which they stood as they remembered the Lord, were even getting drunk.

256

Does your church offer incense and sacrifice everywhere?

John: Malachi prophesied that "from the rising of the sun to its setting my name is great among the nations, and in every place incense is offered to my name, and a pure offering; for my name is great among the nations" (1:11). How would your church's worship fulfill offering incense and sacrificial offerings "in every place"?

Jim: Malachi referred here to a "pure offering" (Malachi 1:11), not a *sacrificial* offering, as you have him saying. The Hebrew word translated "offering" does not necessarily refer to a sacrificial offering for sins, such as the Mass is said to be. Leviticus 6:14-23 uses it with reference to the grain offering, a voluntary act of gratitude, not an atoning sacrifice for sin.

Additionally, though some of Malachi's prophecies refer to the first coming of Christ, most refer to His second coming. Malachi 1:11 speaks of that future time. Then Christ's name will be "great among the nations" (Malachi 1:11), unlike today, when many use His name as a curse word and openly scorn Him.

John: Malachi 1 condemned the Levites' sacrificial offering of animals that were blind, lame, or taken by violence (Malachi 1:7-10,13). These were offered only in the Temple in Jerusalem. Malachi also prophesied that pure incense glorifies God throughout the nations. Does your church offer incense to God as is offered in the New Covenant worship mentioned in Revelation (5:8; 8:3-4)?

Jim: Yes and no. No, in the sense that we do not burn incense. As I pointed out, I believe Malachi 1:11 refers to a future worship by the Jewish people, not by the church.

In another sense, I could answer yes to your question, John, because in the verses you quote from Revelation, the incense is identified as representative of prayer. John writes of "golden bowls full of incense, which are the prayers of the saints" (Revelation 5:8). We do, of course, offer prayer to God.

Is our Lord's body the fulfillment of manna in heavenly worship?

John: When reading Psalm 78, I found an uncanny parallel between it and John 6.

The psalm tells us of the Jews in the desert (during the exodus) who saw God's mighty works, yet they lacked faith (verses 5-17). The unfaithful Jews challenged God, demanding food (verses 18-20), for they did not believe (verses 21-22). God fed them with heavenly bread (verses 23-28) and they ate their fill (verse 29). Despite all this, they sinned (verse 32).

In John 6, the people saw Christ's mighty signs (verse 2), yet they lacked faith (verses 26-29). Christ fed them (verses 5-11) and they ate their fill (verses 12-13,26). The unfaithful Jews challenge Christ, demanding signs and food (verses 30-31), for they did not believe (verses 36,64). Despite all this, they sinned, murmured (verses 41-43,52,60), and left Christ (verse 66).

Manna was called *the bread of angels* (Psalm 78:25; Wisdom 16:20-21) *from heaven* (Psalm 78:24; John 6:31), but our Lord's body is *true bread from heaven* (John 6:32,49-51). Do you believe that our Lord's body is the New Testament fulfillment of manna in heavenly worship?

Jim: No. I believe the Lord Himself is the "bread of God...which comes down from heaven, and gives life to the world" (John 6:33). Jesus said, "I am the bread of life" (John 6:35).

John: Many Old Testament events and signs were figures or types for New Testament events, such as Noah's ark, crossing the Red Sea, and circumcision, and were fulfilled in baptism (1 Peter 3:18-21; 1 Corinthians 10:1-2; Colossians 2:11-15). The bronze serpent was a type for Christ's crucifixion

(John 3:14-15). Does the Old Testament manna have any New Testament fulfillment?

Jim: When the Jews asked, "What work do you perform?" (John 6:30), suggesting Jesus give them bread from heaven as Moses had done, Jesus answered, "I am the bread of life" (John 6:35). It would be reasonable to conclude that the manna has its fulfillment in Christ.

Is John 1 figurative, implying Jesus is not God?

John: Jim, I asked you whether John chapter 1 can be taken figuratively in the same way you take John chapter 6. Yet you gave no limits to figurative interpretation. Are you implying that John 1 can be taken figuratively to mean Christ is not God but only man?

Jim: Perhaps some definitions would help. As evangelicals use the term, taking the Bible *literally* means understanding it in its grammatical and historical context. We seek to take each word, phrase, and sentence as it was intended by the author. We interpret them in their normal, usual, and customary manner as they were understood at the time that they were written. Where the author employs plain language, we take it as such. Where the writer indicates that figurative language is being employed, we interpret it accordingly.

Context is the key to knowing whether an author is writing in plain or figurative language. When John wrote that the Word "became flesh" (John 1:14), he was speaking of the incarnation in plain language. When Jesus said, "I am the bread of life; he who comes to me shall not hunger," (John 6:35), He was using figurative language.

John: I find the language "became flesh" (John 1:14) no more plain than "eat my flesh" (John 6:56). Moreover, nowhere else is "the Word"—Greek *Logos*—so closely connected to God as in John 1:1, evidence that John is using figurative language. But does that make this interpretation accept-able?

Jim: It is not the words of the short phrases you quote that determines whether they are figurative or plain language, but the context. There is some picturesque wording in John 1, but I don't think the overall context of John chapter 1 would support treating "and the Word became flesh" (John 1:14) as figurative.

John: Many early Christians had problems with a literal reading of John 1—Theodotus, Arius, Apollinarius, Sabellius, Nestorius, and Eutyches—to name a few founders of here-sies. In our day, we have Unitarians, Mormons, Jehovah's Witnesses, and so on. How do you respond to people who read John 1 figuratively?

Jim: People sometimes come to the Scriptures with their own theology and try to impress it upon the text. I believe John 1 speaks for itself, telling of the incarnation and that Christ was both God and man.

What precedence is there for the "miracle" of the incarnation?

John: The doctrine of the incarnation affirms that Jesus Christ is a divine person with two complete natures—inner essences—one human, one divine. Yet Christ's disciples only saw outward appearances, the "accidents" of His humanity. When Jesus appeared after the resurrection, He invited Thomas to touch the wounds left by the spikes and spear (John 20:26-28). But this was only evidence of Christ's human nature. What precedence is there for the imperceptible "miracle" of the incarnation?

Jim: I disagree with your analysis. Though "born in the likeness of men" (Philippians 2:7), Jesus' divinity could not be con-tained. Everything about His life sparkled with the super-natural. Even His enemies recognized this. The 12 saw Him with their own eyes "walking on the sea" (Matthew 14:26).

Peter, James, and John were with Him on the Mount of Transfiguration when "his face shone like the sun, and his garments became white as light" (Matthew 17:2). How can you say they saw only His human nature with their eyes?

John: Our Lord's flesh was quite powerful: "the crowd sought to *touch* him, for power came forth from him and healed them all" (Luke 6:19), even raising the dead (Luke 7:14). If you had the opportunity to touch Christ's healing flesh, would you?

Jim: I don't think we should conclude that everyone who touched Jesus' flesh was healed. Did not Jesus say to the woman healed by touching him, "Daughter, your faith has made you well" (Luke 8:48)? We are called to touch Jesus through faith in Him. In this way we receive salvation and ultimately, in the next life, are healed of every infirmity.

John: To receive our Lord's flesh hidden in communion is an act of faith for us. John 6 speaks of touching Christ's body to obtain eternal salvation. Are you willing to risk your eternal salvation and that of your family and congregation on a fallible figurative interpretation of John 6?

Jim: If your understanding of "Christ's healing flesh" is correct, then presumably every Catholic who receives the Eucharist would be physically healed of every infirmity. This, of course, as we know, does not happen. Also, just for the record, I am not trusting my "fallible interpretation" of John 6 for salvation. I am trusting Christ.

There are a lot of issues here, John. I know discussing them is hard for you, as it is for me. One thing that has struck me, however, is that we are dealing with issues that truly divide evangelicals and Catholics. Others have addressed them in books, but there has not been an immediate response from the other side. This is difficult, but it may be groundbreaking.

John: I agree. I will like to see how people reading this will respond, especially those outside our sphere of influence.

Jim: If I am able to get a flight, I will be speaking next week at the Word of Life Conference Center in Schroon Lake, New York. Few planes are getting out of here right now. Wherever I am, I'll be picking up my email, so go ahead and send me your next letter when it is ready.

Letter 39

TUESDAY, SEPTEMBER 18, 2001

Dear Jim,

I pray your trip goes smoothly. With air travel disrupted, I wouldn't be surprised that you encounter delays. I'm sure you'll take advantage of them to pray, read, and study, perhaps even our current topic.

Worship and the Trinity

Worship is a key difference. Historically, after the Judaizers, the first heretics challenged the doctrine of the Trinity and the *miracles* of the incarnation and Eucharist. But the Holy Spirit inspired great witnesses of truth to correct false interpretations of Scripture.

Irenaeus (†202), bishop of Lyons, fought *Gnosticism,* a dualism where matter is evil and spirit is good. Gnostics interpreted John 1 and 6 figuratively: since matter is evil, God wouldn't assume human flesh; God only appears to become and suffer as man. Moreover, a good God wouldn't allow evil matter (bread and wine) to become divinized flesh.

Irenaeus successfully countered these errors, teaching:

> When, therefore, the mixed cup and the baked bread receives the Word of God and becomes the Eucharist, the Body of Christ, and from these the substance of our flesh...nourished by the Body and Blood of the Lord.
>
> *AGAINST HERESIES,* 5.2.2-3[153]

Theodotus taught *Adoptionism,* that the Virgin Mary bore just the man, Jesus; God began dwelling in Jesus at His baptism, making Him the Christ; finally, God resurrected Christ, adopting Him as His son. Against Theodotus, *Hippolytus* (†235) defended Christ's divinity while teaching that bread and wine consecrated by the bishop became Christ's body and blood.[154]

Arianism was the most widespread heresy in the early Church, claiming that Christ is not one substance with the Father, but midway between Creator and creature. *Athanasius* (†373), in the East, and *Hilary* (†367), in the West, championed the truth, interpreting John 1 and 6 literally:

> For He Himself says: "My Flesh is truly Food, and My Blood is truly Drink. He that eats My Flesh and drinks My Blood will remain in Me and I in Him" (John 6:56-57). As to the reality of His Flesh and Blood, there is no room left for doubt, because now, both by the declaration of the Lord Himself and by our own faith, it is truly Flesh and it is truly Blood.
>
> HILARY, *THE TRINITY,* 8.14[155]

> After the great and wonderful prayers have been completed, then the bread is become the Body, and the wine the Blood, of our Lord Jesus Christ...[when] the Word comes down into the bread and wine—and thus is His Body confected.
>
> ATHANASIUS, *SERMON TO THE NEWLY BAPTIZED*[156]

Athanasius also corrected *Apollinarius,* for heretically teaching that the divine Word replaced Christ's human spirit, meaning Christ was not fully man.

More Heresies

Sabellius taught *Modalism,* in which Father, Son, and Spirit are merely three names or manifestations of the one God. Against this error, *Epiphanius* (†403) taught:

> We see that the Savior took [bread] in His hands...
> and giving thanks, He said: "This is really Me." And
> He gave It to His disciples and said..."This is really
> Me;" and none disbelieves His word. For anyone who
> does not believe the truth in what He says is deprived
> of grace and of Savior.
>
> THE MAN WELL-ANCHORED, 57[157]

Nestorius taught two persons in Christ, that the person of the
Word dwelt in the person of Jesus, making Christ a God-bearing
man rather than the God-man. His principal antagonist, *Cyril*
(†444), also interpreted John 6 literally:

> "And he that eats Me," He says, "that person shall
> live" (John 6:57). But we eat, not assimilating the
> divinity—away with such a folly!—but the flesh
> proper to the Word.
>
> AGAINST THE BLASPHEMIES OF NESTORIUS, 4.5[158]

Later, *Eutyches* taught *Monophysitism*, that Christ's human
nature was absorbed by the Logos. So, Christ had only one
nature—divine. *Pope Leo the Great* (†461) defended the literal
reading of John 1 and 6:

> When the Lord says: "Unless you shall have eaten the
> flesh of the Son of Man and shall have drunk His
> blood, you shall not have life in you" (John 6:54), you
> ought to so communicate at the Sacred Table that you
> have absolutely no doubt of the truth of the Body and
> Blood of Christ. For that which is taken in the mouth
> is what is believed in faith.
>
> SERMONS, 91.3[159]

Clearly, the great defenders of the incarnation and Trinity
also believed that we consume Christ's body and blood in the
consecrated bread and wine. Could it be that the Holy Spirit

guided these saints "into all the truth" (John 16:13) regarding the Trinity and incarnation, but permitted erroneous Eucharistic worship?

While Mormons and Jehovah's Witnesses don't accept a triune and incarnate God, their worship is similar to yours. Are you trying to have it both ways: a Mormon worship but a Christian incarnation and Trinity?

Interpreting John 6

For a safe and trustworthy interpretation of John 6, ask someone who knew the evangelist Ignatius of Antioch (A.D. 110):

> Those who hold heterodox opinions...abstain from the Eucharist and from prayer, because they do not confess that the Eucharist is the Flesh of our Savior Jesus Christ.
>
> *LETTER TO THE SMYRNAEANS*, 6.2[160]

The great witnesses of Christian orthodoxy are Catholic in worship. The Holy Spirit guided their scriptural interpretation, safeguarding the faith for future generations like our own. Perhaps our Eucharist is more elaborate; nevertheless, it is faithful to the early Christian interpretation of the Bible.

We keep returning to our original issue—whom should one trust: one's own interpretation, *Sola Scriptura;* or biblical interpretation consistent with Spirit-inspired Tradition and Spirit-guided Magisterium?

I found your answers to my questions somewhat vague and evasive. Does this mean that enough truth is getting through to your conscience and heart? May the Holy Spirit lead us—and those who will read this later—to see *His* truth through our faulty and inadequate witness.

In Christ's truth,

John

Letter 40

Dear John,

I was able to catch a flight. I am now at the Word of Life Conference Center in the Adirondack Mountains of New York. The Fall colors are just beginning to show. The air is mild and breezy. It's such a peaceful setting it is hard to realize that our country is still reeling from last week's terrorist attacks. As I expected, many attending the conference were directly affected. I had dinner with a young man from Staten Island who lost several friends in the collapse of the World Trade Center. We were joined at the table by the chaplain of the Air National Guard squadron that scrambled F-16 fighter jets in a failed effort to intercept the hijacked planes. His unit is now flying patrol over New York and Boston. Despite the immensity of the tragedy, these Christians exhibited the "the peace of God, which passes all understanding" (Philippians 4:7).

Why I Left the Roman Catholic Church

I was surprised that you found my answers vague and evasive. I assure you that it is not because I am wavering in my position about the Eucharist. As a Catholic seeking God, I studied the New Testament, looking for the religious beliefs I had been taught as a youth. To my surprise, I could find no solid evidence for the liturgy of the Mass, a clerical priesthood with the sole right to celebrate the Lord's Supper, or an example of anyone adoring consecrated

267

bread and wine. After careful study, I concluded that Christ meant for us to take bread and wine as symbols.

This created a problem for me as a Catholic. Each Sunday, as you know, the priest holds the host in front of those receiving communion and says, "The body of Christ." Each is required to reply, "Amen," meaning, "Yes, it is so." As you also know, no one may receive the Eucharist who does not believe in the real presence of Christ in the host. I decided that I would continue to attend Mass, but not receive communion.

The second issue, the one that finally drove me out of the Catholic Church, was the sacrifice of the Mass. It seemed incompatible with the gospel of Jesus Christ. How could I tell God that I was trusting Christ and what He finished on the cross and still participate in an ongoing sacrifice for sin?

About that time, some evangelical Christians invited me to the Lord's Supper at their church. I went, planning only to observe. We sat in a circle, a group of about 60. There was a small loaf of bread and a cup of wine on a table in the center. We sang some hymns. One of the men then stood up and led us in praise. This was followed by an elderly gentleman reading from the Scriptures. He then spoke with affection about the grace of God in sending the Lord Jesus to die for us. My mind and spirit were drawn back to that great event. The worship continued in this manner for about 30 minutes. Participation was spontaneous. The love of these Christians for Christ was evident. I had never experienced anything like it.

After a time, someone gave thanks for the bread. He broke the loaf, and they passed it, each person taking a small portion. Another gave thanks for the cup of wine, and they likewise passed it.

At first I felt uncomfortable, seeing several men taking the role that the priest alone held at the Mass. Yet Peter had written concerning all believers, "You are a chosen race, a royal priesthood, a holy nation, God's own people, that you may declare the wonderful deeds of him who called you out of darkness into his marvelous light" (1 Peter 2:9). *Could this have been what he meant?* I thought.

I left the Roman Catholic Church a short time later. It was the most difficult decision in my life, but in the 24 years since, I have not looked back. I remain confident that I made the right choice.

The "Church Fathers" Don't Agree

Before concluding our discussion of worship, I want to respond to your last letter. Your sampling of quotes from the so-called Church fathers does not tell the whole story. The spectrum of their beliefs was wide, encompassing both our views. Consider, for example, Tertullian (A.D. 160-220), the first important writer in the Latin language. Some Roman Catholic theologians, such as Jesuit priest John Hardon, list him as one of the 88 fathers of the Church. Commenting on John 6, Tertullian wrote, "The Word had become flesh, we ought therefore to desire him in order that we may have life, and to devour him with the ear, and to ruminate on him with the understanding, and to digest him by faith."[161] Here he agrees with the evangelical position, viewing John 6 as speaking of faith in Christ, not in the Lord's Supper. Additionally, transubstantiation was not the dominant view of the early church. The Roman Catholic Church did not even define it as dogma until the thirteenth century.

No One Is Beyond Error

I disagree with your contention that if the Holy Spirit has guided a writer into truth concerning the Trinity and incarnation, the same writer must necessarily be correct about the Eucharist. Tertullian again is a fitting example. Though he was the first Latin writer to formulate an effective theology of the triune nature of God and to introduce the Latin word *trinitas* (trinity) to denote it, in his latter years he embraced the errors of Montanism. Being right about one thing does not guarantee being right about everything.

I also question your statement, "For a safe and trustworthy interpretation of John 6, let's turn to someone who knew the evangelist Ignatius of Antioch."[162] Does who you know really make you worthy of trust? Were there not false teachers in the apostolic church? John says there were, and he knew them (1 John 2:18-19). One was Cerinthus, the Gnostic heretic. Judas Iscariot was a disciple of Christ. Who would consider him a trustworthy guide? Even Rome acknowledges that its Church fathers are not always reliable. Pope Leo XIII wrote that they "have sometimes expressed the ideas of their own times, and thus made statements which in these days have been abandoned as incorrect."[163] Catholic author W. A. Jurgens, whom you have been quoting, cautions against over-reliance on the Church fathers: "...we must stress that an isolated patristic text is in no instance to be regarded as a 'proof' of a particular doctrine. Dogmas are not 'proved' by patristic statements but by the infallible teaching instruments of the Church."[164]

As you state in your last letter, your confidence, as Jurgens', is in the Roman Magisterium. As for me, I shall continue to look to the Holy Spirit to lead me through the Word of God.

In Christ's love,

Jim

TOPIC 5
Mary, Angels, and Saints

*What is
their relation
to a Christian?*

Letter 41

TUESDAY, OCTOBER 2, 2001

Dear John,

With this letter we begin the fifth of the six topics we have selected to discuss. It is probably best that I go first in that the evangelical position is fairly simple as compared to that of Roman Catholicism. Here is a brief summary of how I see it.

> Mary was a godly Jewish woman who yielded her life to God's will (Luke 1:38). We consider her blessed, for God chose her to bear the Christ-child (Luke 1:48). Angels are messengers of God sent forth to execute His purposes (Hebrews 1:14). Saints are God's people. The word *saints* conveys the concept of separation from evil, hence holy and consecrated to God. Scripture uses the term to designate all true believers, not a class of exceptional individuals. See, for example, 1 Corinthians 1:2.

I assume you are in basic agreement with these beliefs. On other issues I know we disagree. Evangelical Christians, for example, do not venerate Mary, angels, or saints. We do not pray to them or consider them advocates or mediators between God and us.

Please let me know which issues you would like to discuss further.

In Christ's love,

Jim

Letter 42

WEDNESDAY, OCTOBER 3, 2001

Dear Jim,

Your letter came yesterday, the day Catholics thank God for the protection of His angels. We also celebrated yesterday the anniversary of the foundation of Opus Dei in 1928. Although this topic is straightforward, it contains many emotional issues that could blur our discussion. Let's pray for special light to avoid this possible pitfall.

Prayer

Catholics and Protestants often use similar words, but with different meanings. Protestants tend to associate prayer exclusively with divine worship. Catholics see prayer as conversation and dialogue [CCC 2653], including angels, saints, living family members, friends…I speak to you without worshiping you.

What does prayer mean to you? How do you converse with fellow Christians, friends, angels, and saints?

Honoring and Imitating Saints

The Old Testament honored saints (Abraham, Moses, David, Isaiah, and so on) as examples for us to imitate. Yet, New Testament saints are greater (Matthew 11:11). Should we not honor and imitate them, too?

Intercession of Angels

Intercession can also have different meanings. One is exclusive to Christ: "No one knows the Father except the Son and any one to whom the Son chooses to reveal him" (Matthew 11:27). But a broader type of intercession includes praying for others, witnessing "that all might believe" (John 1:7), making disciples, teaching (Matthew 28:18-20), and so on.

From Genesis to Revelation, the Bible shows angels interceding for us in this broader way. What do you mean by *intercession,* and how does this apply to angels?

Graven Images

God prohibited any "graven image, or any likeness of anything" (Exodus 20:4). I know you condemn Catholic statues with this. However, I would like to know if this also applies to picture books and children's Bibles, to photographs of loved ones etched (engraved) on silver film, statues of famous people or heroes?

Mary's Other Children

You've often reminded me that Mary had other children. Yet nowhere does the Bible explicitly mention them. You seem to disregard other possible explanations for Jesus' "brothers" without dealing with the textual evidence of Scripture. Is this not adding to Scripture, thus invoking the condemnation of Deuteronomy 4:2 and Revelation 22:18-19?

These are a few of the questions on which to focus our discussion. I'll be out this weekend giving a retreat for college men. I *pray* you to pray to God for me and for those making this retreat.

In Christ Jesus,

John

Letter 43

THURSDAY, OCTOBER 25, 2001

Dear John,

Sorry for the delay in getting back to you. I have had a busy teaching schedule lately, including a conference in West Virginia. I passed through Los Angeles on the way and would have liked to have seen you. I was traveling with Steve Caldwell, whom you met in January. Unfortunately, we had just a short layover—at least we thought we did. As it turned out, the air strikes in Afghanistan began the day before we left. Security at airports was at an all-time high. A long delay at LAX caused us to miss our connecting flight to Pittsburgh. United Airlines was able to put us on a flight to Washington, D.C., and the next morning we rented a car and drove the rest of the way. These were small inconveniences, however, given the difficult times through which we are passing. I trust you had less trouble traveling to your retreat.

Prayer

You asked in your last letter what prayer means to evangelicals such as me. We understand prayer to be speaking to God. We do not pray to anyone else, for in the Bible, there are no examples of prayer to Mary, deceased Christians, or angels. The most common New Testament word for prayer occurs only with reference to speaking to God. Jesus instructed, "Pray then like this: Our Father who art in heaven..." (Matthew 6:9).

Prayer can take the form of confession, praise, thanksgiving, or supplication. As Christians we pray to the Father in the name of Jesus. Our Lord promised, "Truly, truly, I say to you, if you ask anything of the Father, he will give it to you in my name" (John 16:23). The Holy Spirit aids us in our prayers. Scripture says that "through him [Jesus] we both have access in one Spirit to the Father" (Ephesians 2:18).

Saints

Neither do we find in the Bible a special class of Christian heroes canonized as saints. Every true Christian, according to the New Testament, is a saint. The word refers to those set apart for God's purpose, sacred in His sight. Because of their wonderful position in Christ, all true Christians are "holy and blameless" (Ephesians 1:4) before God. The New Testament makes more than 50 references to Christians as saints (for example, Romans 15:26; 2 Corinthians 1:1; Ephesians 1:1-15; 4:12; and Colossians 1:2).

You asked whether we honor and imitate New Testament saints. It depends on what you mean. Scripture tells us to "honor all men" (1 Peter 2:17). We also seek to follow the example of the godly men and women who have gone before us (2 Thessalonians 3:7; Hebrews 13:7). We are to "imitate good" (3 John 11). If, however, you are talking about venerating people, treating them as our special intercessors, praying to them, bowing down before their statues, or looking to them for special favors, I would answer no. We see such activities as going beyond honor and bordering on idolatry.

Statues

You are correct in saying that we do not use statues and other images in our worship. We base this on the Ten Commandments.

> You shall not make for yourself a graven image, or any likeness of anything that is in heaven above, or that is in the earth beneath, or that is in the water under the

earth; you shall not bow down to them or serve them; for I the LORD your God am a jealous God....

EXODUS 20:4-5

Because of this command, you will not find statues in evangelical churches or in Jewish synagogues. We understand this prohibition to apply to images used in religious devotion, not to pictures in children's storybooks or to the family photo album. The context makes this apparent. The command says we are not to "bow down" (Exodus 20:5) to these images.

Intercession and Angels

The New Testament word translated "to intercede" means "to plead with intensity" or "to speak to someone on behalf of someone else." I find your definition of *intercession*—which includes additional activities such as witnessing, making disciples, and teaching—too broad to be useful. Neither could I find support for such a definition in the lexicons I consulted.

We do not look to angels as our intercessors. Angels are messengers of God, "ministering spirits sent forth to serve, for the sake of those who are to obtain salvation" (Hebrews 1:14). Our intercessor with the Father is His beloved Son, our Lord Jesus. The Bible says with reference to Christians that "he always lives to make intercession for them" (Hebrews 7:25). John wrote that "we have an advocate with the Father, Jesus Christ the righteous" (1 John 2:1). Paul said, "There is one God, and there is one mediator between God and men, the man Christ Jesus" (1 Timothy 2:5). God has also given us the Holy Spirit to intercede for us in prayer (Romans 8:26-27).

Mary and Her Children

I think we are in agreement that there is much we can learn from Mary's life and much we should imitate. The Bible portrays her as a faithful follower of God. This is evident in the narratives of the birth of Jesus (Matthew 1–2; Luke 1:26–2:40). When the

———

angel Gabriel informed Mary that God had selected her to bear the Son of the Most High, she replied, "Behold, I am the handmaid of the Lord; let it be to me according to your word" (Luke 1:38). Though bearing the incarnate Christ was an immeasurable privilege and blessing, being with child before the consummation of her marriage to Joseph took great faith and humility.

The first time I read the entire Bible, however, I was surprised how little it says about Mary. After the birth of Jesus, there are only about eight events in which she is mentioned. Most of these are very brief, such as the incident about Jesus being left in Jerusalem at age 12 (Luke 2:41-51), Mary's request of Jesus at the marriage feast at Cana (John 2:1-11), and her accompanying Jesus on a visit to Capernaum (John 2:12).

Mary seems to have misunderstood Jesus for a time. Mark records that early in Jesus' public ministry, His family "went out to seize him, for they said, 'He is beside himself'" (Mark 3:21). Jesus' family found Him in Capernaum, surrounded by a crowd teaching inside a dwelling. Scripture says, "His mother and his brothers came; and standing outside they sent to him and called him" (Mark 3:31). The crowd relayed the message to Jesus, saying, "Your mother and your brothers are outside, asking for you" (Mark 3:32). Jesus' reply may indicate there was a breach between Him and His family at that time. He answered, "Who are my mother and my brothers?" (Mark 3:33). Then "looking around on those who sat about him, he said, 'Here are my mother and my brothers! Whoever does the will of God is my brother, and sister, and mother'" (Mark 3:34-35).

At the end of Jesus' ministry, we find Mary standing faithfully at the foot of the cross (John 19:25-27). The last reference to her in the historical narrative of the New Testament mentions Mary praying in the upper room with the Lord's disciples (Acts 1:14).

This is the extent of what is said about Mary in the Gospels and the book of Acts. The epistles do not mention her by name, though Paul briefly alludes to her role in the incarnation twice

(Romans 1:3; Galatians 4:4). Nothing is said about her later years or her death.

In your last letter you said the Bible does not explicitly mention that Mary had other children. You even go so far as to claim that I am adding to Scripture when I say otherwise. Yet in addition to the passage quoted above from Mark, the New Testament makes nine other explicit references to Jesus' brothers and sisters (Matthew 12:46; 13:55-56; Mark 6:3; Luke 8:19-20; John 2:12; 7:1-14; Acts 1:14; 1 Corinthians 9:5; Galatians 1:19). When Jesus taught in the synagogue of His hometown, the people of Nazareth were astonished. Knowing His family well, they asked, "Where did this man get this wisdom and these mighty works? Is not this the carpenter's son? Is not his mother called Mary? And are not his brothers James and Joseph and Simon and Judas? And are not all his sisters with us?" (Matthew 13:54-56). The first Gospel also states that Joseph took Mary as his wife, "but knew her not until she had borne a son" (Matthew 1:25). I think the implication is clear enough.

I am sure this raises other questions, John. Give me a call when you get a chance, and we can discuss this further.

In Christ's love,

Jim

Conversation 9

THURSDAY, NOVEMBER 1, 2001

John: Jim, today is All Saints Day. Today we commemorate all dead Christian men and women who are now living with our Lord in heaven. How appropriate it is that we discuss this topic today!

Jim: Where shall we start?

Where does Scripture say prayer is addressed to God only?

John: You confirmed our different understanding of prayer, quoting John 16:23,26: "If you *ask* anything…I shall *pray* the Father for you." John uses the Greek word *erotao* for "ask" and "pray." It is the only Greek word he uses for prayer. However, in John, priests and Levites also *prayed* to the Baptizer (1:19), the paralyzed man (5:12), and the man born blind (9:15). Greeks prayed to Philip (12:21).

In both the Greek and English texts, *prayer* seems broader than "speaking to God" *only*. Where does Scripture say prayer is addressed to God *only*?

Jim: Words can and often do have two or more distinct meanings. In its most general sense, the English word *pray* means "to entreat, beg, or ask." You used it in this way at the end of your last letter when you wrote, "I *pray* you to pray to God for me and for those making this retreat."

The word *pray* also has a specific theological or religious meaning. I would define it as spiritual communion and communication with God, often performed on one's knees as an expression of worship and submission.

Though the Greek word *erotao* "to ask" is sometimes translated "to pray" (in its general sense of *to entreat),* that does not mean the religious sense is intended in every place the word occurs. Further, the fact that *erotao* is found in the context of asking various individuals different things does not prove that the Bible teaches we should pray to these same individuals in a religious sense.

Consider your four examples of "prayer" to persons other than God. You said, "priests and Levites also *prayed* to the Baptizer" (John 1:19). Did they *pray* to John the Baptist in a religious sense, or simply "ask him, 'Who are you?'" (John 1:19)? Likewise, in your second example, the Jews did not pray to the paralyzed man, but "asked him, 'Who is the man who said to you, "Take up your pallet, and walk"?'"(John 5:12). Far from praying to the man born blind, the Pharisees had nothing but contempt for him. They did not pray to him but "asked him how he had received his sight" (John 9:15). Finally, you say the Greeks prayed to Philip. Scripture says they "said *[erotao]* to him, 'Sir, we wish to see Jesus'" (John 12:21).

The primary Greek word for prayer in the religious sense is *proseuchomai.* Where the context specifies the person to whom the prayer is directed, it is always to God. Jesus taught, "Pray *[proseuchomai]* like this: Our Father who art in heaven…" (Matthew 6:9). He never taught His disciples to pray to Mary or deceased saints.

Doesn't Scripture canonize Abraham as a saintly hero?

John: Abraham exemplifies how the New Testament treats heroes. God is the God of Abraham (Matthew 22:32); friendship with Abraham means friendship with God

(John 8:33-58). Jesus, Stephen, and Paul (Luke 13:16; Acts 3:25; Romans 11:1) acknowledge Abraham as the father of the Jews, Jesus' father (Hebrew 2:16), and our father through faith (Galatians 3:6-29). Jesus encourages us to imitate his deeds (John 8:39-40); Paul, his faith (Romans 4:12), his patient endurance (Hebrews 6:13-20), obedience, and hope (Hebrews 11:8-19); and James, his deeds manifesting faith (James 2:18-24).

Abraham is living (Matthew 22:32) with the saints awaiting redemption (Luke 16:22-30) or heaven (Matthew 8:11). Redemption is Abraham's blessing received through Christ (Galatians 3:14-18,29; Hebrews 6:13-19).

Don't these Scriptures canonize Abraham as a saintly hero?

Jim: I don't think I have a problem with Abraham being called a "saintly hero," if you stick to the definition of canonization that you give here.

Where does Scripture prohibit all images used in religious devotion?

John: Jim, some religious images pleased God: angels alongside the ark (Exodus 25:10-22) and earthly creatures throughout the temple (1 Kings 7:27-29; 9:3). So why do you conclude that Scripture prohibits all images used in religious devotion?

Jim: From the Ten Commandments, in Exodus 20:4-5. This passage prohibits the making and veneration of images. The examples you cite do not prove otherwise. God directed Moses to construct the mercy seat with two cherubim. He said to place the mercy seat with the ark of the covenant inside the Holy of Holies. Essentially, it was never seen again. This room was the dwelling place of God. Entrance was strictly forbidden. Only the high priest could enter, and only once a year on the Day of Atonement. In this way

283

the Lord safeguarded the mercy seat from becoming an object of worship. Likewise, in Solomon's temple there was a large laver resting on 12 bronze oxen (1 Kings 7:23-26). There were also ten bronze stands for smaller lavers. These were decorated with designs of lions, oxen, and cherubim (1 Kings 7:29). They were pedestals that held basins of water for the washing of the priests' hands and feet, not objects of religious devotion and veneration.

John: God worked "special favors" through objects connected with saints. Elijah's cloak parted the river Jordan (2 Kings 2:14), Elisha's bones resurrected the dead (2 Kings 13:21), Paul's handkerchiefs (Acts 19:11-12) and Peter's shadow (Acts 5:15) cured the sick. Do you know of any relic or object connected with a saint from your church (living or dead) that has cured another person while the saint himself was not present?

Jim: No, I do not.

Is prayer intercession?

John: If *to intercede* means "to plea" or "to speak on behalf of someone else" (as you say) and if *prayer* means "to speak to God," then we *intercede* when we pray: "Do not pray for this people, or lift up cry or prayer for them, and do not intercede with me" (Jeremiah 7:16). Doesn't this equate prayer with intercession?

Jim: Yes, we believe in interceding for one another in prayer.

What about angelic intercession?

John: Angels pervade Scripture: Abraham entertains three angels and *prays* them not to destroy Sodom (Genesis 18:1-33). Angels fulfill their mission by ascending and descending Jacob's ladder between God and man (Genesis 28:10-16). God redeemed Israel through an angel (Genesis 48:15-16). The angel told Tobit:

> When you and your daughter-in-law Sarah prayed, I brought a reminder of your prayer before the Holy One....I am Raphael, one of the seven holy angels who present the prayers of the saints and enter into the presence of the glory of the Holy One.
>
> TOBIT 12:12-15

Is this not angelic intercession?

Jim: No. Genesis 18 and 28 portray angels serving as God's messengers, not man's intercessors. The "angel" of Genesis 48 is a reference to God, not a created being. This is evident from the context. The passage reads, "The God before whom my fathers Abraham and Isaac walked, the God who has led me all my life long to this day, the angel who has redeemed me from all evil, bless the lads" (Genesis 48:15-16).

The term "angel" is used of God in several places in Scripture. For example, Exodus states that that "the angel of the LORD appeared" (Exodus 3:2) to Moses in a burning bush. That this is a reference to God is made clear two verses later. There we read, "God called to him out of the bush" (Exodus 3:4).

Your last quotation supports your case better. I cannot accept it as biblical evidence, however, for we do not consider Tobit or the other Catholic apocryphal books you have been quoting (Sirach, Maccabees, Judith, and Wisdom) as part of the sacred Scriptures. There are several reasons. First, Jesus and the apostles never quote any of the apocryphal writers, though they quote almost every book of the Old Testament. Second, the Jews of Palestine never recognized Tobit and the other apocryphal books as Scripture. This is because they were written after Malachi during a period when there was no Jewish prophet. Neither did the early church accept these books. Men such as Jerome, Origen, Athanasius, and Cyril of Jerusalem spoke against them. The character of the books are also different from those of Scripture. They contain fanciful stories and teachings that contradict the Bible. Finally, the apocryphal books do not present themselves as inspired. The author of Maccabees, for example, admits that his book is the abridgement of another man's work. He writes, "all this, which has been set forth by Jason of Cyrene in five volumes, we shall attempt to condense into a single book" (2 Maccabees 2:23). He concludes his second book with an apology: "If it is well told and to the point, that is what I myself desired; if it is poorly done and mediocre, that was the best I could do" (2 Maccabees 15:38).

John: Jim, Luke, too, humbly consulted his sources (Luke 1:1-4) and the prophetic period lasted until John the Baptist (Matthew 11:13), but we've already discussed the issue of the canon.[165] The New Testament Scriptures often reflect the Greek version of the Old Testament—which the apostles used. Revelation 5:8 reflects Tobit's view of angels offering God the prayers of the saints.

Jim: In Revelation there is a picture of the four living creatures and the 24 elders holding bowls full of incense. These represent "the prayers of the saints" (Revelation 5:8). As you mention, these bowls are presented to the Lord. I wouldn't use this figurative picture to argue that angels are our intercessors, serving as mediators between God and us. To the contrary, angels are God's messengers, His agents "sent forth to serve, for the sake of those who are to obtain salvation" (Hebrews 1:14).

John: Our Lord says the angels of children "always behold the face of my Father who is in heaven" (Matthew 18:10). If children cannot understand and believe their angel's message, why would God give them angels if not to intercede for them before God?

Jim: Because He has given them someone far greater than any mere angel to intercede for them, the Lord Jesus Christ, God's beloved Son.

John: Scripture shows Mary dialoguing with God through the angel Gabriel (Luke 1:28-38). Does Scripture prohibit replying to God through angels?

Jim: I don't believe there is a verse that says, "Thou shalt not pray through angels." The biblical formula for Christian prayer, however, is to pray in the Spirit to the Father in the name of the Son (Ephesians 2:18). This is far superior than going to God through a created being, such as an angel, man, or woman. We should want to avail of God's best, not some proposed means that does not have a biblical basis.

John: In the parable of the rich man and Lazarus, the rich man asks Abraham to intercede for his brothers (Luke 16:19-31). If Christ prohibits praying to saints, why would He teach this and give us a bad example by conversing—praying in the broad sense—with two Old Testament saints, Moses and Elijah (Luke 9:30)?

Jim: The Lord is the God of the living, not the dead (Matthew 22:32). It is appropriate, therefore, for Jesus to converse with Moses and Elijah at the Transfiguration. These men were alive with God in heaven. As for interceding through saints in heaven based on the story of Luke 16:19-31, does the passage not show that Abraham was unable to intercede for this man? There was nothing he could do for him.

Does reference to Jesus' brothers imply Mary had other children?

John: Jim, you must know that Hebrew and Aramaic, which Jesus spoke, have no word for *cousin*. Instead, they call *cousins* and other close relatives *brothers* and *sisters*, as Abraham calls his nephew Lot *brother* (Genesis 13:8).

Isn't it odd that the Virgin Mary's sister was also named Mary (wife of Clopas, John 19:25)? Now it wouldn't be so odd if they were cousins. Mary of Clopas was the mother of James and Joseph (Matthew 27:56). Can you explain

287

how *Jesus' brothers* James and Joseph (Matthew 13:55), born of the Virgin Mary's "sister," implies she had other children?

Jim: Though Aramaic does not have a unique word for *cousin*, it can certainly distinguish between a brother and cousin. Speakers simply referred to cousins as "my uncle's son" (*bar dodi* = literally: "son of my uncle"). Hebrew uses a similar phrase. For example, Jeremiah writes of "Hanamel my cousin [uncle's son]" (Jeremiah 32:8). Additionally, it is not certain that Jesus always taught in Aramaic. He would have also been fluent in Greek, having lived His life in "Galilee of the Gentiles" (Matthew 4:15).

Finally, we must ask, Is the fact that Jesus taught in Aramaic relevant? The Holy Spirit chose Greek to be the language of the inspired New Testament Scriptures. Greek has one word for brother (*adelphos*), another word for cousin (*anepsios*), and a third word for kinsman or relative (*sungenis*). The Bible, for example, says that Mark was "the cousin of Barnabas" (*anepsios*, Colossians 4:10). Elizabeth was Mary's "kinswoman" (*sungenis*, Luke 1:36). In 17 verses, by contrast, the inspired writers of the Greek New Testament refer specifically to Jesus' brothers or sisters (various forms of *adelphos*). Four of these are quotations of statements by Jesus (Matthew 12:48-49; Mark 3:33; Luke 8:21). Five are the quotations of others (Matthew 13:55-56; Mark 3:32; Mark 6:3; Luke 8:20). Eight are part of the Greek narrative, not a translation from Aramaic (Matthew 12:46; Luke 8:19; John 2:12; 7:3,10; Acts 1:14; 1 Corinthians 9:5; Galatians 1:19). All 17 specify through the precision of the Greek language that these individuals were not Jesus' cousins but His brothers and sisters.

You ask if I find it odd that Mary and her sister had the same first name. It may be unusual, but it happens even today, typically with different middle names. Mary was a common name among the Jews in honor of Miriam,

Moses' sister. There are five Marys in the New Testament. That two sisters would both be called Mary is less odd when upon closer examination we see that they have variations of the same name. Luke refers to the Lord's mother as *Mariam* (Luke 1:27) and her sister as *Maria* (Luke 24:10). Both are translated into English as Mary.

As you point out, Clopas and Mary had two sons, "James and Joseph" (Matthew 27:56). Jesus' brothers are listed as "James and Joseph and Simon and Judas" (Matthew 13:55). Cousins having the same name is not unusual, usually given to honor other family members. James and Joseph were common Jewish names. James is a derivation of Jacob, the nation's patriarch. Joseph was Jacob's favorite son. There are 14 Josephs mentioned in the Bible. We would expect one of Jesus' brothers to be named Joseph, since that was his father's name.

John: The *Catechism of the Church* states:

> Against this doctrine the objection is sometimes raised that the Bible mentions brothers and sisters of Jesus (cf. Mark 3:31-35; 6:3; 1 Corinthians 9:5; Galatians 1:19). The Church has always understood these passages as not referring to other children of the Virgin Mary. In fact James and Joseph, "brothers of Jesus," are the sons of another Mary, a disciple of Christ, whom St. Matthew significantly calls "the other Mary" (Matthew 13:55; 28:1; cf. 27:56). They are close relations of Jesus, according to an Old Testament expression (cf. Genesis 13:8; 14:16; 29:15; etc.).
>
> [CCC 500]

Scripture also chastises Herod for marrying Herodias, "his brother Philip's wife" (Mark 6:17). Yet Herod's mother was Malthace and Philip's, Mariamne. Scripture still calls them *brothers* (*adelphos*). Could Jesus' *brothers* (*adelphos*) have possibly come from different mothers?

Jim: If they had different mothers, then they wouldn't be brothers, because Joseph was not the father of Jesus. Further, in the example you give, Herod and Philip had the same father, Herod the Great, so they were half-brothers. Nevertheless, the Greek uses *adelphos*. Similarly, with Jesus, "James and Joseph and Simon and Judas" (Matthew 13:55) are identified as "his brothers" (*adelphoi*, Matthew 13:55), when in fact they are His half-brothers, Jesus not being the biological son of Joseph.

Would God just *use* Mary?

John: Jim, would Jesus ever say to His mother, "What you would have gained from me is Corban" (that is, given to God, see Mark 7:11-12)? Would God just *use* Mary to bear Him in her womb and then deny any special relationship to His mother?

Jim: No, I wouldn't think so.

Is implying Mary is a harlot offensive to Jesus?

John: The "until" of Matthew 1:25—that Joseph "knew her not *until* [Greek *eos*]…"—is similar to Jesus' promise to remain with us "*until* [Greek *eos*] the completion of the age" (Matthew 28:20, Darby Translation). This doesn't imply He will abandon us afterwards—at least I hope not!

What you seem to imply is that Mary plays the harlot by having children by another lover (Joseph in this case) after having Jesus by the Holy Spirit, since:

> If a man divorces his wife and she goes from him and becomes another man's wife, will he return to her?…You have played the harlot with many lovers; and would you return to me? says the LORD.
>
> JEREMIAH 3:1

If someone implied this of your mother, wouldn't you take offense? Isn't doing the same to Mary a great offense to Jesus?

Jim: Does my claim that Mary had children by Joseph after the birth of Jesus really make her a harlot and Joseph "another lover"? Before drawing such conclusions, note that under Jewish law, Joseph and Mary were already husband and wife. Scripture identifies Joseph as Mary's "husband" (Matthew 1:19), Mary as Joseph's "wife" (Matthew 1:20). Recall that "the angel Gabriel was sent...to a virgin betrothed to a man whose name was Joseph" (Luke 1:26-27). As betrothed, they had made a legally binding marriage contract, sealed by the presentation of a dowry. All that remained was for Joseph to take Mary into his house and celebrate the wedding feast. During this betrothal period, if "a betrothed virgin" (Deuteronomy 22:23) were to have sexual relations with some other man, the two of them were to be punished as adulterers (Deuteronomy 22:23-24). The second man has "violated his neighbor's wife" (Deuteronomy 22:24). Consequently, Joseph was not "another lover," but Mary's legal husband even at the time she conceived the Christ-child.

Frankly, I think your whole line of reasoning should be abandoned. We cannot apply the terms of human relations to this extraordinary case. Mary and the Holy Spirit were not lovers, were not married, and did not have sexual relations. No divorce occurred, so Jeremiah 3:1 does not apply. Neither should we question the propriety of Joseph and Mary having children. They were legally married, of which the Lord says, "they become one flesh" (Genesis 2:24). After the birth of Jesus, they had children. What's wrong with that?

John: Mary's reply to Gabriel implies she and Joseph were committed to virginity: "How can this be [How can I become the Messiah's mother], since I do not know man" (the literal translation of Luke 1:34, comment added)? If Mary committed herself to virginity, then to accuse her otherwise would be offensive, would it not?

Jim: During the betrothal period, a man and woman did not live together or have sexual relations. In the Jewish custom of marriage, first the couple is betrothed by contract. Later the groom comes with his family and friends to the bride's home and receives his bride into his family. They return to his father's house and celebrate a great wedding feast. The consummation of the marriage follows. When Mary told Gabriel, "How can this be, since I do not know man?" she was referring to the fact she and Joseph had yet to have sexual relations. This cannot be construed as a vow of lifelong celibacy.

John: Jim, thank you for bearing with me through these questions. I appreciate your responses. They reveal how differently we approach and understand Scripture.

Jim: It's been good talking with you, John. I suggest we break from our normal pattern and give you a chance to explain your beliefs concerning Mary, angels, and saints. It may make more sense to get your views on the table before discussing this topic further. Roman Catholic doctrine in this area is far more extensive than that of evangelicals. In your next letter, in addition to your appraisal of my position, why don't you summarize your own? We can go on from there.

Letter 44

WEDNESDAY, NOVEMBER 7, 2001

Dear Jim,

How are things in the McCarthy house? I just finished a private tutorial for a priest exploring possibilities related to future studies. I find one-on-one exchanges so beneficial, no matter with whom, because their challenging questions are unavoidable, forcing me to think. That's what I like about our conversations, too.

Scriptural Accounting

In Letter 43, you wrote: "The first time I read the entire Bible, however, I was surprised how little it says about Mary." Yet, you cited 227 Bible verses (ignoring repeat citations), 206 of them referring just to Mary. In Letter 3 on *Sola Scriptura*, you cite only 28 verses; on Church authority (Letter 18), 119 verses (if disregarding citations of whole chapters); on initial salvation (Letter 23), 82 verses; on worship (Letter 38), 31 verses. Mary has more references by far!

Then there are the Old Testament prophesies (such as a virgin "shall conceive and bear a son," Isaiah 7:14). If you add citations from Pope John Paul II's encyclical on Mary[166] and Scott Hahn's book analyzing the biblical types of Mary (for example, Bathsheba, Esther) and anti-types (such as Eve, Miriam),[167] we would amass 866 non-overlapping Scripture verses with little effort.

Wow! Or should I say, How ridiculous! We're analyzing Mary as though she were an object. Atheists approach God this way, demanding that we Christians "prove" God's existence as physicists prove that subatomic particles exist. Mary is not an electron, but a person!

Mary as a Person

Let me explain. Imagine you were 15 years old again and you say to your mother: "Carol—oops, please pardon me for calling you by your first name. I'm just not convinced you are my mother. I remember little from when I was born and so—although you, Dad (I mean Jeff) and others say that you are my mother…still, until I prove it to myself, I plan on calling you by your first name. I hope you don't mind…"

How would your mother react? Not very happily, I'm sure!

Doubting God's existence affects our relationship with Him… profoundly! If someone sincerely doubted God's existence, he should pray, "God, if You're there, help me to get to know You. Tell me about Yourself…perhaps through Scripture." This is the only way to enter into a relationship with Him. One should take the same approach in getting to know any *personal* being, including Mary, the saints and angels: treating them as *personal* beings and not as objects or particles. Any Christian can pray, "Heavenly Father, help me to learn to know and love Your angels and saints as You desire," and to Jesus Christ, "Help me to learn to know and love Your Mother as is pleasing to You. Do You want me to treat her as You would? As my own mother?"

How we treat Mary affects our relationship with Jesus. If He intended the words, "Behold, your mother" (John 19:27), for all Christians—all disciples whom He loves (John 19:26)—then to reject Mary as our mother is to disobey and thus reject Christ. This is why I asked you whether you were implying Mary played the harlot, because such implications would severely affect our relationship to Christ.

Love and Language

Moreover, love transforms language. That's why we must avoid defining terms too strictly. When you fell in love with your wife, did you not say things like, "I adore you…I worship the ground you walk on"? When your daughters were born, did you say, "I cherish these children"? Nobody takes that to mean you worship them as God (although it is possible to worship another human being, it is rare at this level). Still, the Catholic Church avoids using this kind of language in our relationship to angels, saints, and Mary to avoid any possible confusion with divine worship.

Jim, would you be offended if your daughters kept a photograph (a graven image) of Mom in their bedrooms or in their wallet? No. It would please you because love is not competitive. If you held a photograph of your wife and daughters to your heart, kissed it, and put a fresh flower beside it, would that be idol worship? Hardly! These are acts of love.

Love transforms the way we read Scripture. Love moved Paul to see Jesus Christ as the New Adam when he read Genesis (Romans 5:12-21; 1 Corinthians 15:20-50). Scripture alone never suggested this interpretation. Likewise, John's love moved him to identify the ark of the New Covenant with a woman, the mother of the Redeemer (Revelation 11:19–12:6).

> It is God Himself who, through his angel as intermediary, greets Mary.…*Full of grace, the Lord is with thee*.…Mary is full of grace because the Lord is with her. The grace with which she is filled is the presence of him who is the source of all grace. "Rejoice…O Daughter of Jerusalem…the Lord your God is in your midst" (Zephaniah 3:14,17a). Mary…the ark of the covenant, the place where the glory of the Lord dwells. She is "the dwelling of God…with men" (Revelation 21:3). Full of grace, Mary is wholly given over to him who has come to dwell in her and whom she is about to give to the world.
>
> [CCC 2676]

Honoring God's Works

Would God be offended by us acknowledging the beauty and greatness of His work? How absurd! "On thy wondrous works, I will meditate" (Psalm 145:5).

Again, imagine taking a tour through Rembrandt's studio. As he guides us through his studio, he notices that you don't look at any of his paintings and asks why. "Oh, you're the greatest painter ever! I just want to admire you. I wouldn't want to offend you by looking at and honoring any of your works instead of you." Rembrandt would be offended! By marveling over his works, Rembrandt would be honored. So it is with God!

It is difficult criticizing your position because your approach is so different. It may be clinically objective, so I'm trying to expose the underlying relational meaning. For example, if you were to say to one of your daughters, "You've got a pimple on your nose," technically it may be correct, but your daughter may storm out of the room crying, "He associates the pimple's ugliness with me...can't he see anything else?" However, if you were to say, "Hey, gorgeous...be careful. I wouldn't want that small sore on your nose to become infected. Let's have the doctor check it out." Then she'd think you cared.

Jim, you are so lucky to have a wonderful family. I hope my references to them in this way don't offend them. My hope is that they—God's gifts to you—may help you to understand the deeper, interrelational meaning of our discussion.

Catholic Summary on Mary, Angels, Saints

Since Catholics view the church as a family, we naturally approach this topic in the same way. Moreover, "What the Catholic faith believes about Mary is based on what it believes about Christ, and what it teaches about Mary illumines in turn its faith in Christ" [CCC 487]. Thus, we believe:

That our teaching is rooted in Scripture. To worship angels or saints—including Mary—as divine would be heretical, an excommunicable offense.

Angels are spiritual beings who live in God's constant presence, yet with a mission to protect and care for us, interceding on our behalf.

Saints are our older brothers in the faith. After they die, their relationship with Christ and us becomes even deeper. If Christians can pray for one another while alive, much more can they do so after being completely united with Christ in heaven. God testifies of their holiness and draws us to imitate their example by working miracles through their intercession, but always with God's power.

Mary is considered blessed because of her response of faith (Luke 1:41-45). Scripture clearly states her virginity and maternity to the Lord, the second person of the blessed Trinity. She is the New Eve, and ark of the covenant, which prefigures Mary, her holiness, Immaculate Conception and Assumption into heaven. God calls Christians to fully identify ourselves with Christ by imitating how He honored Mary, treating her as our mother.

Jim, let me know what issues concern you and I'll do my best to respond.

In Christ's all-embracing love,

John

Letter 45

WEDNESDAY, NOVEMBER 14, 2001

Dear John,

I remember you telling me that you had consecrated your life to Mary. I am not surprised, then, that discussing our differences concerning her raises deep emotions within you. I share your admiration for her. She was an exemplary woman of faith, one blessed by God with the privilege of bearing Jesus. I believe, however, that is about as far as God's Word would have us go. You may find this approach too clinical, yet when discussing doctrine, I think it is important that one remains objective.

The summary of your beliefs in your last letter was helpful. I would be grateful if you would expand on the following issues.

Praying to Creatures

Christians have direct access to God through the Lord Jesus, yet the Catholic Church also tells its people to pray to Mary, angels, and saints. For example, one of the most common Catholic prayers to Mary is the *Memorare:*

> Remember, O most gracious Virgin Mary, that never was it known that anyone who fled to your protection, implored your help, and sought your intercession was left unaided. Inspired by this confidence, I fly to you, O Virgin of virgins, my Mother. To you I come; before you I stand, sinful and sorrowful, O

Mother of the Word Incarnate, despise not my petitions, but in your mercy hear and answer me.

Why not direct all your prayers straight to God?

Venerating Creatures

I have often watched Catholics kneeling before a statue of Mary or one of the Catholic saints, bowed in fervent veneration. As we have seen, the Ten Commandments state, "You shall not make for yourself a graven image, or any likeness of anything that is in heaven above...you shall not bow down to them or serve them; for I the LORD your God am a jealous God" (Exodus 20:4-5). Why then does the Catholic Church promote the veneration of the images of Mary and the saints in heaven?

Exempting Mary from All Sin

As I understand the doctrine of the Immaculate Conception, it teaches that Mary lived a perfectly sinless life. She is the "All-Holy." The doctrine of the Assumption of Mary says that at the end of her life on earth her body did not decay. God took it up into heaven. As far as I know, there is no mention of either of these doctrines in the Bible. Could you explain them and their basis?

Bestowing Titles on Mary

In your last letter, you call Mary the "New Eve" and "ark of the covenant." The Roman Catholic Church also calls her the "Queen of Heaven and Earth," "Mediatrix of All Grace," and "Co-redemptrix" of the human race. I don't find anything remotely like this in the Bible. What is the source of these titles?

As we discuss these matters, John, I will try to be sensitive. With God's help we will have a good exchange of ideas.

In Christ's love,

Jim

Letter 46

Dear Jim,

I'm flying back from Seattle. People seem more responsive since September 11, perhaps discovering how short life is. Have you noticed any difference in your ministry?

Our current topic is daunting; we could easily do a book just on this. Yet, many differences disappear by treating angels, saints, and the Virgin Mary as real people. I'll try to introduce you to them, but you must venture to get to know them yourself. It will help to remember we understand terms such as *prayer* and *intercession* differently.

Catholics *don't* "pray," but converse!

For example, if we take your definition of prayer as speaking *only* to God,[168] then we don't "pray" to angels, saints, and Mary. Catholics are prohibited from addressing them as Father, through Christ in the Spirit (Ephesians 2:18). In this sense, we pray to God *alone.*

However, we do converse with angels and saints as we would with earthly family or friends: as John with the angel in Revelation, as Mary with Gabriel (Luke 1:28-38), as our Lord with Moses and Elijah (Luke 9:30). As family and friends don't compete with God, neither do angels and saints. Two of our Lord's three parables on prayer portray prayer as conversation with ordinary people [CCC 2613].

Share, not "intercede"!

Angels and saints don't directly "intercede" for us. Their "intercession" is secondary because their power comes from God. They can only *share* with others what they have received through Christ's primary intercession. It is similar to us *sharing* with others the gospel that we've received. That's why I brought to your attention many examples of secondary intercession.[169] You claim this isn't intercession. Fine. Then—according to your definition—we agree: angels, saints, and Mary don't "intercede." Nevertheless, it pleases God when angels and saints *share* their gifts with us, as parents rejoice seeing children *share* gifts with siblings.

Consecration: Something Very Personal

Yes, I consecrated myself to Mary. I'm reticent about subjecting this very personal act to "clinical scrutiny." Let me just say this: As I read John 19:25-27, I sensed our Lord speaking to me from the cross. At that point I made a special commitment to accept Mary into my home...into my heart, promising Jesus to always treat His mother as my own.

Angels and Saints

Jewish tradition interpreted Exodus 3–4 as an angel appearing and dialoguing with Moses. You reject this interpretation,[170] but Scripture confirms it (Acts 7:35). Moreover, that same angel "spoke to him at Mount Sinai" (Acts 7:38), giving us "living oracles" and "the law" (Acts 7:38,53).

Every Christian is a saint to the extent the Spirit *sanctifies* him (2 Thessalonians 2:13) in Christ's blood (Hebrews 13:12) through baptism (1 Corinthians 6:11; Ephesians 5:25-26). Nevertheless, we are not wholly sanctified (1 Thessalonians 5:23) until we fully yield our bodies to righteousness (Romans 6:19), abstaining from unchastity (1 Thessalonians 4:2-7) and all other sins (1 Corinthians 6:9-10). Only God can assure us of our full sanctification. God usually testifies to a person's holiness by working miracles through His intercessions, as He did, for example, with Elijah's miraculous mantle (2 Kings 2:1-14) and Elisha's bones (2 Kings 13:21).

The saints in heaven are our older brothers and sisters in the faith. While alive, "the prayer of a righteous man has great power" (James 5:16; see also Matthew 21:22). They don't lose that power when they are fully united to Christ in heaven; rather, their prayers become more powerful. Saints are now equal to angels (Luke 20:36; Revelation 22:8-9), so we can treat them as angels, asking for their prayers as we did before they died.

Mary's Spiritual Maternity

Mary is a great saint because she was a woman of great faith:

> Filled with the Holy Spirit [Elizabeth] exclaimed... "Blessed are you among women....*blessed is she who believed* that there would be a fulfilment of what was spoken to her from the Lord."
>
> LUKE 1:41-42,45

All generations of Catholics venerate her by calling her blessed (Luke 1:48). Throughout the Bible her faith reappears:

- in her commitment to virginity after marrying Joseph (Luke 1:27)—despite her calling to be God's mother (Luke 1:31-35);

- in believing that she could conceive and bear a son without loss of virginity (Luke 1:38);

- in embarking on a long journey to Bethlehem when nine months pregnant, not knowing where or when Christ would be born, just trusting the Lord;

- in holding, nursing, and meeting all Jesus' infant needs...yet worshiping Him as God!

+ at the wedding feast of Cana (John 2:1-12): Mary asks Jesus to work a miracle...but she is the first!

+ at the foot of the cross, she believed, like Abraham, that God could raise her only son (Hebrews 11:17-19).

So when Jesus says, "Whoever does the will of God is my brother, and sister, and mother" (Mark 3:33-35), He really compliments Mary. Fulfilling God's will made Mary Jesus' *spiritual mother and sister*. So when the woman said to Jesus, "Blessed is the womb that bore you, and the breasts that you sucked!" (Luke 11:27), Jesus tells us why: "Blessed rather are those [especially Mary] who hear the word of God and keep it!" (Luke 11:28, comment added). Mary is blessed more for her *spiritual maternity*— for hearing and keeping God's Word—than for her physical maternity.[171]

Mother of God

"Remember your leaders...the outcome of their life, and imitate their faith" (Hebrews 13:7). This encourages us to remember and imitate Mary. By her faith she became the mother of the Lord (Luke 1:43), of the Word incarnate (John 1:13-14), of the Emmanuel, *God with us* (Isaiah 7:14; Matthew 1:23).

Reading Scripture with Love: Eve, Immaculate Virgin

To really get to know Mary, we must love her as Christ did. This helps us to discover Mary in other scriptural passages. Many Church fathers noticeably loved Mary as their mother and identified figures of her in the Old Testament. For example, as Jesus is the new Adam, they saw Mary as the new Eve. As Eve's unfaithful disobedience lead to Adam's demise, Mary's obedience of faith lead to Christ's incarnation and Redemption.

As Eve was an immaculate virgin before the fall, so Mary was conceived immaculate and remained a virgin. In fact, God planned that everyone be conceived immaculate, but Adam's sin foiled that. In choosing her "before the foundation of the world"

(Ephesians 1:4) to be His mother, God restored His original plan. She is not the exception, we are!

The parallel between Genesis 2:23–3:24 and Revelation 11:19–12:17 confirms Mary as the new Eve:

+ Adam calls Eve *woman;* Christ calls Mary *woman* (also, John 2:4; 19:26);

+ God clothed Eve with skins; Mary with the sun;

+ woman with birth-pangs (also, Micah 5:3);

+ the serpent battles the woman and her seed;

+ serpent is cursed;

+ God promises to put enmity between the serpent and the woman; God fulfills that promise;

+ mother of the living; mother of the true living, those who keep God's commandments;

+ Eve and her seed put out of garden; woman and child flee into desert;

+ Eve accompanies Adam at the tree of knowledge; Mary accompanies Jesus hanging on the tree (John 19:25; 1 Peter 2:24);

+ an angel vanquishes man from the tree of life; Satan from heaven.

Reading Scripture with Love: True Ark

Mary is also the ark of the New Covenant. Jesus taught us to think this way, explaining that His body was God's true temple (John 2:19-21). The ark contained three things: "the manna, and Aaron's rod that budded, and the tables of the covenant" (Hebrews 9:4). Mary's womb carried the real manna, Christ's body, the true bread from heaven (John 6:48-51); the true high priest, to whom Aaron's rod pointed (Numbers 17:1-13); and the incarnate Word—not just the *Decalogue,* God's *ten words.*

When John saw the ark of the New Covenant in the heavenly temple (Revelation 11:19)…a great sign appears, a virgin with child (Isaiah 7:14), the mother of the Redeemer (Revelation 12:1,5), the new Eve! Moses covered the Old Testament ark with gold (Exodus 25:10-22); Mary's title—*Kécharitôméne,* "full of grace" (Luke 1:28, Douay-Rheims)—indicates that God fully overshadowed her with pure, sinless favor or grace (*charis*). Scripture requires her Immaculate Conception! How then could she have been a sinner? With God, union (grace) and ill relations (sin) are incompatible!

Mary's Virginity

Every child should be conceived in an act of pure love. To be the product of passion, lust, rape, or incest is a grave injustice to an innocent child. Were Mary to have relations with Joseph (which she had a right to before conceiving Jesus) it would mean her love for God, in which she conceived Jesus, wasn't virginal-spousal. But Jesus had to be conceived in an act of virginal-spousal love; thus Mary had to remain a virgin.

We just take Scripture at its word. Mary is called a virgin before conceiving our Lord (Luke 1:27), and while conceiving and bearing Him: " 'Behold, a *virgin* shall conceive and *bear* a son" (Matthew 1:23). In conceiving Christ, Mary became the ark of the New Covenant. Were Joseph to touch the ark (Mary) in an unpriestly manner, he would have met the fate of Uzzah, who died touching the sacred vessel (2 Samuel 6:1-8). Mary's body was more sacred than the Old Testament ark. "The LORD, the God of Israel, has entered by [the gate of Mary's womb]; therefore it shall remain shut" (Ezekiel 44:2, comment added).

As Adam named Eve *woman* when she was a sinless virgin (Genesis 2:23), so the New Adam named Mary *woman* (John 2:4; 19:26), indicating that she was still a sinless virgin at this point. Love notices these details!

Mary's Assumption

Much can be said about Mary's Assumption. Mary is already seen in heaven (Revelation 11:19–12:17). Several Old Testament saints were assumed into heaven: Enoch (Hebrews 11:5), Elijah (2 Kings 2:1-14), and Moses (Jude 9). Many of the dead also rose after the crucifixion (Matthew 27:52-53). If these were taken up for their example of faith, how much more would Mary have been.

Moreover, as the Old Testament ark was removed, never to be found (2 Maccabees 2:1-8), so Mary's body was assumed into heaven never more to be found on earth.

Queenship

To understand Mary's queenship, I suggest reading 1 Kings 1–2. There, Solomon enthroned his mother, Bathsheba, as Israel's queen-mother, *gebirah*. He promised her, "Make your request, my mother; for I will not refuse you" (1 Kings 2:20). This figure is fulfilled when the new Eve is enthroned in heaven, crowned as the queen-mother of the new people of God (Revelation 12:1,17). Scott Hahn develops the scriptural basis of Mary's queenship.[172]

Veneration

We don't venerate anyone as God. That would be heresy. However, Scripture approves recognizing and respecting the dignity of a creature's office by bowing to him. For example, David bowed to King Saul (1 Samuel 24:8); Bathsheba to her husband, King David (1 Kings 1:16); King Solomon to his mother, Bathsheba (1 Kings 2:19)! God requires Jews to bow to Christians (Revelation 3:9)! Similarly, the Church venerates sacred Scripture as she venerates the Lord's body [CCC 103, 141].

Titles: Mediatrix, Co-redemptrix

Your definition of intercession and mediation empties *Mediatrix* of any meaning. So ignore it! The same with *Co-redemptrix*. As copilots assist pilots in flying an aircraft, so Paul and Mary have secondary roles as "God's co-workers," *syn-ergos* (1 Corinthians 3:9). *Co-redemptrix* just refers to Simeon's prophecy of Mary: "and a sword will pierce through your own soul also" (Luke 2:35). Mary was spiritually crucified with Christ when Jesus' heart was pierced (John 19:34).

The Key to Understanding Mary

There is so much more to say. The key, however, to understanding Mary is developing a personal relationship with her. Try praying, "Lord, teach me to love Your mother as You desire of all Christians. Teach me to call her blessed...."

I'll be attending a five-day silent retreat over Thanksgiving in the Bay Area. Please pray that I use it to deepen my relationship with Christ and that I may become a better witness to His gospel. If possible, I'll try to visit on my way home. Perhaps we can discuss these matters then.

In Christ's love,

John

Conversation 10

THURSDAY, NOVEMBER 29, 2001

Jim: Thanks for visiting Monday, John. It was kind of you to interrupt your trip home to see us. The time discussing this writing project was also helpful. Hopefully we can finish up by early spring.

John: It was great to see you and your wife. I'm sorry I couldn't stay longer. My retreat gave me time to read, reflect, and pray. During it I also discovered some additional Bible verses on this topic. I hope to share them with you.

Do you really just "converse" with Mary?

Jim: You say that you do not pray to Mary and the saints as you would to God, but merely converse with them as with family and friends. The Church's prayers seem to indicate otherwise. Consider once more the *Memorare* in which Catholics address Mary: "To you I come; before you I stand, sinful and sorrowful, O Mother of the Word incarnate, despise not my petitions, but in your mercy hear and answer me." Can this really be compared to the way you converse with family and friends?

John: Jim, we say things to intimate friends we'd never say in public. Yet that's still conversation. Imagine a child saying to his mother, "Mom, I come to you, scraped up and bloodied....I disobeyed Dad, riding my bike down the

308

steep hill. Please clean me up and ask Dad not to yell at me…"?

The *Memorare* is actually inspired by an ancient prayer, the *Sub tuum praesidium,* found on a third-century Egyptian papyrus. Love has inspired conversation with Mary for many centuries.

Jim: Is not the reason that many Catholics pray to Mary rather than directly to God the fact that the Church teaches that Mary is more likely to help them than God? Consider, for example, St. Alphonsus de Liguori. Rome recognizes him as an officially sanctioned teacher of the faith and Doctor of the Church. He offers this prayer, quoting Anselm, another Catholic saint and Doctor: " 'Do thou pity me, my Mother Mary, by interceding for me, or at least tell me to whom I can have recourse, who is more compassionate, or in whom I can have greater confidence than in thee.' Oh, no; neither on earth nor in heaven can I find any one who has more compassion for the miserable, or who is better able to assist me, than thou canst, O Mary." [173]

John: The Catholic Church encourages people to pray directly to God: to the Father, to Jesus Christ, and to the Holy Spirit. As members of Christ's body—the Church—we can *also* pray to Mary and the saints as conversing with other family members.

Can a Pope's decree contradict Scripture?

Jim: The Bible says that "all have sinned and fall short of the glory of God" (Romans 3:23). The only exception mentioned is Jesus (2 Corinthians 5:21; 1 John 1:5). Regardless, in 1854 Pope Pius IX decreed that Mary was exempt.

> We declare, pronounce, and define that the doctrine which holds that the most Blessed Virgin Mary, in the first instant of her conception, by a singular grace and privilege granted by Almighty God, in view of the

merits of Jesus Christ, the Savior of the human race, was preserved free from all stain of original sin, is a doctrine revealed by God and therefore to be believed firmly and constantly by all the faithful.

POPE PIUS IX[174]

How can a Pope decree a dogma that contradicts Scripture?

John: No law requires man to sin to be human. Circumcised Jews need Christ's redemption, because they too are sinners (Romans 3:23)! But, Paul says nothing about Mary or her special relationship to Jesus.

Everybody sins and falls short of God's glory, of God's plan from "before the foundation of the world...[to] be holy and blameless [Latin *immaculatus*]" (Ephesians 1:4, comments added). Like Adam and Eve, Jesus and Mary were made "holy and blameless" in anticipation of the Redemption. *All others* "fall short" of God's glory...of God's favor....a*ll others* are not *Kécharitôméne.*

Jesus "knew no sin" (2 Corinthians 5:21) and "no darkness was in him" (1 John 1:5) because He was the light (John 1:4-5), "full of grace and truth" (John 1:14). Mary was perfected in God's favor and grace, *Kécharitôméne* (Luke 1:28), because she came to the light (John 3:21), who clothed her with the sun (Revelation 12:1). "Her lamp does not go out at night" (Proverbs 31:18).

Sin is a failed relationship, a betrayal of God's *favor* or *grace.* God befriended Mary, "consecrated in the womb" (Sirach 49:7), to be the mother of His Son.

Mary is more blessed than any woman (Luke 1:42), including Eve before the Fall! Mary is blessed because of her faith (Luke 1:45) and "whatever does not proceed from faith is sin" (Romans 14:23).

Jim: None of the verses exempt Mary from sin. To the contrary, Mary herself said, "My spirit rejoices in God my *Savior*"

(Luke 1:47). If God was her *Savior*, then Mary, at least at some point, was a *lost* sinner like the rest of us. How else can this verse be understood?

John: The Church acknowledges Mary needs a savior and redeemer, as did Adam and Eve—even if they had not sinned.

> Through the centuries the Church has become ever more aware that Mary, "full of grace" through God (Luke 1:28), was redeemed from the moment of her conception. That is what the dogma of the Immaculate Conception confesses...she is "redeemed, in a more exalted fashion, by reason of the merits of her Son."
>
> [CCC 491-492]

Salvation is a spousal union with Christ (Ephesians 5:31-32). Even for the sinless, Christ had to take flesh and marry the Church as His bride. In this sense, Jesus saved and redeemed Mary at conception.

How many sources of dogma?

Jim: On August 12, 1950, Pope Pius XII decreed that Rome has the right to declare dogma that is clear neither in Scripture nor Tradition. "God has given to His Church a living Teaching Authority to elucidate and explain what is contained in the deposit of faith only obscurely and implicitly."[175]

One Catholic commentator described this as a "leap ahead in doctrinal development."[176] Pius' intention was to prepare Catholics for the Assumption of Mary as dogma, knowing it was a teaching not explicitly taught in Scripture or in the early church. Three months later on November 1, 1950, Pius decreed:

> By the authority of our Lord Jesus Christ, of the Blessed Apostles Peter and Paul, and by our own

authority, we pronounce, declare, and define it to be a divinely revealed dogma: that the Immaculate Mother of God, the ever Virgin Mary, having completed the course of her earthly life, was assumed body and soul into heavenly glory.

Munificentissimus Deus[177]

Would it be accurate to say that the Roman Catholic Church has three sources of dogma: Scripture, Tradition, and the Roman Magisterium?

John: Dogmas (which is Greek for *teachings*) are revealed teachings requiring religious assent by all Catholics [CCC 88].

The blessed Trinity is the exclusive *source of revelation:* it is from the Father, contained in the Word, and brought to our remembrance by the Holy Spirit (John 14:26). *Sacred Tradition* transmits revelation to the present generation, either by word of mouth or by writings (2 Thessalonians 2:15), accepted by Christians as God's Word (1 Thessalonians 2:13). The *Magisterium*'s mission is to "guard the truth that has been entrusted" to it (2 Timothy 1:14), to "teach what befits sound doctrine" (Titus 2:1), to "exhort and reprove with all authority" (Titus 2:15), and to "charge certain persons not to teach any different doctrine" (1 Timothy 1:3).

The early church took many "leaps of doctrinal development" beyond *Sola Scriptura:* the Trinity, infant baptism, the canon of Scripture, and the prohibition against polygamy. Regarding polygamy that's why Luther authorized Philip of Hesse to take a second wife based on *Sola Scriptura:*

I confess that I cannot forbid a person to marry several wives, for it does not contradict the Scripture. If a man wishes to marry more than one wife...he may do so in accordance with the word of God.[178]

Joseph Smith used a similar argument when defending Mormonism.

In my last letter, I gave some scriptural support for Mary's Assumption. Here's more: "Arise, O LORD, and go to thy resting place [Christ's ascension], thou and the ark [Mary's Assumption] of thy might" (Psalm 132:8, comments added). You may also want to explore how early Christians expressed this doctrine in Kilian J. Healy's book *The Assumption of Mary.*[179]

Jim: You say that the role of the Magisterium is to guard what has been entrusted to it. Yet Pope Pius asserted that the Magisterium can "explain what is contained in the deposit of faith only obscurely and implicitly."[180] In defining as dogma what is only obscure in the revelation received from Christ and the apostles, is not the Magisterium claiming to be able to provide additional and new revelation from God?

John: The church did the same with the doctrine of the Trinity, clarifying and making explicit what was implicit in "the Word became flesh and dwelt among us" (John 1:14). This occurred when heretics attempted to use *Scripture alone* to challenge Christ's divinity or humanity.

Regarding the Assumption, the Magisterium simply clarifies what Scripture has taught implicitly, and Tradition explicitly, for the last 2000 years.

Jim: Aren't you comparing things that are really different? What Christian would say the humanity of Christ is only implicit in Scripture or obscure?

John: Historically, many Christians challenged Christ's humanity——for example, Arius, Apollinarius, Sabellius, Eutyches, and their followers. They failed to see how Christ's divinity was compatible with His humanity. So, the Magisterium clarified this matter with the great councils and papal teaching of the fourth and fifth centuries [CCC 250].

How do you know it's Mary?

Jim: Since the early 1800s, Mary has allegedly appeared in various places in Europe, including Lourdes, France (1858); Knock, Ireland (1879); and Fatima, Portugal (1917). Often she has called Catholics to greater devotion to herself. At Fatima she announced, "God wishes to establish in the world devotion to my immaculate heart. My immaculate heart will be your refuge and the way to lead you to God." How does Rome know these apparitions are actually Mary and not some self-promoting demonic spirit leading people astray?

John: Marian apparitions have a long history. Shortly after the Council of Ephesus in 431, a Roman couple—wealthy and childless—prayed to discern what to do with their wealth. Mary appeared to them, requesting a church be built in honor of her divine maternity; it was to be built on the hill covered with snow. In early August it was blistering hot in Rome, but snow miraculously fell on one of its hills. Mary Majors' Basilica now stands on that spot.

Nobody is required to believe in apparitions. "It is not their role to improve or complete Christ's definitive Revelation, but to help live more fully by it in a certain period of history" [CCC 67]. The Magisterium studies them to "test the spirits" (1 John 4:1), making sure the witnesses are credible and that nothing contradicts Scriptures or defined teachings. Often the Church consults non-Catholic experts and scientists to detect frauds. Scientists are limited to saying that something has an explanation or not. NASA scientists have studied the Shroud of Turin and the miraculous image of Our Lady of Guadalupe. The image from Guadalupe, Mexico, dates back to 1531, when Mary appeared to a poor, native-American convert. Her image was left on his *tilma* (poncho). Scientists cannot explain how the *tilma* has lasted or how the colorful image was made. They find no known pigments or brush strokes.

———

Besides miracles, the Church considers how the apparition affects people's lives. Satan would not approve of marked conversions of sinners to the faith. Prophetic witness is another sign. For example, at Fatima, Portugal, Mary predicted the rise and fall of communism as well as the assassination attempt on Pope John Paul II that occurred on May 13, 1981—64 years to the day after the first apparition in 1917.

What is idol worship?

Jim: Rome says that "Christian veneration of images is not contrary to the first commandment which proscribes idols. Indeed, 'the honor rendered to an image passes to its prototype,' and 'whoever venerates an image venerates the person portrayed in it'" [CCC 2132]. If Exodus 20:4-5 does not forbid the making of statues of Jesus, Mary, and the saints, and the veneration of them by kissing and bowing down to them, to what does the command properly apply?

John: The *Catechism of the Catholic Church* clarifies idol worship:

> The first commandment....requires man neither to believe in, nor to venerate, other divinities than the one true God....
>
> [CCC 2112]

> Idolatry consists in divinizing what is not God. Man commits idolatry whenever he honors and reveres a creature in place of God, whether this be gods or demons (for example, satanism), power, pleasure, race, ancestors, the state, money, etc. Jesus says, "You cannot serve God and mammon" (Matthew 6:24)....Idolatry rejects the unique Lordship of God....
>
> [CCC 2113]

Although it is possible to worship saints and Mary as idols, I don't know a single Catholic who does. I do know many who have abandoned their faith to worship money, fame, pleasure [CCC 1723], even their own spouses and children, as our Lord warned (Luke 14:26). Perhaps you would do better to focus on this form of idolatry. I think it affects many more Christians than does devotion to saints.

How does veneration of Mary differ from goddess worship?

Jim: In the Litany of Our Lady approved by Pope Sixtus, the Church instructs Catholics to entreat Mary through a long list of invocations. These include: Holy Mother of God, Mother of divine grace, Mother of our Creator, Virgin most powerful, Seat of wisdom, Cause of our joy, Ark of the covenant, Gate of heaven, Refuge of sinners, and Queen of Angels. How does this differ from goddess worship?

John: Worshiping God recognizes His absolute dominion over creation. The Holy Spirit commands all generations to venerate Mary as blessed (Luke 1:48). Veneration recognizes the "great things" God did in her (Luke 1:49). Mary's greatness is always that of a creature in reference to her Creator: "My soul magnifies the Lord" (Luke 1:46):

- *Holy Mother of God, of divine grace, of our Creator:* because she is the mother of the Lord, who is the Word, the fullness of grace, "from whom are all things" (1 Corinthians 8:6).

- *Virgin most powerful:* Mary's prayer is directed to Christ the King, who says to her, "Make your request, my mother; for I will not refuse you" (1 Kings 2:20).

- *Seat of Wisdom:* the ark is the mercy seat of divine wisdom.

- *Cause of our joy:* she caused "the babe in my womb leaped for joy" (Luke 1:44).

+ *Refuge of sinners:* Mary is portrayed as a city where one and all were born (Psalm 87:5), a city of refuge for sinners (Numbers 35).

Jim: Among the pagan gods there was generally one great god who had dominion over the lesser gods and goddesses. For the Greeks it was Zeus; for the Romans, Jupiter. They also worshiped a host of lesser gods and goddesses who were limited in their abilities and had very human weaknesses and passions. How is Catholic praise of Mary essentially any different from pagan worship of lesser gods and goddesses?

John: Since evangelical worship doesn't have the Sacrifice of the Mass, adoration of Christ's Body and Blood, vows, promises, incense, veneration of the cross, and so on, all you are left with are hymns and prayers. No wonder Catholic prayer to angels and saints scandalizes you. We don't have such a problem because our worship of God is so much greater than veneration of angels, saints, and Mary. Catholics just don't confuse honor given to Mary with worship given to God.

> The Church rightly honors "the Blessed Virgin with special devotion [which]…differs essentially from the adoration which is given to the incarnate Word and equally to the Father and the Holy Spirit, and [which] greatly fosters this adoration."
>
> [CCC 971]

Jim: Pope Pius IX wrote, "God alone excepted, Mary is more excellent than all, and by nature fair and beautiful, and more holy than the Cherubim and Seraphim. To praise her all the tongues of heaven and earth do not suffice."[181] Do you find precedent in Scripture for praise such as this?

John: Yes, the Holy Spirit praises Mary through Elizabeth, "Blessed are you among women" (Luke 1:42). Mary is more

317

blessed and honored than any woman ever. Mary's praise is greater than any Old Testament women—greater than Judith, for example:

> O daughter, you are blessed by the Most High God above all women on earth; and blessed be the Lord God…who has guided you to strike the head of the leader of our enemies.…May God grant this to be a perpetual honor to you.
>
> JUDITH 13:18-20

Why doesn't Scripture refer to Mary's work of redemption?

Jim: The Roman Catholic Church exalts Mary as *Co-redemptrix*, explaining:

> Mary suffered and, as it were, nearly died with her suffering Son; for the salvation of mankind she renounced her mother's rights and, as far as it depended on her, offered her Son to placate divine justice; so we may well say that she with Christ redeemed mankind.
>
> POPE BENEDICT XV[182]

Why doesn't Scripture make any reference to Mary's sufferings as redemptive?

John: In Colossians 1:24, Paul daringly refers to his own suffering as redemptive: "Now I rejoice in my sufferings for your sake, and in my flesh I complete what is lacking in Christ's afflictions for the sake of his body, that is, the church." Simeon prophesied that Christ was to cause "the fall and rising of many in Israel," as the "sign that is spoken against" (Luke 2:34), then describes Mary's unique redemptive role, that "a sword will pierce through [Mary's] own soul," revealing the "thoughts out of many hearts" (Luke 2:35). This was fulfilled, as my letter explained, when Mary suffered the tremendous sorrows and pains seeing her only

---

son tortured as He hung on the cross. If you put yourself in Mary's shoes and reread the passion account, you would understand this better.

Jim: Rome says that on August 19, 1917, Mary appeared near Fatima, Portugal, to three young children. She allegedly told them, "Pray, pray very much. Make sacrifices for sinners. Many souls go to hell, because no one is willing to help them with sacrifice." John, could you explain how the sufferings of Mary and other Catholic saints contribute to the salvation of souls?

John: When discussing the priesthood of all Christians, I asked whether the priestly sacrifices in 1 Peter 2 and Hebrews 13 detracted from or added to Christ's sacrifice. You agreed that those sacrifices of the Christian priesthood do not.[183]

We see all martyrdom and sacrifices as Paul does, completing "what is lacking in Christ's afflictions for the sake of his body" (Colossian 1:24). Our sacrifices ascend to heaven on behalf of sinners to invoke God's mercy.

Are some Catholics trusting Mary to save them?

Jim: Catholic saint and Doctor of the Church Alphonsus de Liguori suggests this prayer to Mary: "In thee is all my confidence; only grant me the consolation of dying before thy picture, recommending myself to thy mercy, then I am convinced that I shall not be lost, but that I shall go and praise thee in heaven, in company with so many of thy servants who left this world calling on thee for help, and have all been saved by thy powerful intercession."[184] It would appear that he is trusting Mary rather than Jesus for his salvation.

John: Jim, earlier you clarified how many misread Luther's exaggerated claims that multiple murders and adulteries cannot separate a Christian from Christ. Likewise, the piety of some saints can also be misinterpreted or misconstrued. Alphonsus de Liguori clarifies this point:

> Everyone knows that God has given us Jesus Christ... as our principal Mediator...God has also given us Mary to be an advocate with Jesus..."a mediator with Christ the Mediator..." Jesus Christ alone is our Mediator by absolute necessity.[185]

Jim: If Mary is the mediator to the Mediator, is not Rome saying that Catholics go through two mediators to get to God the Father?

John: Mary's role is often compared to a mother's role in the family. Children, especially when they are very young, often fear their father making it hard for them to go directly to him. So, they may approach their mother, asking her to ask Dad. In that sense, a person may feel more at ease to approach Jesus through Mary.

Remember the centurion who sent Jewish elders and then his friends to Jesus, saying through them, "Lord, do not trouble yourself, for I am not worthy to have you come under my roof" (Luke 7:6). Jesus cures the centurion's servant, marveling, "I tell you, not even in Israel have I found such faith" (Luke 7:9). I think the Lord will say the same of us when we approach Him through friends...like Mary.

Jim: Let's look at it going the other way for a moment—that is, from God to us. Pope Pius X wrote, "Now from this common sharing of will and suffering between Christ and Mary, she 'merited to become most worthily the Reparatrix of the lost world and therefore Dispensatrix of all the gifts which Jesus gained for us by His Death and by His Blood....For she is the neck of our Head, by which all spiritual gifts are communicated to His Mystical Body.'"[186] Is Rome saying that not only should Catholics go through

Mary to Jesus to God, but that grace and blessing flows from God through Jesus through Mary to Catholics?

John: God blesses us through Mary, as God blesses others through us, when we evangelize them and when we pray for them. The same thing happens with the saints and angels.

Jim: When Catholics say the Hail Mary, they entreat her, "Pray for us sinners, now and at the hour of our death." The *Catechism of the Catholic Church,* commenting on this prayer, says, "We give ourselves over to her now, in the Today of our lives. And our trust broadens further, already at the present moment, to surrender 'the hour of our death' wholly to her care" [CCC 2677]. Is this not trusting Mary for salvation?

John: Jim, we see no competition between Mary and Jesus. The Holy Spirit moved Elizabeth to cry out, "Blessed are you among women, and blessed is the fruit of your womb!" (Luke 1:42). He blesses Mary before blessing the Son of God. Moreover, Elizabeth said, "Why is this granted me, that the mother of my Lord should come to me?" (Luke 1:43), and not, "What a great honor to have my Lord visit me!" Honoring His mother doesn't offend Jesus. Mary's honor and blessedness comes from her relationship to Jesus and her faith in God.

The passage you cited from *Catechism* goes on to say, "May she welcome us as our mother at the hour of our passing (cf. John 19:27) to lead us to her son, Jesus, in paradise" [CCC 2677].

Jim: Thank you, John, for replying to these questions. They raise some important issues that we evangelicals find difficult to understand. I'll give you my response in my next letter.

Letter 47

Dear John,

Christmas will soon be upon us. What better time to pause and thank "God for his inexpressible gift!" (2 Corinthians 9:15), the Lord Jesus Christ. How wonderful to have peace with God through Jesus!

This is also a fitting season to consider the life of Mary, the mother of Jesus. How odd that such a woman of faith and humility should now be a topic of controversy between Christians. Nevertheless, that is where we find ourselves. Here I will limit my comments to three of your arguments.

Was Mary sinless?

The first regards the 1854 decree of the Immaculate Conception, namely, that Mary "was preserved from all stain of original sin and by a special grace of God committed no sin of any kind during the whole of her earthly life" [CCC 411]. I can only ask: How can this be? Jesus said, "No one is good but God alone" (Mark 10:18). The saints in heaven proclaim to the Lord, "Thou alone art holy" (Revelation 15:4). That leaves no room for Mary being "the All-Holy One" [CCC 2677].

You argued that the Bible supports Mary's perfect sinlessness, citing the angel Gabriel's greeting to her, "Hail, full of grace" (Luke 1:28, Douay-Rheims). This, of course, is repeated millions of times each day by Catholics as they pray, "Hail, Mary, full of grace...." I don't see how you can conclude from this short greeting, however, that Mary was sinless. Additionally, the quote is from a sixteenth-century Catholic translation of a Latin text. Modern translations from the original Greek render the greeting, "Hail, O favored one" (Luke 1:28). This communicates the true nature of Mary's status before God. He *favored* her with the privilege of bearing the Christ-child. Nowhere do the Scriptures exclude her from the stain of Adam's sin or attribute sinless perfection to her.

Is Mary the co-redeemer?

Second, Rome says that Mary was "crucified spiritually with her crucified Son."[187] She "with Christ redeemed mankind."[188] How can this be? Scripture says the price of our redemption was "the precious blood of Christ" (1 Peter 1:19). Yes, Mary experienced much sorrow, as any mother would in seeing her son crucified. But were her sufferings redemptive? The New Testament word for redemption refers to *a release upon payment of a ransom*. Christ accomplished our redemption at the cross. He gave His life for us. Is this not sufficient?

You defended Mary's role as co-redeemer, writing, "Paul daringly refers to his own suffering as redemptive,"[189] quoting Colossians 1:24. Here Paul is speaking of the hardships he experienced in his ministry for the Colossians. Though he acknowledged that the Lord Jesus in heaven identifies with the suffering of his people on earth (Acts 9:4; 1 Corinthians 12:26), Paul makes no reference to these sufferings being redemptive, the payment for the sins of the world.

Is Mary the ever virgin?

Finally, Rome says that Mary is "the Blessed Mary, ever Virgin."[190] Scripture, as I have pointed out, makes numerous references to Jesus' brothers and sisters. You say these are simply his cousins and other close relatives, claiming that the Aramaic and Hebrew languages were inadequate to distinguish brothers from cousins. But is this reasonable? Jews place great emphasis on family relationships, bloodlines, and inheritance rights. Are we to believe that their language could not even distinguish a brother from a cousin or a son from a nephew? What about the Messianic psalm in which by the Spirit David speaks prophetically for Jesus, "I have become a stranger to my brethren, an alien to my mother's sons" (Psalm 69:8)? Could it be more explicit that Mary had more than one son?

Whether Mary remained a virgin after the birth of Christ is not as important as some of the others doctrines we have discussed. I mention it again here because it so clearly illustrates for me the foundational issue that separates us. *We have different sources of authority.* You look to the Catholic Church to determine your doctrine. Rome says, "Jesus is Mary's only son" [CCC 501]. That settles it for you. As the Catholic maxim states: *Roma locuta est; causa finita est*—Rome has spoken; the case is closed. No argument from Scripture will persuade you otherwise.

By contrast, I look to the Scriptures for my doctrine. If it says Jesus had brothers and sisters, I accept it. Give it a try, John. It's really very liberating.

I hope you have a blessed Christmas. Thank you for your friendship and diligent efforts in our dialogue through letters.

In Christ's love,

Jim

Letter 48

TUESDAY, DECEMBER 18, 2001

Dear Jim,

Christmas is a good time "to pause and thank 'God for his inexpressible gift!'" Let's also thank Mary for welcoming Christ into her womb!

Looking back over our last few letters and conversation, I found it ironic that you quoted so many Church documents—to prove them erroneous—and I responded with Scripture. Someone reading this might think that you're the Catholic and I'm the Bible Christian! At least they'd be half right.

Jim I do *accept* Scripture, but read it differently, not as a collection of isolated categorical legal statements. Is the passage "no one is good but God alone" (Mark 1:18) categorical? Barnabas "was a *good man,* full of the Holy Spirit and of faith" (Acts 11:24), and "a *good man* obtains *favor* from the LORD" (Proverbs 12:2). Since God *favored* Mary for believing, overshadowing her with the Holy Spirit, she too would be *good!* But no, these statements contradict the categorical reading of Mark 1:18!

Catholics must read Scripture in a way that is coherent and consistent with the content and unity of the whole of Scripture [CCC 112]. One can prove anything with isolated passages; Catholics may not. You presented ten or eleven citations categorically interpreted; I've responded with an interpretation coherent with the whole Bible, using 145 relevant citations from 38 books of the Bible...with more to come!

Mary's Assumption

Jim, is God prejudiced against women, assuming only men into heaven? God assumed Enoch into heaven because he "walked with God" (Genesis 5:24) and "pleased the Lord" (Sirach 44:16). By this, God attests to his faith (Hebrews 11:5) and repentance (Sirach 44:16). "No one like Enoch has been created on earth, for he was taken up" (Sirach 49:14).

Yet Mary was greater, at least "among women."

David's rejoicing in bringing the ark of the covenant into Jerusalem (2 Samuel 6:15) prefigured our Lord's joy in bringing Mary's body into the heavenly Jerusalem. Let's rejoice with Christ...and watch out, Michal was cursed for not rejoicing (2 Samuel 6:16,23)!

Immaculate Conception

Jesus is greater than Abraham, Jacob, Jonah, Solomon... greater than the temple, the tablets of the law, manna, and Aaron's rod (John 4:11-15; 8:52-58; Matthew 12:6,41-42)... because He is holy (Revelation 15:4), the "high priest, holy, blameless, *unstained*, separated from sinners" (Hebrews 7:26)! But, "if one who is unclean...touches any [holy thing], does it become unclean?" Scripture answers: "It does become unclean" (Haggai 2:13). Didn't Christ need a vessel holier than the Holy of Holies and the ark? Mary became such a vessel when God reestablished His original plan for man, conceiving her immaculate (Ephesians 1:4).

Moreover, when God names someone, it says everything. God changed Abram's name to Abraham, "father of a multitude of nations" (Genesis 17:5). Simon's name became Peter, the *rock* the Church is built on (Matthew 16:18). Mary became *Kécharitômérne* (Luke 1:28), the one God fully favored or graced. Jesus renamed her again as *woman* (John 2:4; 19:26)—Eve's name before the fall.

Where else is *Kécharitômérne* translated *favored?* Long before the Reformation controversy affected translations, Christians translated it *gratia plena* or "full of grace," which is used in the

RSVCE (Revised Standard Version Catholic Edition) and KB (The Knox Bible), modern translations from the original Greek.

Mary is more blessed (Luke 1:42) than the bride of the Song of Solomon: "You are all fair, my love; *there is no flaw in you*...My dove, *my perfect one,* is only one, the darling of her mother, *flawless* to her that bore her" (Song of Solomon 4:7; 6:9).

Co-redemption

Redemption has several dimensions. As revealing the Father (Matthew 11:27) or as the price of our salvation (1 Corinthians 6:20), only Christ could redeem. But since dying on the cross was a spousal act of self-giving (because it was total), it demands a spousal response, our total self-giving (Matthew 10:38; 1 John 3:16). In this sense, both Paul and Mary were co-redeemers, to "complete what is lacking in Christ's afflictions" (Colossians 1:24) because they carried in their "body the death of Jesus" that we may have life (2 Corinthians 4:10).

Mary's participation in Christ's Redemption (Romans 5:11) is similar to Eve's participation in Adam's anti-Redemption: "as sin came into the world through one man...Adam" (Romans 5:12,14). Both Mary and Eve played crucial roles.

> But the blessed Virgin's salutary influence on men...
> flows forth from the superabundance of the merits of
> Christ, rests on his meditation, depends entirely on it,
> and draws all its power from it.
>
> [CCC 970]

Her Virginity

Virginity is a sign of singular dedication and sinlessness, whereas harlotry portrays idolatry, infidelity, and sin. The "virgin Israel" who would "encompass" the Messiah (see Jeremiah 31:21-22) prefigures Mary, whose womb is an enclosed garden (Song of Solomon 4:12) belonging only to God (Song of Solomon 2:16).

Gabriel echoed the angel's message to Samson's mother, "Behold, you are barren and have no children; but you shall con-

ceive and bear a son" (Judges 13:3). Mary's Magnificat (Luke 1:46-
55) echoes the song of Hannah (1 Samuel 2:1-10), who rejoiced
over bearing a son after being unable to do so. In other words,
these words would apply to Mary only if she had no expectation
of children. As the *Catechism* confirms:

> The deepening of faith in the virginal motherhood
> led the Church to confess Mary's real and perpetual
> virginity even in the act of giving birth to the Son of
> God made man. In fact, Christ's birth "did not
> diminish his mother's virginal integrity but sanctified
> it." And so the liturgy of the Church celebrates Mary
> as *Aeiparthenos,* the "Evervirgin."

[CCC 499]

Mary's Feminine Influence

Personally, I owe so much to Mary, my spiritual mother! Just
as Jean's feminine presence has made you a better person, Mary
has done likewise for me.

I doubt I'd still be Catholic or even Christian without her. In
my youth, I was very rational, heady, and self-righteous, with little
patience for the unorthodox. I was often critical toward those who
inconvenienced me. Mary's feminine way taught me to have more
heart and understanding, in other words, she taught me to
love...to love Jesus Christ and to love others, with compassion for
the weak, and ultimately to give my whole life to God. Without the
Virgin Mary, I'd have been a heartless priest and, although I have
a long way to go, Mary still encourages me. She taught me the
meaning of chastity and fidelity to my commitment to serve God
with virginal love.

Jim, your love for Jean doesn't detract from your love for God.
No, it probably strengthens it. So does my love for Mary. As you
took Jean into your home, I strive to be a "beloved disciple" and
take Mary into mine (John 19:26-27).

You quoted Augustine, *Roma locuta est; causa finita est*—Rome spoke; case closed, describing the pope's approval of the council that resolved the canon of Scripture.[191] Rome resolved the debate on which books belong in the Bible...something Scripture *alone* could not.

I still think we need a separate book to deal with all the issues and scriptures regarding Mary. I am beginning to see how the early Christians applied Scripture to Mary. But now we must move on to our next topic.

May the child Jesus bless your family's Christmas,

John

TOPIC 6
Final Salvation

*What does it
take to make it
to heaven?*

Letter 49

WEDNESDAY, DECEMBER 26, 2001

Dear Jim,

I hope your Christmas was pleasant. Our Christmas Tijuana service project was cancelled, but I still have a retreat for this weekend.

One topic we still have pending is that of final salvation: What does it take to go to heaven? Catholics believe:

> Heaven is not so much a place, but the consummation of our betrothal to Christ. When we die, we will be judged on our love [CCC 1022]. Our actions in this life—good deeds and sacraments—show God that we want to marry Him, i.e, be with Him forever in heaven.
>
> Hell manifests God's love and mercy. The damned choose hell, rejecting heaven and their threefold relationship to God. One doesn't go to heaven by default. Wasting talents—the graces God offers us—or not responding to the needs of others, risks eternal damnation.
>
> God is all-holy; nothing unholy can enter His presence; so, complete holiness is needed to enter heaven; thus, we must be purged of any remaining unholiness, or choose hell. This purification process is called purgatory.
>
> After having believed and been baptized, we are still free to sin and abandon God's favor, like the

prodigal son. If we do sin, God gives us the sacrament
of confession to reconcile ourselves to Christ.

Jim, I hope this helps. I think we are making much progress in
our mutual understanding and respect of each other.

In Christ peace,

John

Letter 50

Dear John,

I am returning with my family today from Indianapolis. Along with 1100 others from around the United States and Canada, we were there for a three-day Bible conference. The theme was our common vocation to serve Christ. I taught two workshops titled "Christ's Design for the Church." We had a great time, especially seeing old friends and making new ones.

The subject before us, John, is all-important. At stake is eternal salvation: Who is truly a Christian? Who will enjoy heaven with God forever? If we get this one wrong, we have lost everything. We must tread carefully, therefore, keeping Paul's warning to the Galatians before us: "But even if we, or an angel from heaven, should preach to you a gospel contrary to that which we preached to you, let him be accursed" (Galatians 1:8).

There are five areas in which I would like you to expand your explanation of the Catholic way of salvation.

Confessing to a Priest

As evangelical Christians, we confess our sins directly to God. The Catholic Church, on the other hand, teaches that after baptism, Catholics must confess to a priest every serious sin they commit. Why is this necessary?

Final Steps in Catholic Salvation

As I understand it, the final steps in the Catholic plan of salvation involve final perseverance, the Particular Judgment, purgatory, and the General Judgment. What is your understanding of these, and how do they lead to heaven?

Saving Others by Prayer and Good Works

Rome says it is the custodian of a vast reservoir of merit called the "Church's treasury." It dispenses this as *indulgences,* the yielding of temporal punishment [CCC 1032, 1471, 1476]. The Second Vatican Council explained that Christ earned this merit with the help of others.

> This treasury includes as well the prayers and good works of the Blessed Virgin Mary. They are truly immense, unfathomable and even pristine in their value before God. In the treasury, too, are the prayers and good works of all the saints, all those who have followed in the footsteps of Christ the Lord and by his grace have made their lives holy and carried out the mission the Father entrusted to them. In this way they attained their own salvation and at the same time cooperated in saving their brothers in the unity of the Mystical Body.[192]

What is the biblical basis for people cooperating in saving others by their prayers and good works?

Earning Eternal Life

Would you explain what Rome means when it says that Catholics receive eternal life "as a reward...for their good works and merits"?[193]

Unsure About Heaven

When the *New York Times* asked Cardinal John O'Connor of New York whether he knew if he were going to heaven, he answered:

———

Church teaching is that I don't know, at any given moment, what my eternal future will be. I can hope, pray, do my very best—but I still don't know. Pope John Paul II doesn't know absolutely that he will go to heaven, nor does Mother Teresa of Calcutta....[194]

Why cannot even model Catholics know whether or not they will make it to heaven? Having the assurance from God's Word that we are forgiven, at peace with God, and will spend eternity with Him in heaven is something we cherish as evangelical Christians. I can't image how you can live each day not knowing what your eternal destiny will be.

I heard on the radio last week that the Vatican announced that it will be making Josemaría Escrivá, founder of Opus Dei, a saint. I understand this means they think he is in heaven. How do they know this? What does his sainthood mean for you and Opus Dei as an organization?

In Christ's love,

Jim

Letter 51

Dear Jim,

Happy New Year's! While others were partying, celebrating their desires for the future and drowning past miseries, we at the Center were giving thanks to God and invoking His blessings for the new year.

Right before Christmas, we received news that a cure attributed to God through Blessed Josemaría's intercession had been thoroughly studied by scientific and theological experts and was accepted by the Holy See as miraculous. This is the last major step—before the actual ceremony—in the process of declaring him a saint—that is, the Church "certifies" that he is in heaven with Christ and can intercede for others. Miracles are God's way of ratifying this fact, just as God did by raising the dead with Elisha's bones (2 Kings 13:21) and curing the sick with Paul's handkerchief (Acts 19:11-12).

For us in Opus Dei, this announcement brings us great joy and spurs us on to pray more, especially for world peace and Christian unity, two intentions very dear to Blessed Josemaría.

Assurance of Heaven

We all like to think we're going to heaven. Yet, "many…will seek to enter and will not be able" (Luke 13:24). "Many" have false assurances of heaven. Formulas such as accepting Jesus Christ as one's Lord and Savior are appealing, but give no assurance: "Not every one who says to me, 'Lord, Lord,' shall enter the kingdom of heaven" (Matthew 7:21).

We discussed this in Letters 24 and 25, especially while commenting on 1 John. As I said then, we can be assured of our *knowledge* of God and our status before Him if we have genuine *faith* and do what is right.[195]

What does it take to go to heaven?

Heaven is a great reward (Matthew 5:12), including bodily pleasures, or freedom from toil, pain, and suffering; freedom from sorrow, loneliness, dissension, and sadness. Yet this misses the essence of heaven.

Jesus compares heaven "to a king who gave a marriage feast for his son" (Matthew 22:2). Someone may react, "Great! I like parties...good food...good drink...music and dancing...." But again, that would miss the point.

Who is getting married at this wedding banquet?

The son of the great King...Christ! Yes, but whom is He marrying?

Christ wants to marry you...me...the Church, His bride. Thus heaven is the great wedding feast of the lamb (Revelation 19:7-9). Heavenly bliss is that of a bride on her wedding night...yet lasting forever! [CCC 1027].

Imagine being back in high school and a girl comes up to you and says, "Jim, let's get married. I know you don't love me and I certainly don't love you. But if we got married, then you could move out of your parents' house and I of mine. We could share an apartment, but you could do your thing and I could do mine. What do you say—shall we?" Would you marry her? Of course not! You want to marry someone who loves you and whom you love. The same is true with Christ. To go to heaven means to marry Christ, but one cannot marry Him unless he loves Him, correct?

When we die, perhaps our dialogue with Christ will go something like this:

Christian: "Lord, I want to go to heaven, I understand it is an awesome place."

Jesus: "Oh, so you want to marry Me!"

Christian: "Sure, whatever it takes…now will You let me in?"

Jesus: "But do you love Me? I can't marry anyone who doesn't love Me."

Christian: "I guess so…now may I enter?"

Jesus: "You say you love Me, but can you show Me? We have your life here on videotape, let's watch it together while you point out those things you said and did that show that you love Me…."

That is why when we die, God will judge us on our love [CCC 1022], love shown by deeds. Christ's "Bride has made herself ready; it was granted her to be clothed with fine linen, bright and pure—for the fine linen is the righteous deeds of the saints" (Revelation 19:7-8). That is why Jesus said,

> Not every one who says to me, "Lord, Lord," shall enter the kingdom of heaven, but he who does the will of my Father who is in heaven. On that day many will say to me, "Lord, Lord, did we not prophesy in your name, and cast out demons in your name, and do many mighty works in your name?" And then will I declare to them, "I never knew you; depart from me, you evildoers."
>
> MATTHEW 7:21-23

It's not enough to accept Jesus as Lord; it's not enough to preach Jesus as the Christ, work miracles, baptize, and cast out demons in His name. The key to heaven is *doing* the Father's will.

What is the Father's will? Well, Jesus just enumerated it in the Sermon on the Mount. The Father's will is that we be "poor in spirit," "meek," "merciful," "pure of heart"; that we do and teach "the law and prophets," pray, fast, give alms, lay up "treasures in heaven," seek "his kingdom and righteousness," not being anxious about material things nor judging others, and so on (Matthew

5:3–7:12). Christ "will repay every man for what he has done" (Matthew 16:27). So, let's do the Father's will and enter heaven!

Hell

How can we reconcile hell with a God who is all-loving and all-merciful? Many do not. In fact many Christians do away with the hell that Scripture clearly teaches about.

People go to hell because they choose to [CCC 1033, 1037]. Let's suppose a couple that once loved each other allowed their relationship to grow cold, ending their marriage in a bitter divorce. The last thing they want is to be near the person they hate. They want to get as far away from the other person as possible.

If a person lives divorced from God and dies hating Him, the last thing he would want is to be face to face with God in marital intimacy. He'd flee from God. But where can he go? God is everywhere! "If I ascend to heaven, thou art there! If I make my bed in Sheol [hell], thou art there!" (Psalm 139:8, comment added). Mercifully, God grants the soul who hates Him a place where His presence is minimal. That place is called hell.

The souls in hell take *consolation* in physical punishment. Since they still reflect God's image and likeness, they try to destroy God's image in their soul. Hell is an eternal suicide! Although souls in hell suffer tremendously, they would suffer even more seeing God directly in heaven. God doesn't force anyone to love Him.

So, why doesn't God just allow those souls to cease to exist? Simple! Because to do so, God would have to stop loving those souls. But God's love for those souls is eternal! So He does the next most merciful thing—shielding His presence from them. Therefore, hell is eternal [CCC 1035].

What does it take to go to hell? Be lazy and waste one's talents (Matthew 25:14-30) or ignore the poor and hungry (Matthew 25:31-46).

Purgatory

If heaven consists of intimate, marital union with the all-holy God (Revelation 15:4) as His bride, then to go to heaven, one needs "the holiness without which no one will see the Lord" (Hebrews 12:14). When Moses went to Mount Sinai, the Jewish people had to be consecrated and made holy to talk with God. Whoever was unholy and touched the mountain died (Exodus 19:10-25). Likewise, "nothing unclean shall enter" heaven (Revelation 21:27).

Christ said, "You, therefore, must be perfect, as your heavenly Father is perfect" (Matthew 5:48). If a person is not perfectly holy when he dies, he must become so before entering into God's presence [CCC 1030]. This purification is called purgatory, a kind of prison where we remain "till you have paid the last penny" (Matthew 5:26), rendering "account for every careless word...for by your words you will be justified...[or] condemned" (Matthew 12:36-37).

Whether this purification takes place over time or in the instant we die, we do not know. What we do know is that "the glory of the LORD was like a devouring fire" (Exodus 24:17), capable of purifying us so we can enter heaven:

> Now if any one builds on the foundation with gold, silver, precious stones, wood, hay, stubble—each man's work will become manifest; for the Day will disclose it, because it will be revealed with fire, and the fire will test what sort of work each one has done. If the work which any man has built on the foundation survives, he will receive a reward. If any man's work is burned up, he will suffer loss, though he himself will be saved, but only as through fire.
>
> 1 CORINTHIANS 3:12-15

Confession

So, we want to be free and forgiven of our sins to be able to enter heaven.

In the Old Testament, what happened when a person committed a sin? They were required to confess their sin *to a priest* (Leviticus 4–19). For example, when a ruler sinned, he had to offer a goat and "the priest shall make atonement for him for his sin, and *he shall be forgiven*" (Leviticus 4:26).

In the New Testament, Christ's sacrifice on the cross was our sin offering [CCC 615]. However, Christ—who had the power to forgive sins (Matthew 9:2-8)—gave that power to the New Testament priests-apostles to apply that sacrifice to the person confessing his sins:

> Receive the Holy Spirit. If you forgive the sins of any, *they are forgiven;* if you retain the sins of any, they are retained.
>
> JOHN 20:22-23 [see CCC 1442]

The parallels are not mere coincidence. Old Testament sin offerings are fulfilled in the New. We confess to priests because Christ gave them the power to forgive sins. Had He not, we would never do so. Presbyters (priests) could forgive sin confessed to them (James 5:13-16), a God-given ministry of reconciliation (2 Corinthians 5:18-21).

We can and ought to confess our sins directly to God. However, being human, we tend to live in denial. Paul confronted the Corinthians to arouse "godly grief" and repentance (see 2 Corinthians 7:2-13). God had to send His prophet, Nathan, to David (2 Samuel 12) to confront him about his adultery and murder (2 Samuel 11). David could have confessed directly to God had he been honest with himself. Confession helps us confront and take responsibility for our sins.

David confesses his sin to God through Nathan and God forgives his guilt, but God still punishes David by taking the child's life (2 Samuel 12:14-23). Forgiveness of sin and purification of punishment are not equivalent. The Catholic Church says that this "temporal punishment" for sin "must be purified either here on earth, or after death in Purgatory" [CCC 1472]. Many have experienced a great relief to know their sins have been judged and forgiven now rather than have to wait until the final judgment to discover the verdict.

Indulgences

Indulgence means "forgiveness." It refers to the temporal punishment or purification of sin needed to enter heaven. One way this purification takes place is by suffering:

> Since therefore Christ suffered in the flesh, arm yourselves with the same thought, for whoever has suffered in the flesh has ceased from sin, so as to live for the rest of the time in the flesh no longer by human passions but by the will of God.
>
> 1 PETER 4:1

If we can pray to alleviate another's suffering in this life, why can we not pray to alleviate the suffering of another's purification? The church encourages us to pray for the dead, applying the merits of Christ and the Church to their needs.

Paul prayed for mercy for his dead friend, Onesiphorus (2 Timothy 1:15-18). Septuagint versions of the Bible—the one used by early Christians—show Jews making atonement for the sins of their fellow soldiers who died precisely because they wore tokens of idols (2 Maccabees 12:39-46). Although I know you don't consider this canonical Scripture—yet Augustine did—at least it shows us what Jews believed at the time of Christ.

These scriptures should answer your questions. Yes, let's heed Paul's warning: accursed be anyone who preaches "a gospel contrary to that which we preached to you" (Galatians 1:8). Fortunately, the Church has been gifted "that some should be apostles... some pastors and teachers...to equip the saints...until we all attain to the unity of the faith and of the knowledge of the Son of God...so that we may no longer be children, tossed to and fro and carried about with every wind of doctrine" (Ephesians

4:11-14). Our apostles and pastors ought to guide us to a true interpretation of Scripture, to avoid some partial and "accursed" gospel.

In Christ's love,

John

Conversation 11

WEDNESDAY, JANUARY 9, 2002

Jim: I understand today is a special day for you, John.

John: Yes, it is—it's the centennial of our founder's birth. We are celebrating this in our Centers today and we will have several public Masses in local churches. In Rome, we are hosting a symposium on Blessed Josemaría with the theme "The Greatness of Ordinary Life," because he emphasized that the way to great intimacy with Christ can be found in doing the little things of everyday life with great love of God.

Must Christians confess to a priest?

Jim: As Rome will soon canonize Escrivá, it's appropriate that we discuss how, according to the Catholic Church, he and others obtain salvation. I have several questions.

In your explanation of why Catholics must confess their serious sins to a priest, you wrote, "Presbyters (priests) could forgive sin confessed to them (James 5:13-16)."[196] I question your equating presbyters and priests. The passage you quote reads, "Is any among you sick? Let him call for the elders of the church" (James 5:14). As we have discussed before, "elder" is the translation of the Greek word *presbuteros*, meaning a man of great age or maturity, and sometime translated as "presbyter." The Greeks had a different word for priest, *hiereus*. It is not found in the book of James or any of the other verses you cited from the New Testament. Have you any biblical justification for equating presbyters and priests or a New Testament scripture that says Christians must confess their serious sins to a priest (*hiereus*)?

John: Scriptures are not static legal documents, but the dynamic history of God's family. So, let's examine how the faith was lived, instead of getting hung up on terms.

When Christ said, "If you forgive the sins of any, they are forgiven" (John 20:23), He empowered the apostles to forgive sins, did He not? When God said to Moses, "The priest shall make atonement for him for the sin...and he shall be forgiven" (Leviticus 4:35; see also 5:10,13; 19:22), God also empowered *priests* to forgive the sinner.

An apostle or priest can only judge whether to forgive or retain a sin if we confess it to them. To fulfill these Scriptures, we need to confess our sins to "another" (James 5:16) so that sins we have "committed...will be forgiven" (James 5:15).

Christ came to fulfill the law and the prophets (Matthew 5:17-20). We see James 5 and John 20 fulfilling Leviticus when, confessing our sins to the *presbuteros,* we receive forgiveness from the apostles' successors. How do you see the New Testament fulfilling Leviticus?

Jim: Determining whether James 5:13-16 refers to confession to a priest or not is not a matter of "getting hung up on terms," but a necessary step in correctly understanding and applying the text. We need to know about whom James is speaking. So, my question remains: Do you have any lexical or biblical basis for treating elders and priests as one and the same?

John: The English word *priest* is derived from the Greek word *presbuteros,* not *hiereus,*[197] showing that Christians understood *elder* and *priest* synonymously. Even first-century

Christian writings, such as the *Didache,* encourage confession of sins in church[198] to the presbyters.[199]

Can a person be dejustified and rejustified multiple times?

Jim: The Catholic Church says that through the sacrament of confession "those who through sin have forfeited the received grace of justification, can again be justified."[200] I understand this supposedly takes place every time a person commits a mortal sin, thus forfeiting justification, and then receives the sacrament of confession, being justified again. A person could theoretically repeat this cycle hundreds of times during his lifetime. Now, I know that God is always ready to forgive a repentant sinner, but I question the concept of a person once being justified being dejustified and rejustified. Do you have any scripture to support this Catholic doctrine?

John: "Dejustified" and "rejustified" are not part of my Catholic vocabulary, but sin is. Can we sin multiple times? Can God forgive us multiple times? Scripture says yes: "If we confess our sins, he is faithful and just, and will forgive our sins" (1 John 1:9).

Look at David. By committing adultery with Bathsheba and murdering her husband (2 Samuel 11), David deserved death, forfeiting his justification. But God forgave him (2 Samuel 12:13). Later, David again disobeyed God by numbering the people, for which David deserved death (2 Samuel 24:17). God forgave David when he offered a sacrifice for his sins, and Israel's plague ceased (2 Samuel 24:25). This "cycle" repeats itself all too often in the Bible. God's mercy is an example for us (Luke 6:36), forgiving us more than "seventy times seven" times (Matthew 18:22).

Nevertheless, we should not presume God's forgiveness:

> Do not be so confident of atonement that you add sin
> to sin. Do not say, "His mercy is great, he will forgive
> the multitude of my sins," for both mercy and wrath
> are with him, and his anger rests on sinners.
>
> SIRACH 5:5-6

Thus, confession requires conversion which "entails sorrow for and abhorrence of sins committed, and the firm purpose of sinning no more in the future" [CCC 1490].

How can we make amends for our sins?

Jim: The Bible says, "If any one does sin, we have an advocate with the Father, Jesus Christ the righteous; and he is the expiation for our sins, and not for ours only but also for the sins of the whole world" (1 John 2:1-2). The sacrament of confession seems to deny this truth. For example, the *Catechism of the Catholic Church* says that a person, having confessed his sins to a priest, "must still recover his full spiritual health by doing something more to make amends for the sin: he must 'make satisfaction for' or 'expiate' his sins. This satisfaction is called 'penance'" [CCC 1459]. If the blood of Christ is not sufficient to make satisfaction for our sins, how can anything we do make amends for them?

John: True, Christ's one sacrifice atones for everyone's sins (Romans 3:25). Yet Paul exhorts: "Present your bodies as a living sacrifice, holy and acceptable to God, which is your spiritual worship" (Romans 12:1). Offering "spiritual sacrifices" (1 Peter 2:5) of praise, doing good, and sharing with others (Hebrews 13:15) doesn't detract from or add to the sacrifice of Christ—as you noted earlier.[201]

Scripture tells us how we can atone for sin: "By loyalty and faithfulness iniquity is atoned for" (Proverbs 16:6). "Whoever honors his father atones for sins...almsgiving atones for sin" (Sirach 3:3,30). "Love covers all offenses" (Proverbs 10:12). "Love covers a multitude of sins" (1 Peter 4:8). "Whoever brings back a sinner from the error of his way will save his soul from death and will cover a multitude of sins" (James 5:20).

Finally, the Old Testament sin offerings made atonement for sin. As you can see, this Catholic teaching is not novel....

Jim: You say that Christ's one sacrifice atones for everyone's sin, but then proceed to explain how we too must atone for our sins. Are you saying, then, that Christ made satisfaction for sins at the cross but not *full* satisfaction?

John: Paul's words—"I rejoice in my sufferings for your sake, and in my flesh I complete what is lacking in Christ's afflictions" (Colossians 1:24)—do not say that Christ's sacrifice was inadequate, but invite us to unite ourselves to His sacrifice by our own suffering and prayer, thereby participating in His atonement for sin.

Jim: Perhaps an analogy would help. Someday, by the grace of God, I will make the final payment on my house mortgage. Though I will have faithfully sent the lender a monthly check for years, I will do so no longer. My obligation will be satisfied, my debt paid in full. Similarly, if Christ's blood made full atonement for our sins on the cross, why must Catholics continue to atone for their sins?

John: Christ's cross is a spousal gift of His whole self to us, one sacrifice for all sins. Yet, He calls us to respond as a spouse, by giving our whole self to Him, participating in His suffering.

Jim: I am not referring here to whether a person participates in Christ's suffering but the concept that a sinner, having confessed to a priest, must "make amends for the sin: he must 'make satisfaction for' or 'expiate' his sins" [CCC 1459]. Why must the sinner make satisfaction if Christ made satisfaction?

John: We take responsibility when we acknowledge our sins. Although our satisfaction doesn't pay the debt, it pleases God when we humbly acknowledge our sins by making small sacrifices.

Here's an analogy to follow up yours: A boy was playing in the backyard and hit a ball through the neighbor's window. He goes to his father and says he's sorry, and that he wants to make up for it, but he can't pay for the window. The boy's father pays the neighbor, and the boy takes responsibility for his misdeed by doing some service around the house—perhaps mowing the lawn. That's why we do childlike satisfaction.

What must one do to be saved?

Jim: You wrote, "The key to heaven is *doing* the Father's will."[202] In his book *A Catechism for Adults*,[203] Catholic priest Father William J. Cogan lists ten things a Catholic must do to be saved. He says one must 1) believe; 2) be baptized; 3) be a loyal member of the Church; 4) love God; 5) love his neighbor; 6) keep the Ten Commandments; 7) receive the sacraments, especially Holy Communion; 8) pray; 9) do good works; and 10) die in a state of grace. Is this a good summary, or are there additional things a Catholic must also do to be saved?

John: Although just a summary, it expresses fairly well what "genuine" Christian faith is. As I said in my letter, we must do God's will to be saved (Matthew 7:21), as summarized in the Sermon on the Mount.

Is 1 Corinthians 3:12-15 really referring to purgatory?

Jim: In 1 Corinthians 3:12-15, Paul uses an allegory to remind Christians that in the future the Lord will review their service for Him. Paul imagines each person's ministry as a building constructed of various materials: "gold, silver, precious stones, wood, hay, stubble" (1 Corinthians 3:12). He then pictures this building passing through fire, thus revealing "what sort of work each one has done" (3:13). Each one, Paul writes, "will receive a reward" (3:14) for what survives. Catholic purgatory, on the other hand, is a real place where God punishes and purifies people, not imaginary buildings. The Second Vatican Council (1962-1965) said this occurs "in the next life through fire and torments or purifying punishments."[204] Surely, this is not what Paul is speaking about in 1 Corinthians 3:12-15, is it?

John: Purgatory is not so much a place, but a process of purification [CCC 1031]. Perhaps this causes you some confusion.

Paul speaks of "the Day"—the Day of Judgment—when "each man's work will become manifest...it will be revealed with fire, and the fire will test what sort of work each one has done" (1 Corinthians 3:13). Fire is just a metaphor; it purifies and tests our faith (1 Peter 1:7), burning away any "work" that is not "holy" (1 Corinthians 3:17), or not "gold, silver [or] precious stones" (1 Corinthians 3:12).

Like Paul, the Church does not describe the exact process of this spiritual purification, but insists that we need "the holiness without which no one will see the Lord" (Hebrews 12:14).

Can't we be certain of heaven from Scripture?

Jim: The Catholic Church says that it is impossible for anyone to know with certainty that he or she is going to heaven "unless he shall have learned this by special revelation."[205] I think we both agree that the Bible is a form of special revelation. It says, "He who has the Son has life; he who has not the Son of God has not life. I write this to you who believe in the name of the Son of God, that you may know that you have eternal life" (1 John 5:12-13). Why can't a person who meets the requirements of these verses—

trusting in the Lord Jesus Christ for salvation—know with certainty that he has eternal life?

John: As I pointed out in Letter 24, 1 John uses the verb "to know" some 37 times. *To know one has eternal life* requires knowledge of the Trinity, of Christian living, and of "the truth," not walking in darkness and worldliness, but loving God and others with deeds.[206]

Thus, Catholics can *know that we have eternal life,* but with the humble knowledge that we are also sinners, for "if we say we have no sin, we deceive ourselves" (1 John 1:8). We don't presume God will give us the gift of eternal life, although we confidently rely on His mercy.

Is eternal life a free gift or merited reward?

Jim: Scripture teaches that "the free gift of God is eternal life in Christ Jesus our Lord" (Romans 6:23). How then can Rome say that Catholics through their good works "truly merit...eternal life"?[207]

John: Of course heaven and eternal life are gifts. We do not earn them. We confidently rely on God's mercy without presuming it. If one were absolutely certain of eternal life, then it is no longer a gift but a right! But we agreed that faith doesn't give us the right to heaven.[208]

God gives us the grace to believe, without forcing us to. God gives us the grace to do good works—to love Him—but never forcing us to do them. Finally, God never forces heaven on us, but He freely invites us to enter a spousal relationship with Him forever. God will not force us to say yes; He just gives us the grace to be able to choose to believe and love.

Thus, having invited us to His heavenly banquet, we do say yes by our act of faith and our good works. *Merit* means that we are free and responsible when saying yes to God's gift.

Jim: The *Catechism of the Catholic Church* says that *merit* means "the recompense owed" [CCC 2006]. So when Rome says that Catholics through their good works "truly merit... eternal life,"[209] is it not saying that heaven is an earned reward, a recompense owed for good works performed?

John: I think you would agree that your three daughters are precious gifts from God, not only to you and Jean, but also to the world. Yet you and Jean had to cooperate to bring those gifts into being: you had to love each other, marry, and become one flesh. Had you not cooperated in this fashion, God would never have given those gifts for you to receive.

Similarly, Catholics see eternal life as God's gift requiring our cooperation.

Jim: I am not so much asking whether we must participate in *receiving* eternal life, but whether it is an earned reward. In a book bearing the imprimatur of the late Cardinal Cooke of New York, Catholic priest Father Matthias Premm wrote, "It is a universally accepted dogma of the Catholic Church that man, in union with the grace of the Holy Spirit must merit heaven by his good works....we can actually merit heaven *as our reward.* There are few truths so infallibly attested by Scripture....Heaven must be fought for; we have to earn heaven."[210] Is this not Catholic belief?

John: Jim, your question emphasizes man's work while ignoring the Holy Spirit's work in this process. As the *Catechism of the Catholic Church* states:

> The merit of man before God in the Christian life arises from the fact that God has freely chosen to associate man with the work of his grace. The fatherly action of God is first on his own initiative, and then follows man's free acting through his collaboration, so that the merit of good works is to be

attributed in the first place to the grace of God, then to the faithful.

[CCC 2008]

We should focus more on God's work and less on man's.

Jim: I am quoting Roman Catholic sources. The emphasis is where they place it. Recently the Catholic Church restated this, saying, "...eternal life is, at one and the same time, grace and the reward given by God for good works and merits."[211] The Roman Catholic Council of Trent anathematized anyone who denied this.

John: John 3:36 appears to say that we merit eternal life by faith. Nevertheless, faith cannot obtain eternal life unless the Holy Spirit first moves us to make a free act of faith. Works that merit eternal life are first God's, because He works in us so we can "work out" our own salvation (Philippians 2:12-13).

Jim: Let me then return to my original question with regard to how eternal life can be "the free gift of God" (Romans 6:23) and something Catholics "truly merit"[212] both at the same time. Perhaps you could explain what the Council of Trent meant when it said:

> To those who work well right to the end and keep their trust in God, *eternal life should be held out,* both as a grace promised in his mercy through Jesus Christ to the children of God, and *as a reward* to be faithfully bestowed, on the promise of God himself, *for their good works and merits*[213] (emphasis added).

John: Paul wrote:

> You stand fast only through faith. So do not become proud, but stand in awe. For if God did not spare the

natural branches [the Jews], neither will he spare you.
Note…God's kindness to you, *provided you continue
in his kindness; otherwise you too will be cut off.*

ROMANS 11:20-22, comment added

Non-Jewish Christians must do works of kindness to
avoid being cut off from God's gift of eternal life. Jesus said,
"He who endures to the end will be saved" (Matthew
24:13).

Are good Muslims also saved?

Jim: The Second Vatican Council said that God's plan of salvation includes those who sincerely practice Islam [CCC
841].[214] Does this not contradict Jesus, who said, "I am the
way, and the truth, and the life; no one comes to the Father,
but by me" (John 14:6)?

John: God "desires all men to be saved and to come to the knowledge of the truth" (1 Timothy 2:4), but one cannot enter
heaven without a spousal relationship to Jesus Christ. The
one Church is Christ's bride.

If a non-Catholic dies and goes before Jesus, saying, "I
want to go to heaven," our Lord could say, "To enter heaven
you must be My bride, a member of the Catholic Church."
If the person replied, "Jesus, had I known that, I would've
joined the Church long ago; please, have mercy and let me
become Catholic," I think our Lord would. This applies to
Muslims, Jews, and to non-Catholic Christians too [CCC
838-845].

However, if a person replied, "I want heaven, but I hate
the Church and all it stands for. I opposed it all my life…."
Our Lord can do nothing for him because his dispositions
are incompatible with heaven.

That's why the *Catechism* says, "Outside the Church
there is no salvation" [CCC 846-848] and "All men are called
to this catholic unity of the People of God" [CCC 836].

Thus, we should make Christ known, giving each the opportunity to say yes to Christ and embrace salvation before they die:

> God "desires all men to be saved and to come to the knowledge of the truth" (1 Timothy 2:4); that is, God wills the salvation of everyone through the knowledge of the truth. Salvation is found in the truth. Those who obey the prompting of the Spirit of truth are already on the way of salvation. But the Church, to whom this truth has been entrusted, must go out to meet their desire, so as to bring them the truth. Because she believes in God's universal plan of salvation, the Church must be missionary.
>
> [CCC 851]

Jim: Vatican II stated that divine salvation includes "those who, without any fault of theirs, have not yet arrived at an explicit knowledge of God, and who, not without grace, strive to lead a good life."[215] Does this mean that anyone, regardless of his religious beliefs or lack thereof, who sincerely wants to spend eternity with God and tries to live a good life will go to heaven?

John: Paul refuses to judge even himself (1 Corinthians 4:3). The Church refuses to judge who makes it to heaven and who doesn't. Nevertheless, she gives us hope that those who have missed the opportunity to know and fall in love with Jesus Christ in this life still will have the possibility of heaven. As Peter said, "Truly I perceive that God shows no partiality, but in every nation any one who fears him and does what is right is acceptable to him" (Acts 10:34-35).

This gives us hope that those who have not known Jesus but fear and respect God and try to do what is right in their lives will be acceptable to Him and enter eternal life.

Jim: I'm not sure *trying* to do what is right is the standard God uses. Let me think about it and give you my response in my next letter.

Letter 52

SATURDAY, JANUARY 26, 2002

Dear John,

We have discussed some important differences concerning salvation, ones that have divided Christianity for centuries. God has helped us to do this without acrimony or offense. My prayer is that we will be able to continue and hopefully see a breakthrough.

Here I would like to move our discussion one step further by sharing three of my concerns about Catholic salvation. I also want to respond to some of your comments.

Confession to a Priest

I feel the Roman Catholic priesthood hinders people from going to God for salvation. Like Mary, priests are mediators. Their principal function is to offer the Sacrifice of the Mass and to forgive sins, both necessary for Catholic salvation. As we have already discussed the Eucharist, I will limit my comments here to the sacrament of reconciliation.

Rome commands the faithful "to confess every serious sin at least once a year" [CCC 1457] to a priest. You say this is supported by James 5:13-15. When I objected to you substituting "priests" for "elders" in the text, you replied that the English word *priest* is derived from the Greek word *presbuteros.* The derivation of a word, however, does not determine its meaning. We must look to Greek usage during the first century to determine the meaning of a New Testament word. Then we must select a word with the

359

corresponding meaning in our language to translate it. *Presbuteros* means "older man" or "elder," not "priest."

Further, the Bible distinguishes between the offices of elder and priest, and so should we. In Judaism, elders were the heads of tribes, clans, and families. Priests, by contrast, were mediators, representing the people before God and offering sacrifices. This distinction persisted throughout biblical times, though it became somewhat blurred in the first century when the chief priests joined the Pharisees on the council of the elders (Luke 22:66).

On Pentecost, Christ's apostles received the baptism of the Holy Spirit. The church was born and a new order inaugurated. Over each local church the apostles appointed several men, giving them the title of *elder* (Acts 14:23; Titus 1:5). These men were shepherds, caring for the needs of the people (Acts 20:28; 1 Peter 5:1-4). Scripture does not call them priests. They did not function as mediators. In the apostolic church, as I discussed earlier, all Christians were priests, having equal and direct access to God (Ephesians 2:18; 1 Peter 2:4-10; Revelation 1:6).

A final point: You say the *Didache* encourages Christians to confess their sins to the presbyters. The passages you cited, however, simply say that Christians should confess their sins regularly. They don't say to whom. Evangelicals believe Christians should confess their sins regularly to God (Psalm 32:5; Hebrews 4:16; 1 John 1:9; 2:1-2).

Working for Salvation

When I think of Catholic salvation, I think of all that one must *do* to be saved. Catholic priest Father William J. Cogan listed ten things. You added the instructions of the Sermon on the Mount, containing some 60 others. Let's assume for a moment that you are right—that salvation is achieved by doing the will of God. May I ask then: Can you do it? Can you consistently "love your neighbor as yourself" (Mark 12:31)? Can you, as Jesus taught, "be perfect, as your heavenly Father is perfect" (Matthew 5:48)?

I know you try, John, and try sincerely. But Jesus didn't say *try* to love your neighbor, or *try* to be perfect. He told the lawyer who thought he could obtain eternal life through keeping the commandments, "Do this, and you will live" (Luke 10:28). And the man would have obtained eternal life, if he could *do* it. But who can? Who can be perfect as God is perfect?

Scripture answers, "None is righteous, no, not one" (Romans 3:10). That is why God sent His Son to save us. We are sinners— lost sinners, all of us. We can't measure up to God's standard for even an hour. That is why the Bible answers the question "What must I do to be saved?" (Acts 16:30) with the gospel: "Believe in the Lord Jesus, and you will be saved" (verse 31).

I am deeply concerned, John, that when I ask practicing Catholics how they hope to get to heaven, only about 30 percent even mention Christ. Even less say anything significant about the cross. Most talk about all that the Church requires them to do to get to heaven. "I try to live a good and decent life," is a typical response. "I go to church." "I try to be kind to everyone." "I do my best." There is too much *I* and not enough *Christ* in their answers. It tells me in whom they are trusting for their salvation.

Only when a person stops working for his salvation can he truly trust Christ for it. He needs to come to the end of himself, and like the tax collector who went up to the temple to pray, cry out, "God, be merciful to me a sinner!" (Luke 18:13). Only then does the cross make sense, and he can place his faith in Jesus to save him.

Who makes satisfaction for sins?

We didn't seem to connect on whether Christ made full or partial satisfaction for sins. You argued that Catholics should make amends for their sins, but you would not acknowledge that this implies Christ did not make *full* satisfaction. The *Catechism of the Catholic Church* does the same. It says that a sinner, after receiving absolution in confession, must do "something more to make amends for the sin: he must 'make satisfaction for' or 'expiate' his sins" [CCC 1459]. In the next paragraph it says Christ "alone expiated our sins once for all" [CCC 1460]. Are these not contradictory?

The Bible teaches that since Christ made complete satisfaction for sin, we do not need to make amends for our sins, neither here on earth nor later in purgatory. Christ "made purification for sins" (Hebrews 1:3). "By a single offering he has perfected for all time those who are sanctified" (Hebrews 10:14). Jesus paid it all. One of our best-loved hymns expresses this well. Titled "It Is Well With My Soul," the third verse reads:

> My sin, oh, the bliss of this glorious thought,
>
> My sin not in part but the whole,
>
> Is nailed to the cross and I bear it no more,
>
> Praise the Lord, praise the Lord, O my soul![216]

I hope we can sing this together someday, John.

In Christ's love,

Jim

Letter 53

Dear Jim,

Your last letter gave me hope. Although it appears we are still far apart, we are challenging each other to address serious issues in a charitable and Christian way, tearing down the walls that separate us, seeking "that all of you agree and that there be no dissensions among you, but that you be united in the same mind and the same judgment" (1 Corinthians 1:10).

Confession to a Priest

You see priesthood as a hindrance for salvation, but God doesn't. He called the apostles (and me) to serve as priestly mediators, administering His Word and forgiveness to others: "You did not choose me, but I chose you and appointed you....If you forgive the sins of any, they are forgiven" (John 15:16; 20:23). God chose us as He did the Old Testament Levites.

The Levitical priesthood complemented—not eliminated—the priesthood of every Jew to offer spiritual sacrifices of thanksgiving and contrition (Exodus 19:3-6; Psalm 50:14,23; 51:17, and so on). The New Testament ministerial priesthood also complements—not eliminates—the priesthood of every Christian. Isaiah's prophecy makes this clear:

> I am coming to gather all nations and tongues...that
> have not heard my fame or seen my glory; and they

> shall declare my glory among the nations....And
> some of them also I will take for priests and for
> Levites, says the LORD.
>
> ISAIAH 66:18-21

Non-Jews becoming ministerial priests! Why? To preach and absolve sin—to be New Covenant Levites.

When our Lord cured the lepers, He sent them to the priests (Luke 5:12-14; 17:12-19). Scripture associates sin with disease (Psalm 107:17), especially leprosy (Numbers 12:1-16; Deuteronomy 24:8-9). Jesus forgave their sin and healed their disease. He still sent them to the priests: to prepare us to send people to the Church to be cleansed of spiritual diseases and truly forgiven (Matthew 18:15-18)!

So, not in isolation but in this context do I interpret James 5, identifying priest and presbyter.

God's Frustrated Call

Jim, among other things, God calls us to be poor of spirit, meek, merciful, pure...perfect (Matthew 5:1-48; 6:14-15), to obey the commandments (Matthew 19:17-19) and love one another (John 13:34-35; 15:12-17). Would God command us to do something just to prove it is impossible? Are you saying we shouldn't try to obey God? Isn't this "relaxing" God's commandments, vacating them of any substance (Matthew 5:19)?

Would you ask your daughters to respect their mother, drive safely, avoid sex until marriage, and so on just to show that they can't do it? No way! You expect them to try to obey, knowing that they may mess up occasionally due to weakness.

How are we saved, then? "He who believes in the Son has eternal life; he who does not obey the Son shall not see life" (John 3:36).

Would our Lord call us to believe and obey while knowing full well we can't possibly do so? If so, then we are all damned. How absurd!

Catholic Salvation

True, we can't believe, obey, or do good works without God's help. Faith is "the work of God" (John 6:29). The Holy Spirit moves us to believe and do good works, guiding us toward salvation. Yes, sometimes we choose not to follow His inspiration. When that happens to me, I go to God immediately, ask pardon for my sin, and confess it to another priest as soon as possible. Trusting in His mercy, I begin again.

Differing Paradigms and Notions of Gift

Why don't we connect? Perhaps because we use different paradigms: You see salvation as God paying off business debt; Catholics see it as a spousal relationship with Christ. Thus, we interpret Scripture differently.

Your notion of gift seems one-directional, as coming from God and requiring no response from us. We see God calling us to use His gift for the good of others.

For example, suppose you bought some flowers for Jean. Would she take them from you and hide them in her closet, saying, "They're mine...I'll enjoy them by myself"? No, that would be selfish! Rather, she would take the flowers with gratitude, cut and trim the stems, place them in a vase, arrange them to bring out their beauty, and place the vase in a prominent place where all can enjoy the flowers. In a sense, she would give back to you the very gift you gave her, only with her own creativity attached.

If salvation were God's gift for you to enjoy by yourself with no obligations associated with it, wouldn't it become something selfish?

Merit

Merit simply means that something depends on our personal responsibility—our free choice. If someone asked Jean, "Who is responsible for the flowers in the dining room? she'd reply that you are: You bought them and gave them to her. If someone asked you, "Who's responsible for the flowers on the table?" you'd reply, "Jean is." She trimmed the stems, arranged them in a nice vase, and placed them on the table. You "merited" a kiss from her for your gift; she "merited" a kiss from you for her presentation.

Salvation involves more than flowers, it involves a gift of self: God gives a threefold gift of self to us and we respond, giving ourselves to Him. Salvation is a spousal gift.

A woman demonstrates love for her husband by details of affection and service. By these, the woman *merits* her husband's love and service in return—to live in his house and receive his support. But all this presupposes their original *gift* of self in marriage and their ongoing *free gift* of love. She doesn't *earn* her husband's support as some kind of business transaction…that would be harlotry!

I know it is a different way of looking at things, but it's perfectly consistent with Scripture. As you see, the *Catechism of the Catholic Church* doesn't contradict itself. Let's pray that we can both see God's wonderful plan of salvation clearly. I look forward to your presentation.

In Christ's love,

John

Letter 54

THURSDAY, JANUARY 31, 2002

Dear John,

You posed an interesting question in your last letter. Speaking of the Ten Commandments, you asked: Would God command us to do something just to prove it is impossible? Allow me to restate this, so as to avoid having to qualify my answer. Did God give the Jews the Ten Commandments to prove to them that they could not keep them? I believe so, for an essential step in receiving "the righteousness of God through faith in Jesus Christ" (Romans 3:22) was for a Jew to come to the end of himself. He needed to see himself as God saw him—a sinner with no righteousness of his own. The same is true of us. Here's how evangelical Christians see salvation.

> Only when we realize the futility of trying to find acceptance with God through living a good life can we cast ourselves upon God's mercy, trusting Jesus as our Savior. When a person does this, the Lord forgives him and declares him righteous in His sight. Concurrent with this is the rebirth and baptism of the Holy Spirit. The person becomes a member of the body of Christ, a child of God. This is a permanent relationship that nothing can sever. God has promised, "I will never fail you nor forsake you" (Hebrews 13:5). God guarantees the person a place in heaven.

I will explain this more fully in my next letter. I welcome your questions.

In Christ's love,

Jim

Letter 55

FRIDAY, FEBRUARY 1, 2002

Dear Jim,

Last night we had an all-night vigil in front of the Blessed Sacrament. College students and residents here took one-hour turns accompanying our Lord throughout the night, trying to say *yes* to Christ's "Could you not watch with me one hour?" (Matthew 26:40). In my hour, I prayed for you, your family, and our final salvation, asking Christ's guidance in this important issue.

Your letter was shockingly frank. What you say seems to empty 90 percent of Scripture of any meaningful content. Perhaps that is why many of the scriptures I have cited don't answer your questions—because they exist just to show us the futility of our efforts. I hope you can show me otherwise.

Obedience of Faith

Paul begins and ends Romans describing faith as an "obedience of faith" (Romans 1:5; 16:26). Scripture details God's will with many exhortations and commands. You say God does this to prove that we cannot possibly fulfill His will. You condemn Christians—especially Catholics—who believe in Christ and then try to obey God, relying on the Holy Spirit's strength and guidance to do so. You imply that *obedience* opposes faith, whereas Scripture says *disobedience* opposes faith.

For example, you seem to ignore the Scriptures I cited: "He who does not obey the Son shall not see life" (John 3:36); and,

"Not every one who says to me, 'Lord, Lord,' shall enter the kingdom of heaven, but he who does the will of my Father who is in heaven"(Matthew 7:21). How can anyone go to heaven if he is unable to obey or do God's will?

When was Abraham saved?

In Letter 23, you say that Abraham believed God. "Thereafter God considers him perfectly righteous in his sight."[217] When did Abraham's once-in-a-lifetime event occur, and what made it saving?

"De-justification"

In Conversation 11, you asked whether committing a mortal sin forfeits our justification. But John wrote, "If any one sees his brother committing what is not a *mortal sin,* he will ask, and God will give him life for those whose *sin is not mortal.* There is *sin which is mortal*" (1 John 5:16).

Do you believe that after Abraham was saved, he was no longer free to commit *mortal* sin, a sin that could sever him from God and from receiving life?

Does heaven require holiness?

Jim, you say that all true believers are not just called to *be,* but we *already are* saints (meaning holy ones).[218] But in Letter 47 you say God alone is holy, leaving no room for Mary to be a saint, a holy one.[219] What kind of holiness is needed to be a saint and enter heaven?

These are my questions for you. I hope your answers will resolve them.

In Christ's saving love,

John

Letter 56

FRIDAY, FEBRUARY 8, 2002

Dear John,

You've asked some great questions! I think you are beginning to understand what I have been saying about salvation. Not that you agree—I know you don't. But the fact that you are finding what I am saying "shocking," completely out of phase with your understanding of Scripture, actually gives me hope. You should be shocked. What I believe is radically different from Roman Catholicism. Indeed, it is at odds with every other religion on earth. For the most part, as I understand it, they all basically say the same thing: *Those who sincerely seek God and do good in this life will be accepted by Him in the next.*

A Unique Way of Salvation

Biblical Christianity stands apart. It says, "None is righteous, no, not one" (Romans 3:10). It exalts God as dwelling in unapproachable holiness. It indicts man as fallen, sinful, and guilty before Him. It proclaims our only hope is "Jesus who delivers us from the wrath to come" (1 Thessalonians 1:10). It offers reconciliation to God, not by what *we* have done, but by what *He* has done for us. It is salvation by grace, not merit; received by faith, not works. It is of God, not of us.

I know of no similar teaching in any of the world's faiths. Nor would I expect it, for such is foolishness to this world (1 Corinthians 3:18-31). Instead, I find man-made religions that cater to

370

our pride. They tell us we are basically good and promise that if we practice religion, do our best, and amend for our sins, God will receive us into His kingdom. Even Judaism and Christianity, though they began with the truth, have not escaped the corrupting hand of man. Consider the religious history of the Jews.

God Declares Abraham Righteous

Judaism began with divine revelation. God appeared to Abraham and called him to leave his country. The Lord promised to make him a great nation and to bless the people of the earth through him (Genesis 12:1-3). Abraham obeyed him. Years later, however, aged, childless, and perplexed, he began to wonder how this might be. The Lord led him out into the night air, saying, "Look toward heaven, and number the stars, if you are able to number them....So shall your descendants be" (Genesis 15:5). It is here that we read the astounding words that Abraham "believed the LORD; and he reckoned it to him as righteousness" (Genesis 15:6). Scripture emphasizes that this act of faith was the moment when God justified Abraham (Romans 4:1-3). It determined his eternal salvation and serves as an example of how to be saved for all who would come after him (Romans 4:1-25; Galatians 3:6-9). This is what I believe, John—justification by faith.

You say I teach that obedience opposes faith. To the contrary, I believe faith brings obedience. Consider Abraham once more. In time, God gave Abraham a son, Isaac, whom he loved dearly, the son of promise. Some 20 years later, however, Scripture says, "God tested Abraham" (Genesis 22:1). He asked him to sacrifice Isaac on Mount Moriah. But as Abraham raised the knife to slay his son, God stopped him, saying, "Because you have done this, and have not withheld your son, your only son, I will indeed bless you" (Genesis 22:16-17). This is what I believe, John: True faith is exhibited by obedient good works. Earlier I expressed the relationship of faith, justification, and good works as:

faith ➤ justification, new and eternal life ➤ good works

—

Israel Seeks to Establish its Own Righteousness

Over the next 400 years, Abraham's descendants grew into a great people two million strong, the nation of Israel. Times became difficult, however, when the Egyptians cruelly enslaved them. In their despair, Israel cried out to the Lord. God sent Moses to deliver the people and bring them to the land He had promised to Abraham. Along the way, God tested them. Their actions revealed they lacked the faith of Abraham. They grumbled when food or water became scarce. They disobeyed God's instructions. They clung to idols hidden among their possessions, such as a detestable deity of the Ammonites (Acts 7:42-43). At one point, they threatened to stone Moses.

When Israel finally arrived at Mount Sinai, the unexpected happened. The Lord proposed a new covenant (Exodus 19:5-6). A formal contract containing 613 commands, including the familiar Ten Commandments, it specified how the Jews were to live. The terms were fair but exacting. God promised that if the people obeyed these commands, He would bless them beyond any nation on earth. Correspondingly, if they failed, He would curse them with plagues, drought, and wars (Leviticus 26:1-46).

What were they to do? Should they accept the terms of the contract? Was the Lord testing them yet again? Their track record was abysmal; the consequences for failure frightening. Regardless, something about the offer appealed to them. Maybe it was the chance for a new start. Maybe they sincerely thought they could please the Lord now that they knew exactly what He wanted them to do. Whatever the reason, they told God, "All that the LORD has spoken we will do, and we will be obedient" (Exodus 24:7).

It didn't last six weeks. While Moses was away, the Israelites built for themselves a golden calf representing God, proclaiming, "Tomorrow shall be a feast to the LORD" (Exodus 32:5). It quickly degraded into a drunken orgy. The punitive clauses of the covenant of law became operative. On top of Mount Sinai, the Lord told Moses, "I have seen this people, and behold, it is a stiff-necked people; now therefore let me alone, that my wrath may burn hot against them and I may consume them" (Exodus 32:9-10). Only through the earnest pleading of Moses, reminding God of His previous and still-valid covenant with Abraham, did the Lord spare Israel (Exodus 32:13; Galatians 3:17).

Israel's Decline into Apostasy

The incident of the golden calf typified Israel's conduct. They became notorious in the region, known for every form of gross idolatry, immorality, and violence. The Scriptures record their sins in unblushing detail. Their history illustrates that rules and rituals cannot make bad people good. Despite warnings and chastisement, Israel remained unchanged. Nevertheless, throughout their history a small minority believed. These included individuals such as Rahab, Ruth, Hannah, Samuel, David, and Daniel.

When Jesus began His ministry in the first century, the Pharisees had the people in their grip, scrutinizing every aspect of Jewish life. Jesus refused to submit. He accused them of having turned Judaism into a vain form of worship, marked by religious hypocrisy (Mark 7:6-7). He called the Pharisees "whitewashed tombs, which outwardly appear beautiful, but within they are full of dead men's bones and all uncleanness" (Matthew 23:27).

As John before Him, Jesus preached a message of repentance. He used the Ten Commandments to show His people their need of salvation. "You have heard that it was said to the men of old," 'You shall not kill; and whoever kills shall be liable to judgment.' But I say to you...whoever says, 'You fool!' shall be liable to the hell of fire" (Matthew 5:21-22). He continued, "You have heard that it was said, 'You shall not commit adultery.' But I say to you that every one who looks at a woman lustfully has already committed adultery with her in his heart" (Matthew 5:27-28). Bottom line, He told them, "None of you keeps the law" (John 7:19).

The True Purpose of the Law

Jesus' teaching confirms that God never intended for anyone to be saved through keeping the law. "Why then the law?" (Galatians

3:19), Paul asks for us. He explains that God gave the law to serve as a benchmark, a standard of the perfection God requires. Too high for any fallen child of Adam to meet, it was intended to help the Jews see their sinfulness and the necessity of coming to God through faith in the promised Messiah (Galatians 3:19-29). "Through the law comes knowledge of sin" (Romans 3:20).

So why didn't the law accomplish its purpose, bringing the Jewish nation to faith in Jesus? Paul answers, "Because they did not pursue it through faith, but as if it were based on works" (Romans 9:32). "For, being ignorant of the righteousness that comes from God, and seeking to establish their own, they did not submit to God's righteousness" (Romans 10:3). In their sinful pride, they had turned Judaism into a religion preaching salvation through faith in God *and* righteous living under the law.

As mentioned previously, however, a few were saved. They received the law as it was intended—a revelation of the holiness of God and a moral code of conduct for the nation. They understood that the law was not intended to save them but to point them to one who could. Paul wrote, speaking of himself and his believing Jewish brethren, "The Law has become our tutor to lead us to Christ, so that we may be justified by faith" (Galatians 3:24 NASB).

Christendom Follows Israel

Given what Judaism had become and the ruling Jews' opposition to Jesus, it is little wonder that He chose to start afresh, instituting the church. It began well, but early on, even while the apostles were alive, false teachers began introducing law-keeping for righteousness. They taught that justification came through faith in Jesus but had to be maintained by adherence to the laws of God. This heresy spread quickly, especially in the churches of Galatia. Paul saw where it was leading, and warned the Galatian believers in the sternest of words (Galatians 1:8-9). It was the reason for the Council of Jerusalem (Acts 15:1-29). But this did not stop it, for the sinful heart of man insists on proving his self-worth. Thirteen years later, Paul was still fighting it in Ephesus

(1 Timothy 1:6-11). He prophesied that this problem would still be with us in the last days (2 Timothy 3:1-13).

I fear that much of Christendom today, including many Protestant denominations, has gone the way of Judaism. It has become a religion of misguided people who think peace with God can be achieved through religious practices and moral living. In the so-called "Christian countries" of the world, relatively few people have any real knowledge of the Scriptures or can explain the gospel of Jesus Christ. Many of these, frustrated with the inability of their churches to bring them a life-changing experience of God, have given up, concluding that God is unknowable or doesn't exist.

Christendom may fail, but Christ will not. "I will build my church," Jesus promised, "and the gates of hell shall not prevail against it" (Matthew 16:18 KJV). Even today in every corner of the world men and women are returning to the Scriptures. In the revelation received from Christ, they are finding the gospel for themselves, "the power of God for salvation to every one who has faith" (Romans 1:16).

Questions and Answers

You have asked several good questions, John, that I will try to answer before closing.

What made Abraham's faith genuine and saving? Rather than depending on his own thinking and righteousness, Abraham trusted God. His faith had divine revelation as its basis, the promise of God as its content, and the Lord Himself as its object.

Could Abraham have committed a sin that would have severed him from God and eternal life? No. He had not been saved from eternal judgment by his own righteousness; neither was he being kept from it by his own righteousness. The same is true of born-again believers today. There is no "mortal sin" that can result in their damnation. "It is God who justifies; who is to condemn?" (Romans 8:33-34). Should a child of God go astray, the Father promises to discipline him as a son whom He loves. He will never, however, forsake him (Hebrews 12:5-11; 13:5). The verse that you cited, 1 John 5:16, is not talking about a true Christian, but a false one who has left the faith, most likely for Gnosticism. This is the sin of apostasy, an informed and hostile rejection of Christ, a sin for which there is no remedy. For this reason, John describes it as a sin unto death or mortal sin.

What kind of holiness did Abraham or other saints need to enter heaven? God's holiness. "You, therefore, must be perfect, as your heavenly Father is perfect," said Jesus (Matthew 5:48). Though impossible in ourselves, this holiness is available to us through the gospel, "even the righteousness of God through faith in Jesus Christ for all those who believe" (Romans 3:22 NASB).

Let's talk soon and discuss these things further. Please give me a call when you get a chance.

In Christ's love,

Jim

Conversation 12

John: Jim, belated Valentine's Day! Did you do anything special yesterday for your wife and daughters?

Jim: I got the girls each a large gingerbread heart. They really enjoyed them. Jean and I went out to Starbucks after dinner. We had a nice time talking and planning for the future.

Is faith a free act?

John: Jim, I still detect some stereotyping of Catholicism in your writing. Your insistence on faith emphasizes that salvation is a free gift from God. We agree here. Faith is absolutely necessary for Catholics, too. Works acknowledge our freedom in obeying and loving God. Yet the Holy Spirit initiates every deed done for love for God.

Catholics believe that faith is a free act on our part— that God doesn't force us to believe—do you?

Jim: Yes, we agree that faith is necessary for salvation and that it is a free act, not something that God forces on us. I do not think, however, we both agree that salvation is a free gift received by faith apart from meritorious works. Roman Catholicism teaches that only *initial* salvation received at baptism is free [CCC 2027]. It says that Catholics must strive to persevere to the end and achieve *final* salvation.

They obtain heaven as an eternal reward *for good works* they accomplished on earth with God's help [CCC 1821]. Rome says "by those very works…[they] have truly merited eternal life, to be obtained in its due time, provided they depart this life in grace."[220] I trust you do not consider this stereotyping, but the authentic Catholic position.

John: But I do. It is Christ who says those who endure to the end will be saved (Matthew 10:22).

I gave the example of how a woman's love, affection, and service *merits* her husband's love in return. She *merits* living in his house and receiving his support. She doesn't *earn* her husband's support as some kind of business transaction—as I said, that would be harlotry—but expresses an ongoing, mutual, *free gift* of love.[221] Do evangelicals believe that this kind of free exchange of love is possible between God and man?

Jim: Yes, but it is only possible once we have been reconciled to God through the Lord Jesus Christ. The use of the word *merit* with regard to this is unbiblical. You describe salvation as a woman's love meriting her husband's love in return. Roman Catholicism defines merit as "divine reward for the practice of virtue."[222] It is a "recompense owed" [CCC 2006]. God, however, doesn't owe us anything. It is "by grace you have been saved through faith; and this is not your own doing, it is the gift of God" (Ephesians 2:8).

What makes Abraham's faith "genuine"?

John: Jim, let's look to Abraham, who "serves as an example for all who would come after him as to how to be saved." In Genesis 12:1-4, God asked Abraham to leave his land and family and to go to Bethel, promising to make his descendents into a great nation. Already an old man (75 years old) with no children, Abraham believed and obeyed.

Now, Christ said, "Every one who has left houses or…children or lands, for my name's sake, will receive a hundredfold, and inherit eternal life" (Matthew 19:29). So, Abraham had faith to inherit eternal life. But you seem to say Abraham's faith was not "genuine" until 11 years later. Why? What makes his faith disingenuous?

Jim: You will have to ask God, John. Only He knows what was in Abraham's heart. I only know what Scripture tells me. It says God declared Abraham righteous at a later time (Genesis 15:6). Apparently something was lacking when Abraham first left his home in Ur of the Chaldeans. For the same reason, I would not apply Matthew 19:29 to every case, as if leaving one's home was a meritorious act that automatically earns eternal life. Judas Iscariot, for example, left his home to follow Jesus, and we know he did not inherit eternal life (Mark 14:21; John 17:12). I would see it as an action of faith which, when truly done for Jesus' sake, would be evidence of true faith.

John: But Scripture explains:

> By faith Abraham obeyed when he was called to go out to a place which he was to receive as an inheritance; and he went out, not knowing where he was to go….For he looked forward to the city…whose builder and maker is God….But as it is, [Abraham and his descendents] desire a better country, that is, a heavenly one. Therefore God is not ashamed to be called their God, for he has prepared for them a city.
>
> HEBREWS 11:8,10,16, comment added

If Abraham's leaving home moved God to prepare heaven for us, isn't that saving faith?

Jim: When Scripture says that God "has prepared for them a city," this is not a *result* of Abraham's faith. God has prepared heaven for all who have faith in Him. Abraham will be able to enjoy it because he had faith and God justified him.

John: How about when Abraham returned to Bethel a second time and called upon the name of the Lord (Genesis 13:4)? Paul said, "Every one who calls upon the name of the Lord will be saved" (Romans 10:13). Was this not saving faith?

Jim: I don't know what was deficient in Abraham's faith. God did not justify him until later (Genesis 15:6). Paul said he was concerned that some of the Corinthians may have "believed in vain" (1 Corinthians 15:2). Simply having *faith*—for example, believing God exists—does not necessarily save. We must have faith in God as the object of our salvation, trusting Him to deliver us from the punishment of sin. The content of our faith must be the gospel—"that Christ died for our sins in accordance with the scriptures, that he was buried, that he was raised on the third day" (1 Corinthians 15:3-4). Also, it must be faith in Christ alone. Faith mixed with works doesn't save.

Was Abraham free to apostatize?

John: In Genesis 15:1-6, God renewed His promise a third time to make a great nation of Abraham, and Abraham believed again. You say this was "the moment when God justified Abraham." Was Abraham *free* to apostatize, to reject his faith, so that—no matter what he did thereafter—he would still go to heaven?

Jim: The nature of genuine faith is that it endures. We know Abraham had true faith, for God justified him. We can conclude, therefore, that Abraham's faith would endure, and indeed it did endure. It doesn't make sense to ask what happens when real faith, the kind of faith that endures, does not endure.

As for real faith and going to heaven, God promises that the person He declares righteous will go to heaven. "Those whom he justified he also glorified" (Romans 8:30). Nothing can separate God's elect from him (Romans 8:31-39). "Who shall bring any charge against God's elect? It is God who justifies; who is to condemn?" (Romans 8:33-34). I should also add that once we are born again, our relationship with God is secure in Christ, not in ourselves. Jesus promised, "My sheep hear my voice, and I know them, and they follow me; and I give them eternal life, and they shall never perish, and no one shall snatch them out of my hand. My Father, who has given them to me, is greater than all, and no one is able to snatch them out of the Father's hand" (John 10:27-29).

John: Yet, when Abraham was 99, God renewed His promise to give him numberless descendents. But now, Abraham must circumcise himself to ratify the covenant in faith: "Any uncircumcised male who is not circumcised in the flesh of his foreskin shall be cut off from his people; he has broken my covenant" (Genesis 17:14).

Had Abraham cut himself off from God's covenant and people by refusing circumcision, would he still have received eternal life?

Jim: This is essentially the same question as your previous one. From my perspective, it is self-contradictory. Abraham had genuine faith. Genuine faith endures. It doesn't make sense, therefore, to ask what would happen if his faith failed. Also, I want to emphasize again that it is God who keeps us, not ourselves (1 John 5:18; Jude 1).

Would Abraham have been saved had he not sacrificed his son?

John: In Genesis 22, God asks Abraham to sacrifice his only son, Isaac:

> By faith Abraham, when he was tested, offered up
> Isaac, and he who had received the promises was ready
> to offer up his only son....He considered that God was
> able to raise men even from the dead.
>
> HEBREWS 11:17-19

Would Abraham have gone to heaven had he failed the
test, refusing to sacrifice Isaac?

Jim: Yes, for God had justified Abraham, declaring him righteous in His sight. The purpose of the test was not for God
to learn if Abraham had faith or for Abraham to merit
heaven. The purpose was to demonstrate to others, especially later generations who would read the biblical record,
that Abraham was a man of genuine faith in a right relationship with God. James pointed this out in James 2:21-24.

John: Let's look at what James said:

> Was not Abraham our father justified by works, when
> he offered his son Isaac upon the altar? You see that
> faith was active along with his works, and faith was
> completed by works.
>
> JAMES 2:21-22

So, the work of sacrificing Isaac completed Abraham's
faith, justifying him.

Jim: Abraham's obedience on Mount Moriah demonstrates to
others that Abraham was a man of genuine faith in a right
relationship with God. That is the sense in which James
commented that Abraham was "justified by works" (James
2:21). His works *showed* him to be righteous, not to God,
who already knew, but to other men and women. James is
talking about the *evidence* of genuine faith being shown by
good works. He is not talking about good works being the
cause of justification. Paul said, "If Abraham was justified

382

by works, he has something to boast about, but not before God" (Romans 4:2). In other words, Abraham would really have had a story to tell if he could brag that he had been justified by his good works. He couldn't tell such a story, however, in the presence of God, for God knew better. The next verse says, "For what does the scripture say? 'Abraham believed God, and it was reckoned to him as righteousness' " (Romans 4:3).

John: James clarified the context: "Blessed is the man who endures trial, for when he has stood the test he will receive the crown of life which God has promised to those who love him" (James 1:12). Scripture also asks: "Was not Abraham found faithful when tested, and it was reckoned to him as righteousness?" (1 Maccabees 2:52). How would you answer that?

Jim: I would answer that this is another example of how the apocryphal books of the Catholic Bible contradict God's Word.

Along with faith, are works of obedience required to enter heaven?

John: Jim, I keep asking you about John 3:36, "He who does not obey the Son shall not see life," and Matthew 7:21. Both passages seem to require, along with faith, works of obedience to enter heaven. Do you?

Jim: The question you asked earlier and introduced with John 3:36 and Matthew 7:21 was, "How can anyone go to heaven if he is unable to obey or do God's will?"[223] You may not have recognized it as such, but I devoted almost my entire last letter to answering that question. In short, we can go to heaven by trusting Jesus. I might point out that this is not contrary to the will of God, but is His expressed will. Jesus said, "This is the work of God, that you believe in him whom he has sent" (John 6:29).

The question you ask here is somewhat different: Are faith and works required to enter heaven? I would answer no. We are justified by faith, not faith plus works. "To one who does not work but trusts him who justifies the ungodly, his faith is reckoned as righteousness" (Romans 4:5). The thief on the cross is a good example of this. He believed and died moments later, Jesus having assured him of heaven, saying, "Truly, I say to you, today you will be with me in Paradise" (Luke 23:43).

Finally, allow me to comment on the two verses you feel I have been avoiding. The first begins, "He who believes in the Son has eternal life" (John 3:36). I think I have quoted numerous verses that make the same point. The second part of the verse says, "He who does not obey the Son shall not see life, but the wrath of God rests on him." This refers to the person who rejects Christ, refusing to obey His call to "repent, and believe in the gospel" (Mark 1:15).

Matthew 7:21 reads, "Not every one who says to me, 'Lord, Lord,' shall enter the kingdom of heaven, but he who does the will of my Father who is in heaven." This verse emphasizes that not everyone who *says* that Jesus is his Lord is going to heaven. True faith is required for salvation. The outward evidence of new life in Jesus is obedience to the will of God.

John: Are you saying that commandments and exhortations in Scripture are there to describe the "outward evidence" of justification? Thus, if one fails to show this "outward evidence"—not forgiving his neighbor (Matthew 6:14-15), for example, or failing to feed the hungry, or shelter the homeless (Matthew 25:31-46)—then he lacks *genuine* faith and is not really saved. Is that correct?

Jim: Yes, "faith by itself, if it has no works, is dead" (James 2:17).

John: Our Lord said, "If you love me, you will keep my commandments" (John 14:15). Love fulfills all commandments

(Roman 13:8-10), whereas transgressing one commandment is equivalent to transgressing them all (James 2:10).
Would you say disobeying even one commandment shows
"outward evidence" that he lacks love and thus is not really
saved?

Jim: Thankfully, God is not that harsh. We all sin. What the
Scriptures say is that a born-again Christian's life will not
be *characterized* by sin. He will not *practice* sin. "No one
who is born of God will continue to sin, because God's
seed remains in him; he cannot go on sinning, because he
has been born of God" (1 John 3:9 NIV).

What happens to Christians who continue to sin?

John: Jim, in Conversation 5, you said, "The Christian must learn
to live a holy life, walk by the Spirit, replace sinful practices with godly disciplines, and yield each day to God."[224]
You then quoted Wuest, saying that we must coopcrate
with the Holy Spirit. What happens when Christians fail
to walk by the Spirit, continuing in sin?

Jim: It depends on what you mean. A true Christian may
stumble and sin. This will hinder his fellowship with God,
but it will not sever his relationship with his heavenly Father
(Hebrews 13:5). When a Christian sins, he should repent
and confess the sin to God (1 John 1:9). Should he fail to do
so, God will discipline him as a loving father does his son
(Hebrews 12:5-11). If what you mean by continuing in sin
is living the life of a reprobate, we would understand that as
evidence that the person is still a slave to sin, and not a true
born-again Christian (1 John 2:4-6). Jesus said, "If the Son
makes you free, you will be free indeed" (John 8:36).

How do you forgive sins in your church?

John: Christ gave power to forgive sin to the apostles (John
20:22-23) and to His church (Matthew 18:17-18), just as

He had to the Levitical priests (Leviticus 4–19). How is this power exercised in your church?

Jim: In Matthew 18:15-20, Jesus explained the process the church is to follow when confronting a person practicing sin. He said four steps are to be taken if the person will not repent: 1) a private first warning by one person, 2) a second warning by two or three Christians, 3) a third warning by the entire church, 4) the excommunication of the person from the fellowship of the church. The authority to "bind" or to "loose" refers to the power to impose or to remove an order of excommunication. "If you forgive the sins of any, they are forgiven; if you retain the sins of any, they are retained" (John 20:23). We try to follow this process in our church. Only rarely does it go to the third and fourth steps.

Are you holy, perfect?

John: In Conversation 5, you acknowledged that you were saved and had eternal life. In Letters 41 and 43 you say that all Christians are saints, holy. Now you say that to have eternal life one has to be perfect as God is perfect. Are you now perfect and holy—that is, are you a saint?

Jim: Yes, John, I am, at least in the eyes of God, and that's the only place that really counts. Scripture says that in Christ a Christian is "holy and blameless before him" (Ephesians 1:4). This is a hard concept to grasp from a Catholic perspective, but let me try to explain.

In Catholicism you are told that through baptism you have been *made* holy through the infusion of sanctifying grace. You become more holy through continued reception of the other sacraments and the performance of good works. You lose this holiness should you commit a mortal sin. It is restored in the sacrament of reconciliation. In the Day of Judgment, God will determine whether you are righteous or not, rewarding or punishing you accordingly.

Evangelical Christians, on the other hand, believe that our holiness is not in ourselves but in Christ. He took our sin as His own that we might receive God's righteousness as our own. Scripture says, "God made him who had no sin to be sin for us, so that in him we might become the righteousness of God" (2 Corinthians 5:21 NIV). We refer to this as imputed righteousness. God reckons or assigns His righteousness to us.

John: Assurance of salvation and holiness means you can judge yourself now for all eternity. But Paul refused to judge himself, saying: "Do not pronounce judgment before the time" (1 Corinthians 4:5). Shouldn't we follow this recommendation?

Jim: Only God knows the heart. It would be wrong for me go around saying this person is absolutely saved and that person is not. But this does not negate the promises of God to the person who trusts Christ as Savior. He can rejoice in his salvation (Romans 4:7-8).

John: In Letter 47, you said that since God alone is holy (Revelation 15:4), there is no room for Mary being holy.[225] Yet, you say you are. Can't Mary—whom all generations call blessed because of her faith (Luke 1:45,48)—be holy and immaculate in God too?

Jim: That's a good question, John. I hope it will clarify an important issue. I said that only God is holy in response to the Catholic Church's claim that Mary lived a perfectly sinless life. She was a sinner, like the rest of us (Romans 3:23). She was received into heaven not because she lived a perfect life but because she had genuine faith. God assigned to her the righteousness of God, even as Abraham.

Did Moses mediate between Israel and God?

John: Jim, you say, "Only through the earnest pleading of Moses, reminding God of His previous and still valid covenant with Abraham, did the Lord spare Israel." This sounds like intercession. Was Moses a mediator between Israel and God?

Jim: Yes, Scripture refers to Moses as a mediator with regard to the giving of the Old Covenant (Galatians 3:19). He went between God and the people of Israel (Exodus 20:19). Christ is the mediator of the New Covenant (Hebrews 8:6). With regard to salvation, however, "there is one mediator between God and men, the man Christ Jesus" (1 Timothy 2:5).

John: Thank you, Jim, for bearing with me. It is not easy to understand the issues that divide us, but now it is easier.

Letter 57

Dear Jim,

Friday's conversation was quite interesting. There is so much more to discuss.

Agreements

You seem to draw near the Catholic view of salvation, but then back away. We agree that salvation is God's free gift from God, not purchased in a business transaction but received from God through a free act of faith; that Church leaders have some authority to confront sinners; that persons with faith will produce good works, at least as "outward evidence" of their salvation. You balked at admitting that good deeds can signify our ongoing free cooperation with God's grace and salvation, or that believers remain free to reject salvation.

In Conversation 6, I clarified that Catholics—like you—believe their holiness and justification exist only in relation to Christ.[226] We also agree that God alone knows a person's heart, making it wrong to say that one is "absolutely saved," but we can rejoice in God's faithfulness to His promises.

Commandments and Life

If asked the question, What, if any, "good deed must I do, to have eternal life?" (Matthew 19:16), you would answer, "We are justified by faith, not faith plus works." But Christ answered: "If you would enter life, keep the commandments" (Matthew 19:17). But that's impossible, you say, because God gave "the Jews the Ten Commandments to prove to them that they could not keep them."

Moses said, "For this commandment which I command you this day *is not too hard* for you....But the word is very near you; it is in your mouth and in your heart, so that *you can do it*" (Deuteronomy 30:11,14). It takes effort, but if you trust the Holy Spirit guiding you, you *can* obey God:

> See, I have set before you this day life and good, death and evil. If you obey the commandments of the LORD your God which I command you this day, by loving the LORD your God, by walking in his ways, and by keeping his commandments and his statutes and his ordinances, then you shall live....But if your heart turns away...you shall perish....I have set before you life and death, blessing and curse; therefore choose life, that you and your descendants may live.
>
> DEUTERONOMY 30:15-19

Abraham and *Sola Scriptura*

Your approach to Abraham demonstrates the problem with *Sola Scriptura*. One can easily miss (perhaps unconsciously) many pertinent scriptures that convey the complete gospel by focusing on the one or two passages to one's liking. Then one "legalizes" those choice passages.

Certainly Abraham believed and was declared righteous. But true faith began years earlier and continued years later; his faith-journey was expressed in deeds (including circumcision and sacrificing his only son); those works moved by faith justified him. Faith did not take away his freedom, but helped him endure to the end and be saved (Matthew 10:22).

To maintain your position, you must contradict Matthew 19:29, Hebrews 11:8-16, Romans 10:13, Genesis 17:14, James 1:12; 2:21-22 and 1 Maccabees 2:52.

Purgatory and Merit

To no surprise, you don't believe in purgatory, since you view yourself perfectly holy. Anyone not perfectly holy is not yet saved and has no chance of heaven. It's legally black or white; no in between: "once saved, always saved" means Christians are not free to choose to cut themselves off from God and His covenant.

That's why *merit* makes no sense to you, for because you are already saved, nothing you do could affect your future salvation. For Catholics, *merit* simply means we continue to have free responsibility after initial salvation. You erroneously view merit as some kind of coercion of God, as debt owed to man. Trust me, that's not what Catholics believe!

The Prodigal Son

Scripture exemplifies a Catholic understanding of redemption: from Adam—who failed his test and lost friendship with God—to the prodigal son (Luke 15:11-32). This younger son was in good standing with his father (i.e., God). Yet he took his inheritance (i.e., salvation received from his father) and wasted it on sinful living (you call apostasy, "dejustification"). He lived cut off from his father until he came to his senses and repented. His father was loving and merciful and forgave him (you call this "rejustification"). Perhaps you would say the son was never really saved—in other words, the son never really was his father's son until he was forgiven his grave sin. And if he returned to his sinful ways ("living with harlots") and died that way, in your mind, he will still go to heaven!

> If a righteous man turns from his righteousness and commits iniquity...he shall die for his sin, and his

righteous deeds which he has done shall not be remembered.

EZEKIEL 3:20

Denying the freedom to apostatize implies God's mercy is not free, but guaranteed; not a grace, but a right. That's exactly the same evil you accuse Catholics of. It's amazing—we agree even in our errors! However, Hebrews 6:4-6 shows "saved" Christians ("partakers of the Holy Spirit") committing apostasy.

I would encourage you to re-evaluate how you read Scripture, especially regarding Abraham. As you can see, Catholics just use a very different approach.

You and your family will always be in my prayers. Please continue to pray for me.

In Christ's love and mercy,

John

Letter 58

TUESDAY, FEBRUARY 26, 2002

Dear John,

Thank you for your many prayers and recent letter. It has been some time, however, since we have been able to just sit and talk. I hope to be in Los Angeles later this week. Is there any chance you could join me for lunch on Friday?

Our discussion of final salvation has clarified some important similarities and differences. In this concluding letter on the topic, I wish to respond to two of your points.

Gift or Reward?

You say we agree that "the free gift of God is eternal life" (Romans 6:23), and we receive it through faith. Yet you continue to argue that justification is by faith plus works. Can you not see that if good works are required for salvation, then heaven is no longer a gift? Scripture says, "Now to one who works, his wages are not reckoned as a gift but as his due" (Romans 4:4). That is why I object to Rome saying Christians receive eternal life "as a reward... for their good works and merits."[227]

You say I misrepresent Catholic merit, making it a debt God owes man. You write, "Merit simply means we continue to have free responsibility after initial salvation."

I checked several Catholic sources, seeking clarification. The word *merit* comes from the Latin *merces*, meaning "hire, pay, reward." The *Catholic Encyclopedia* defines it as "that property of a good work which entitles the doer to receive a reward from him in whose service the work is done."[228] The *Pocket Catholic Dictionary* explains, "It is Catholic doctrine that by his good works a person in the state of grace really acquires a claim to supernatural reward from God."[229] Merit is a *"recompense owed"* [CCC 2006]. What is owed to the Catholic who dies in a state of grace is heaven. "Eternal life is the reward for the good deeds performed in this world."[230] As quoted earlier, "It is a universally accepted dogma of the Catholic Church that man, in union with the grace of the Holy Spirit must merit heaven by his good works....Heaven must be fought for; we have to earn heaven."[231] This doesn't sound like the free gift of God to me.

Possible or Impossible?

You raised some interesting points about the Ten Commandments from Matthew 19 and Deuteronomy 30. Here, at least, we agree that we disagree.

You say we can and must obey the Ten Commandments if we are to attain heaven. That's what Jesus meant, you say, when He told the rich young ruler, "If you would enter life, keep the commandments" (Matthew 19:17).[232]

If so, why did Jesus rebuke the Jews, saying, "None of you keeps the law" (John 7:19)? As you pointed out yourself, "Whoever keeps the whole law but fails in one point has become guilty of all of it" (James 2:10). Not even Moses could keep it. God barred him from entering the promised land because of a single act of disobedience (Numbers 20:8-12). Does this not tell us something?

As for the rich young ruler, I believe Jesus was testing him. Their conversation began when the man asked, "Teacher, what good deed must I do, to have eternal life?" (Matthew 19:16). The Lord listed several of the Ten Commandments, summarizing them, "You shall love your neighbor as yourself" (verse 19).

The man proudly replied, "All these I have observed; what do I still lack?" (verse 20).

Jesus charged him, "If you would be perfect, go, sell what you possess and give to the poor, and you will have treasure in heaven; and come, follow me" (verse 21). The man departed crestfallen, "for he had great possessions" (verse 22). As he went, Jesus said, "It is easier for a camel to go through the eye of a needle than for a rich man to enter the kingdom of God" (verse 24).

Jesus' disciples were astonished. "Who then can be saved?" they asked (verse 25).

"With men this is impossible," the Lord answered, "but with God all things are possible" (verse 26).

It is impossible for anyone to keep the Ten Commandments and thereby merit eternal life. Further, when we seek righteousness before God through our deeds, we are telling God we want to be judged by our performance. This can only bring condemnation (Galatians 3:10; 5:2-5).

Likewise, Deuteronomy 30 does not teach that the Jews had the ability to keep the law and thereby attain their final salvation. Rather, Moses began the chapter speaking of the future restoration of the Jews. At that time God will gather Israel from the ends of the earth, changing them within (Deuteronomy 30:1-10). "The LORD your God will circumcise your heart and the heart of your offspring," wrote Moses, "so that you will love the LORD your God with all your heart and with all your soul, that you may live" (Deuteronomy 30:6). This circumcision of the heart, not water baptism, is the New Covenant fulfillment of the circumcision of the flesh (Deuteronomy 30:6; Jeremiah 31:31-34; Romans 2:29).

In the remaining verses of Deuteronomy 30, Moses addressed the Jews of his day. He told them that they too could choose life and receive the blessings of the Old Covenant (Deuteronomy 30:11-20). He assured them that God was not asking them to do something too difficult for them or to comprehend some great truth out of reach to the common man (Deuteronomy 30:11-13). Rather, "The *word* is very near you," Moses wrote, "it is in your mouth and in your heart, so that you can do it" (Deuteronomy 30:14).

What is this "word" by which they might live? The New Testament provides the answer, interpreting Deuteronomy 30:12-14 for us:

> "The word is near you, in your mouth and in your heart"—that is, the word of faith which we are preaching, that if you confess with your mouth Jesus as Lord, and believe in your heart that God raised Him from the dead, you will be saved; for with the heart a person believes, resulting in righteousness, and with the mouth he confesses, resulting in salvation.
>
> ROMANS 10:8-10

In Christ's love,

Jim

CONCLUSION
Letters 59 and 60

Exchanged
Simultaneously

Letter 59

TUESDAY, MARCH 19, 2002

Dear Jim,

We've tried to resolve our disagreements calmly and intellectually, but I sense our hearts still need conversion. Perhaps we need to follow our Lord's suggestions better, to pray and fast for this intention (Mark 9:29).

Failed Approach?

Intellectually, this discussion has been very humbling. I tried to address your concerns with ample scriptural arguments, to show how Catholic teachings fulfill and accomplish "the law and the prophets" (Matthew 5:17-18). When that failed, I presented early Christian writers moved by the Spirit; their interpretations seemed very Catholic.

Occasionally I redirected some of your "trick" arguments back toward you to share how it feels. I meant no offense. Overall, I thank you for helping me deepen my faith and develop new approaches to explaining perennial Catholic doctrine. Actually, we agree on more things than not: our differences arise mostly from the different meanings of words developed by Catholics and Protestants, rarely from Scripture. Much misunderstanding is really miscommunication.

Please forgive me. I did try to "checkmate" you early on with some of my questions and arguments, principally out of pride,

---

thinking I could and because I feared your potential traps. Later, I felt you weren't listening and considered abandoning the project as futile, much like Jonah. The Spirit gave me reassuring evidence that He wanted us to continue. With time I learned to relax, trusting God more and trusting you, too.

Recent Attacks

Lately, I've noticed a return to attacking Catholic positions instead of addressing my concerns regarding yours. For example, you insisted Catholics believe in *merit* as recompense owed. You fail to recognize that the *Catechism* quote [CCC 2006] refers to human societies and communities. The next paragraph clearly states that this notion does *not* apply to God: "With regard to God, there is no strict right to any merit on the part of man" [CCC 2007]. Is this not what I tried to say, or is my explanation of *merit* heretical? Repeatedly, I brought up how the Holy Spirit uses *true* merit-language in Scripture [CCC 2009];[233] yet you didn't address this.

Your legalistic approach to Scripture—and now to Catholic sources[234]—is a barrier to mutual understanding and unity.

Supporting Unity and Catholics

Although Christ prayed for and insisted on Christian unity (John 17:11,20-26), in the last 500 years, Satan has successfully divided Christianity into tens of thousands of independent churches. Would the great twentieth-century horrors have occurred had Christianity remained united against the evil one? I doubt it. Unity protects us from him (John 17:15). Now is the time to abandon past prejudices, listen to the Spirit, and work for unity. Our dialogue is a good first step, but more is needed.

Would you make an effort to support Catholics in their faith, challenging them to discover the biblical basis of their beliefs? You could do so much good here. Scripture does witness to Catholic beliefs (John 5:39). Being truly open means listening to the

Church's positive message and acknowledging the valid points it makes from Scripture.

Prayerful Re-examination

As we come to a close, let's prayerfully re-explore the lynchpins of our positions; I have challenged you to find any scriptural basis for *Sola Scriptura,* and for salvation as a single, irrevocable, life decision; you challenge Catholics to greater confidence in God's mercy without judging ourselves righteous (Luke 18:9-14).

Although we agree in most, let's seek God's help to resolve several interpretations in dispute, Galatians 3:16-22 and 2 Thessalonians 2:15;[235] Matthew 16:19;[236] Romans 3–5 and James 2;[237] John 6;[238] references to Jesus' *brothers;*[239] and the purpose of God's precepts and whether He "laid down precepts that are to be fully obeyed" (Psalm 119:4 NIV).[240]

Key to understanding Catholicism is seeing the link between one's relationship to God and family relationships. You have repeatedly ignored this analogy. Perhaps reading Scripture in this family context will help you to appreciate the Catholic approach to Scripture as legitimate.

You and your family continue to be in my prayers. May the Spirit grace each of us with a true conversion of heart, to ultimately share common faith and worship, crowning our relationship with true friendship in Christ.

In Christ's love,

John

Letter 60

TUESDAY, MARCH 19, 2002

Dear John,

Well, with God's help we made it! Sixty letters, 12 conversations, and more than 100,000 words have passed between us. Though we have yet to resolve our differences, we have explained our beliefs, faced the hard issues, listened to one another's criticisms, and tried to understand. Our friendship is still intact, maybe even strengthened. Thank you, John, for your diligent work, patience, and concern.

In this last letter, I ask that you reconsider the topics of authority and salvation.

Authority

Unity will continue to evade us unless we can settle the authority question. From it flows every other belief. The solution, as I see it, lies in Scripture, for we both accept it as the inspired Word of God. We use it, however, differently.

I go to the Bible *for* my beliefs, expecting Scripture to clearly and firmly establish the Christian faith. You come to the Bible *with* your beliefs, looking for confirmation of the dogmas of Roman Catholicism. At times you seemed satisfied if a doctrine were consistent with the Bible in the sense that it simply did not contradict Scripture as you understand it. The Roman papacy and Mary's Assumption are examples. When arguing for your beliefs, often the emphasis was on citing numerous references rather than carefully applying Scripture in context. You used Old Testament truths concerning Israel, for example, to explain the New Testament church. Many of your proofs are simply allegories that draw parallels between two things—for example, circumcision and infant baptism, Eve and Mary, or the spousal relationship and the way of salvation. If you were to require a higher level of evidence from the Bible for a doctrine, it would be a step in the right direction.

Your unquestioning loyalty to Rome, however, makes me question if you can interpret Scripture objectively. Throughout our discussions, you sought, as instructed by your church, "to show how a doctrine defined by the Church is contained in the sources of revelation...'in that sense in which it has been defined by the Church.'"[241] But what if the true meaning of Scripture were contrary to that sense? Is this possible? Would you be able to recognize it if it were so? Would you be willing to adopt it as your own, despite what Rome says?

If you can answer yes to these questions, you are beginning to understand what we mean by *Sola Scriptura*. To answer no is the essence of Roman Catholicism.

Salvation

I remember asking an elderly priest visiting Fatima if he thought he were going to heaven. "Of course!" he roared, clearly amused at anyone asking him such a question. "I've been a priest for 40 years," he added with a grin. Apparently that was reason enough.

Contrast this with Paul's words in Philippians 3. Born of solid Jewish stock, he scrupulously observed the traditions of Judaism. He was as a model of devotion and zeal. As to righteousness under the law, he was "blameless" (Philippians 3:6). Then through a series of events recounted in Acts 9, he came to see that he was completely wrong. He renounced all reliance on the practice of religion and his good works for salvation. He placed his faith fully in Christ to save him. Paul wrote,

Whatever things were gain to me, those things I have counted as loss for the sake of Christ. More than that, I count all things to be loss in view of the surpassing value of knowing Christ Jesus my Lord, for whom I have suffered the loss of all things, and count them but rubbish so that I may gain Christ, and may be found in Him, not having a righteousness of my own derived from the Law, but that which is through faith in Christ, the righteousness which comes from God on the basis of faith.

PHILIPPIANS 3:7-9 NASB

I hope that someday, John, you will do the same, trusting Christ alone for your salvation. I close with a prayer, borrowed from a ninth-century scribe who appended it to a manuscript of the Psalms.

Mercy to him who wrote, O Lord,
Wisdom to those who read.

In Christ's love,

Jim

Scripture Index

(Those cited by John are *italicized*)

Subject Index

References to the *Catechism of the Catholic Church*

(Those cited by John are italicized; endnote's number in {})

67 *314*	**6 8 3** *146, 205*
69 *46*	**6 8 4** *205*
78 *65*	**7 9 0** *146*
80 *58*	**8 3 0** *11*
83 *48*	**8 3 6** *356*
87 9 4	**838-845** *356*
88 *312*	**8 4 1** 356
89-90 *59*	**846-848** *356*
95 *63*	**8 4 6** 201
1 0 0 94	**8 5 1** *357*
1 0 3 *306*	**888-892** *{86}*
11 3 69	**8 9 0** *100*
109-119 *94*	**9 7 0** *327*
1 0 9 *94*	**9 7 1** *317*
11 2 *325*	**1 0 2 2** *333, 340*
11 9 *95*	**1 0 2 7** *339*
1 2 0 *52*	**1 0 3 0** *342*
1 3 1 *94*	**1 0 3 1** *352*
1 3 3 *16*	**1 0 3 2** 336
1 3 5 *16*	**1 0 3 3** *341*
1 4 1 *306*	**1 0 3 5** *341*
1 6 1 *157*	**1 0 3 7** *341*
2 5 0 *314*	**1 0 8 5** 237
411 322	**11 2 4** *59*
491-492 *311*	**11 2 8** 176
4 8 7 *296*	**11 2 9** 187, 201
4 9 9 *328*	**1 2 1 3** 200
5 0 0 *289*	**1 2 1 5** *146*
5 0 1 324	**1 2 4 3** *146*
6 1 5 *343*	**1 2 6 2** *146*

Notes

1. Ignatius of Antioch (†110), quoted in *Catechism of the Catholic Church*, 2ⁿᵈ ed. (United States Catholic Conference, Inc. and Libreria Editrice Vaticana, 1997), paragraph 830. See also *The Martyrdom of Saint Polycarp*, 8.1 (†155). Henceforth in this book the numbered paragraphs of the *Catechism of the Catholic Church* will be referenced simply with CCC in square brackets. For example, [CCC 830] refers to numbered paragraph 830 of the *Catechism*.

2. Augustine, *City of God*, book 9, chapter 5; quoted from Philip Schaff, editor, *A Select Library of the Nicene and Post-Nicene Fathers of the Christian Church* (Grand Rapids: Eerdmans Publishing Co, 1886).

3. Augustine, *City of God*, book 11, chapter 3; quoted from Gerald G. Walsh, S.J., Demetrius B. Zema, S.J., Grase Monahan, O.S.U., Daniel J. Honan, translators, *The City of God* (New York: Doubleday, 1958).

4. Cyril of Jerusalem, *Catechetical Lectures* 4:17, quoted from Philip Schaff, editor, *A Select Library of the Nicene and Post-Nicene Fathers of the Christian Church* (Grand Rapids: Eerdmans Publishing Co, 1886).

5. Augustine, "Letter of Augustine to Januarius," quoted from W. A. Jurgens, editor, *The Faith of the Early Fathers* (Collegeville, MN: The Liturgical Press, 1979), vol. 3, p. 3.

6. Jim, Letter 3, p. 20.

7. Jim, Letter 3, p. 22.

8. John, Letter 4, p. 35.

9. B. B. Warfield, "Inspiration," *International Standard Bible Encyclopedia* (Grand Rapids: Eerdmans Publishing Co., 1939), p. 1473.

10. Second Vatican Council, "Dogmatic Constitution on Divine Revelation," no. 9.

11. First Vatican Council, session 3, "Dogmatic Constitution on the Catholic Faith," chapter 2. Also: Second Vatican Council, "Dogmatic Constitution on Divine Revelation," no. 10.

12. Second Vatican Council, "Dogmatic Constitution on Divine Revelation," no. 21. Stated also at the Council of Trent: "…truth and rule are contained in written books and unwritten traditions…" Council of Trent, session 4, "First Decree: Acceptance of the Sacred Books and Apostolic Traditions."

13. Jim, Letter 5, p. 39.

14. The RSV version of *The Holy Bible* does not use italics or brackets. In this book, all bracketed text of Bible quotations [ ] indicates comments added by the author to the reference and all *italics* used indicates emphasis added by the authors.

15. John and Jim, Conversation 1, p. 27.

16. John, Conversation 1, pp. 30-31.

17. Jim, Conversation 1, p. 32.

18. Quoted from W. A. Jurgens, editor, *The Faith of the Early Fathers* (Collegeville, MN: The Liturgical Press, 1979), vol. 3, p. 263.

19. Quoted from W. A. Jurgens, editor, *The Faith of the Early Fathers* (Collegeville, MN: The Liturgical Press, 1979), vol. 1, pp. 89-91.

20. W. A. Jurgens, editor, *The Faith of the Early Fathers* (Collegeville, MN: The Liturgical Press, 1979), 3 volumes.

21. John, Letter 8, p. 48.

22. John, Letter 4, p. 34.

23. John, Letter 8, p. 53.

24. John, Letter 8, p. 49.

25. John, Letter 8, pp. 49-50.

26. John, Letter 8, p. 50.

27. John, Letter 2, p. 16.

28. John, Letter 8, pp. 49-50.

29. John, Conversation 2, p. 64.

30. Jean Bainvel, *The Catholic Encyclopedia* (New York, NY: Robert Appleton Co., 1912), "Tradition," vol. 15, p. 9.

31. John, Conversation 2, p. 61.

32. John, Conversation 2, p. 65.

33. Jim, Letter 5, p. 40.

34. Jim, Letter 5, p. 40, quoting Hebrews 4:12.

35. Jim, Conversation 1, p. 23.

36. Jim, Letter 5, p. 38. See also Conversation 1, pp. 27-28.

37. First Vatican Council, session 4, "First Dogmatic Constitution of the Church of Christ," chapter 3.

38. Quoted from W. A. Jurgens, editor, *The Faith of the Early Fathers* (Collegeville, MN: The Liturgical Press, 1979), vol. 1, 43-43b, p. 19; 48, p. 20.

39. *Letter to the Romans*, Address, quoted from W. A. Jurgens, editor, *The Faith of the Early Fathers* (Collegeville, MN: The Liturgical Press, 1979), vol. 1, 52, p. 21.

40. Quoted from W. A. Jurgens, editor, *The Faith of the Early Fathers* (Collegeville, MN: The Liturgical Press, 1979), vol. 1, 20, p. 10. See also 44.1, 21, p. 10.

41. *Sermo* 131.10, in W. A. Jurgens, editor, *The Faith of the Early Fathers* (Collegeville, MN: The Liturgical Press, 1979), 1507, vol. 3, p. 28.

42. *Sermo* 46, *On Pastors.*

43. *The Code of Canon Law,* cc. 1024-51.

44. *The Code of Canon Law,* c. 378.

45. John, Letter 13, p. 86.

46. See quotes in John, Letter 13, pp. 86-87.

47. Second Vatican Council, "Dogmatic Constitution on Divine Revelation," no. 23.

48. Pope Pius XII, *Humani Generis,* no. 21; quoting Pope Pius IX.

49. John, Letter 13, pp. 87-88.

50. Quoted from W. A. Jurgens, editor, *The Faith of the Early Fathers* (Collegeville, MN: The Liturgical Press, 1979), vol. 1, 580, p. 232.

51. John, Letter 13, pp. 85-86.

52. John, Conversation 3, p. 97.

53. John, Letter 13, p. 88.

54. John, Letter 13, pp. 87-88, referring to Acts 15.

55. John, Letter 13, p. 86.

56. John, Letter 13, p. 87, referring to 1 Timothy 4:15, etc.; Conversation 3, p. 93. See also 1 Timothy 5:22.

57. Jim, Conversation 3, pp. 91-92; Letter 14, pp. 103-04.

58. He is referring to the passage quoted above in John, Letter 13, p. 93.

59. *Letter to the Corinthians,* 44.1, Francis W. Glimm et. al., translators, *The Apostolic Fathers* (New York: CIMA Publishing Co., Inc., 1947), p. 43.

60. John, Conversation 3, p. 96, referring to 1 Peter 5:13.

61. John, Letter 13, p. 84, referring to Deuteronomy 34:9; pp. 84-85, referring to Matthew 23:1-3.

62. Jim, Letter 14, p. 105, referring to Acts 5:29.

63. John, Letter 13, p. 88, referring to Matthew 16:19.

64 John, Letter 13, p. 87, referring to Acts 15:5.

65. Old Testament excommunication, see John, Letter 13, p. 83, referring to Deuteronomy 17:8-13; and New Testament excommunication, as Matthew 18:15-17 states, quoted from John, Letter 13, p. 87.

66. John, Letter 13, p. 84, referring to Numbers 20:10-13; Conversation 3, p. 100.

67. Jim, Conversation 1, p. 26.

68. Jim, Conversation 1, p. 24.

69. Jim, Letter 3, pp. 20-21.

70. Jim, Letter 1, p. 15; Letter 3, p. 20; Conversation 3, p. 95.

71. Jim, Conversation 3, p. 94.

72. Jim, Letter 12, p. 79; Conversation 3, pp. 99-101; Letter 14, p. 105; Letter 16, p. 111.

73. John, Letter 13, p. 83.

74. Jim, Letter 3, p. 21.

75. Jim, Letter 12, p. 80; Conversation 3, pp. 99-101; Letter 14, p. 105.

76. Jim, Letter 14, p. 105.

77. Jim, Letter 14, p. 105.

78. Jim, Conversation 1, p. 26.

79. Jim, Conversation 1, p. 24.

80. John, Letter 13, p. 86; Conversation 3, pp. 91, 100.

81. Jim, Conversation 3, pp. 91-92; Letter 14, pp. 103-04.

82. John, Letter 13, p. 89 and Letter 15, p. 108.

83. *Letter of Augustine to Generosus,* 53.1.2, quoted from W. A. Jurgens, editor, *The Faith of the Early Fathers* (Collegeville, MN: The Liturgical Press, 1979), vol. 3, 1418, p. 2.

84. Confraternity of Christian Doctrine, *New American Bible: St Joseph Medium Size Edition* (New York: Catholic Book Publishing Co., 1970), note of Titus 1:5-9.

85. Perhaps we could begin with the *Catechism* [CCC 1539-1547].

86. See Second Vatican Council, Dogmatic Constitution on the Church, *Lumen Gentium,* no. 25. See also CCC 888-892, 2032-2040.

87. John and Jim, Conversation 4, pp. 127-28.

88. See CCC 1776-1802; 1897-1904; 1949; 2214-2220; especially 2242 and 2313.

89. Jim, Conversation 4, p. 129, quoting Matthew 18:15-20.

90. Jim, Conversation 4, p. 130.

91. John, Letter 15, p. 108, quoting John 20:21, where I showed how Paul and Barnabas didn't fill the requirements in Acts 1:15-26.

92. See, for example, *Letter to the Magnesians*, 2, 3.1, 6.1, 13.1 quoted from W. A. Jurgens, editor, *The Faith of the Early Fathers* (Collegeville, MN: The Liturgical Press, 1979), vol. 1, 43a-47a, pp. 19-20. I quoted in part in Letter 13, pp. 88-89.

93. John, Letter 13, p. 89.

94. Conversation 4, p. 132.

95. John, Letter 13, pp. 85-86; Conversation 3, p. 99.

96. Jim, Conversation 3, p. 102.

97. Martin Luther, *A Letter to Melanchthon*, Letter no. 99, August 1, 1521.

98. Jim, Conversation 4, p. 127.

99. John, Letter 13, p. 84.

100. John, Letter 13, p. 84; John, Conversation 3, p. 100.

101. John, Letter 13, p. 88.

102. John, Letter 22, p. 145.

103. Martin Luther, *A Letter to Melanchthon*, Letter no. 99, August 1, 1521.

104. Jim, Conversation 4, p. 127.

105. R. C. Lenski, *The Interpretation of St. Paul's Epistles to the Galatians, Ephesians, and Philippians* (Minneapolis: Augsburg Publishing House, 1937), p. 422.

106. Kenneth S. Wuest, *Wuest's Word Studies from the Greek New Testament—Philippians* (Grand Rapids: Eerdmans, 1942), vol. 2, p. 75.

107. John Calvin, *Institutes of the Christian Religion*, trans. Allen (Grand Rapids: Eerdmans, 1949), IV: xvi.

108. A summary of their teaching with references can be found in the Church document by the Sacred Congregation for the Doctrine of the Faith, *Pastoralis Actio*, published October 20, 1980, nn. 4-5.

109. Irenaeus, *Detection and Overthrow of the Gnosis falsely so-called* or *Against Heresies*, 2.22.4, quoted from W. A. Jurgens, editor, *The Faith of the Early Fathers* (Collegeville, MN: The Liturgical Press, 1979), 201, vol. 1, p. 87.

110. Jim, Letter 23, p. 153, quoting Romans 3:28.

111. Jim, Conversation 5, p. 158.

112. Jim, Conversation 5, p. 159.

113. Jim, Conversation 5, p. 160, citing 1 John 2:29.

114. Jim, Conversation 5, p. 159.

115. Council of Trent, session 6, "Decree on Justification," chapter 7.

116. Jim, Conversation 5, p. 158.

117. *The Holy Bible, Douay-Rheims Version* (Rockford, IL: Tan Books and Publishers, Inc., 1971).

118. Council of Trent, session 6, "Decree on Justification," chapter 4.

119. Conversation 5, "Right to Eternal Life," p. 163.

120. Response of the Catholic Church to the Joint Declaration on the Doctrine of Justification by the Lutheran World Federation and the Catholic Church, June 25, 1998, paragraph 3.

121. Council of Trent, session 6, "Decree on Justification," chapter 10.

122. CCC 1988, citing 1 Corinthians 12 and John 15:1-4.

123. John, Letter 28, p. 180.

124. To make this point, you use—by my count—verses from Romans 3:1–5:1 and Galatians 2:15–3:29, seven times in Letter 23, ten times in Conversation 5 and 12 times in Letter 25.

125. Jim, Conversation 5, p. 158.

126. Council of Trent, session 6, canon 20.

127. Quoted by William J. Cogan, *A Catechism for Adults* (Youngtown, AZ: Cogan Productions, 1975), p. 30.

128. Council of Trent, session 6, chapter 7.

129. *Jerome Biblical Commentary*, Raymond E. Brown, S.S., Joseph A. Fitzmyer, S.J., and Roland E. Murphy, O.Carm., editors (New Jersey: Prentice Hall, 1968), vol. II, p. 349, commenting on Ephesians 5:32.

130. John, Conversation 6, p. 197.

131. See Bernard Orchard, ed., *A Catholic Commentary on Holy Scripture* (New York: Thomas Nelson & Sons, 1953), p. 1125.

132. *Letter to the Church of Smyrna*, 6.2.

133. Joan Carroll Cruz, *Eucharistic Miracles* (Rockford, IL: Tan Books and Publishers, 1991).

134. Pope Pius XII, *Mediator Dei*, no. 70.

135. Pope Pius XII, *Mediator Dei*, no. 68.

136. John A. McHugh, O.P., and Charles J. Callan, O.P., translators, *The Roman Catechism: The Catechism of the Council of Trent* (Rockford, IL: Tan Books and Publishers, 1982), p. 258.

137. CCC 1322, 1330, 1353, 1359, 1362, 1364, 1369, 1372, 1382, 1407, 1410.

138. The Memorial Prayer of the Third Eucharistic Prayer.

139. Council of Trent, session 22, "Teaching and Canons on the Most Holy Sacrifice of the Mass," chapter 2.

140. John, Conversation 7, pp. 225-26.

141. Pope Pius XI, "Ad Catholici Sacerdotii," December 20, 1935.

142. Second Vatican Council, "Sacred Liturgy," "On Holy Communion and the Worship of the Eucharistic Mystery Outside of Mass," no. 6.

143. A detailed historical and scientific report on the miracle I describe is published in: Bruno Sammarciccia, *The Eucharistic Miracle of Lanciano, Italy*, Rev. Anthony E. Burakowski, trans. (Sanctuary of the Eucharist Miracle, 66034 Lanciano, Italy).

144. *Immanuel's Land*, lyrics by Anne R. Cousin.

145. Jim, Conversation 7, pp. 229-31.

146. Second Vatican Council, "Sacred Liturgy," "General Instruction on the Roman Missal," no. 2.

147. Second Vatican Council, "Sacred Liturgy," "The Constitution on the Sacred Liturgy," no. 47.

148. Pope Pius XII, *Mediator Dei*, no. 68.

149. The Memorial Prayer of the First Eucharistic Prayer.

150. Council of Trent, session 22, "Teaching and Canons on the Most Holy Sacrifice of the Mass," chapter 2.

151. Second Vatican Council, "Dogmatic Constitution on the Church," no. 3.

152. Jim, Letter 38, p. 248.

153. Quoted from W. A. Jurgens, *The Faith of the Early Fathers* (Collegeville, MN: The Liturgical Press, 1970), vol. 1, 249, p. 99.

154. Hippolytus of Rome, *The Apostolic Tradition,* 23.

155. Quoted from W. A. Jurgens, *The Faith of the Early Fathers* (Collegeville, MN: The Liturgical Press, 1970), vol. 1, 870, p. 377.

156. Quoted from W. A. Jurgens, *The Faith of the Early Fathers* (Collegeville, MN: The Liturgical Press, 1970), vol. 1, 805, pp. 345-46.

157. Quoted from W. A. Jurgens, *The Faith of the Early Fathers* (Collegeville, MN: The Liturgical Press, 1970), vol. 2, 1084, p. 69.

158. Quoted from W. A. Jurgens, *The Faith of the Early Fathers* (Collegeville, MN: The Liturgical Press, 1970), vol. 3, 2131, p. 229. See *Commentary on John,* 10.2 on John 15:1, W. A. Jurgens, *The Faith of the Early Fathers* (Collegeville, MN: The Liturgical Press, 1970), vol. 3, 2116, p. 223.

159. Quoted from W. A. Jurgens, *The Faith of the Early Fathers* (Collegeville, MN: The Liturgical Press, 1970), vol. 3, 2214, p. 280.

160. Quoted from W. A. Jurgens, *The Faith of the Early Fathers* (Collegeville, MN: The Liturgical Press, 1970), vol. 1, 64, p. 25.

161. Tertullian, "On the Resurrection of the Flesh," chapter 37, in *The Anti-Nicene Fathers,* vol. 3, *Tertullian,* ed. A. Roberts and J. Donaldson, from *The Sage Digital Library* (Albany, OR: Sage Software, 1996), p. 1068.

162. John, Letter 39, p. 266.

163. Pope Leo XIII, *On the Study of Sacred Scripture,* St. Paul Editions, p. 24.

164. W. A. Jurgens, *The Faith of the Early Fathers* (Collegeville, MN: The Liturgical Press, 1970), vol. 3, p. 359.

165. Topic 1: Jim, Letter 3, p. 22; Conversation 1, pp. 31-32; John, Letter 4, p. 36; Letter 8, p. 52; Letter 10, pp. 72-73. Topic 2: John, Letter 13, p. 89; Letter 19, p. 135.

166. Pope John Paul II, *Mother of the Redeemer* (Boston: St. Paul Press, 1987).

167. Scott Hahn, *Hail, Holy Queen* (New York: Doubleday, 2001).

168. Jim, Letter 43, p. 276; Conversation 9, p. 282.

169. John, Letter 42, p. 275 and Conversation 9, pp. 284-87.

170. Jim, Conversation 9, p. 285.

171. Pope John Paul II develops this theme much more extensively in his encyclical *Mother of the Redeemer* (Boston: St. Paul Press, 1987).

172. Scott Hahn, *Hail, Holy Queen* (New York: Doubleday, 2001).

173. Alphonsus de Ligouri, *The Glories of Mary* (Brooklyn: Redemptorist Fathers, 1931), chapter 1, section 4, p. 79.

174. Pope Pius IX, *Ineffabilis Deus.*

175. Pope Pius XII, *Humani Generis,* no. 21.

176. Francis X. Murphy, *The Papacy Today* (New York: Macmillan, 1981), p. 69.

177. Pope Pius XII, *Munificentissimus Deus,* no. 44.

178. De Wette, II, 459, quoted in Mark P. Shea, *By What Authority?* (Huntington, IN: Our Sunday Visitor, 1996), pp. 101-02.

179. Kilian J. Healy's book *The Assumption of Mary* (Wilmington, DE: Michael Glazier, Inc., 1982).

180. Pope Pius XII, *Humani Generis,* no. 21.

181. Pope Pius IX, *Ineffabilis Deus.*

182. Pope Benedict XV, *Inter Sodalicia.*

183. Conversation 4, p. 126.

184. Alphonsus de Ligouri, *The Glories of Mary* (Brooklyn: Redemptorist Fathers, 1931), chapter 1, section 4, p. 77.

185. Alphonsus Maria de Ligouri, *The Glories of Mary* (Montreal, Canada: Palm Publishers), vol. 2, reply to the Abbé Rolli, p. 217.

186. St. Pius X, Encyclical, *Ad diem illum*, February 2, 1904, quoting St. Bernardine of Siena.

187. John Paul II, Allocution at the Sanctuary of Our Lady of Guayaquil, given on January 31, 1985, reported in the *L'Osservatore Romano*, English edition, March 11, 1985, p. 7.

188. Pope Benedict XV, *Inter Sodalicia*.

189. John, Conversation 10, p. 318.

190. Litany of the Blessed Virgin Mary, approved by Pope Sixtus V.

191. John, Letter 13, p. 89.

192. Second Vatican Council, "Sacred Liturgy," "Apostolic Constitution on the Revision of Indulgences," no. 5.

193. Council of Trent, session 6, "Decree on Justification," chapter 16.

194. *New York Times*, February 1, 1990, B4.

195. John, Letter 24, p. 167-69.

196. John, Letter 51, p. 343.

197. See *Webster's New World Dictionary*, Second College Edition (New York: Simon and Schuster, 1984).

198. *Didache*, 4.14; 14.1-2.

199. Polycarp of Smyrna, *Letter to the Philippians*, 6.1.

200. Council of Trent, session 6, "Decree on Justification," chapter 14. Translation by H. J. Schroeder, *Canons and Decrees of the Council of Trent* (Rockford, IL: Tan Books and Publishers, 1978), p. 39.

201. Conversation 4, p. 126.

202. John, Letter 51, p. 340.

203. Father William J. Cogan, *A Catechism for Adults* (Youngstown, AZ: Cogan Productions, 1975), p. 50.

204. Second Vatican Council, "Sacred Liturgy," Apostolic Constitution on the Revision of Indulgences, no. 2.

205. Council of Trent, session 6, "Decree on Justification," "Canons Concerning Justification," canon 16.

206. John, Letter 24, pp. 167-69.

207. Council of Trent, session 6, "Decree on Justification," "Canons Concerning Justification," canon 32.

208. Conversation 5, p. 163, quoting Romans 6:23.

209. Council of Trent, session 6, "Decree on Justification," "Canons Concerning Justification," canon 32.

210. Matthias Premm, *Dogmatic Theology for the Laity* (Rockford, IL: Tan Books and Publishers, 1967), p. 262.

211. "Response of the Catholic Church to the Joint Declaration on the Doctrine of Justification," June 25, 1998.

212. Council of Trent, session 6, "Decree on Justification," "Canons Concerning Justification," canon 32.

213. Council of Trent, session 6, "Decree on Justification," chapter 16.

214. Second Vatican Council, "Dogmatic Constitution on the Church," no. 16.

215. Second Vatican Council, "Dogmatic Constitution on the Church," no. 16.

216. Lyrics to "It Is Well with My Soul" by H. G. Spafford.

217. Jim, Letter 23, p. 152.

218. Jim, Letter 41, p. 273, quoting 1 Corinthians 1:2.

219. Jim, Letter 47, p. 322, quoting Revelation 15:4.

220. Council of Trent, session 6, "Decree on Justification," chapter 16.

221. John, Letter 53, p. 366.

222. Father John Hardon, S.J., *Pocket Catholic Dictionary* (New York: Image Books, 1985), "merit," p. 259.

223. John, Letter 55, pp. 368-69.

224. Jim, Conversation 5, p. 164.

225. Jim, Letter 47, p. 322.

226. John, Conversation 6, p. 194, although you imply the contrary in Conversation 12, p. 377.

227. Council of Trent, session 6, "Decree on Justification," chapter 16.

228. J. Pohle, *The Catholic Encyclopedia* (New York: Robert Appleton Co., 1911), "merit," vol. X, p. 202.

229. John A. Hardon, S.J., *Pocket Catholic Dictionary* (New York: Image Books, 1985), "merit," p. 259.

230. Ludwig Ott, *Fundamentals of Catholic Dogma* (Rockford, IL: Tan Books and Publishers, 1960), p. 268. See also Council of Trent, session 6, "Decree on Justification," canon 32; and CCC 1821.

231. Matthias Premm, *Dogmatic Theology for the Laity* (Rockford, IL: Tan Books and Publishers, 1967), p. 262.

232. Stated also by the Council of Trent, session 6, "Decree on Justification," chapter 7 and canon 24. See also CCC 2068.

233. John, Conversation 6, pp. 191-92, quoting 2 Timothy 4:8; John 1:12; Matthew 13:44-46; Psalm 18:20-24. Letter 51, pp. 339, 342, quoting Matthew 5:12 and 1 Corinthians 3:12-15. Conversation 11, pp. 355-56, quoting John 3:36; Philippians 2:12-13; Romans 11:20-22; Matthew 24:13. Conversation 12, p. 378, quoting Matthew 10:22.

234. Similarly, please reread your other sources, such as Ludwig Ott, *Fundamentals of Catholic Dogma* (Rockford, IL: Tan Books and Publishers, 1960), p. 267, where Ott describes merit as dependent upon God's free ordinance and God's free gift of grace to perform those works.

235. Galatians 3:16-22 is used by John to challenge *Sola Scriptura* in Letter 8, pp. 49-50; Letter 10, p. 73; and challenged by Jim in Letter 9, p. 68. Second Thessalonians 2:15 is used by John to require Tradition in Conversation 1, p. 28; in Letter 8, p. 51; in Letter 10, p. 73; and is challenged by Jim, Conversation 1, p. 28 and Letter 9, p. 68.

236. John uses this passage to establish papal authority in Letter 13, p. 88 and in Conversation 4, p. 128; Jim expresses his alternative interpretation in Letter 14, p. 104; and John responds to this interpretation in Letter 15, pp. 108-109.

237. Jim tries to show how these two passages are compatible with two distinct meanings of faith, beginning in Conversation 5, p. 159; John gives alternative way of making these two passages compatible with two distinct meanings of *works*, in Conversation 6, pp. 195-96.

238. John applies John 6 to Catholic worship beginning in Letter 33, p. 216; Jim challenges this beginning in Conversation 7, p. 224 through Letter 40, p. 270.

239. Discussed throughout Topic 4.

240. Jim suggests God gives precepts to show the futility in trying to obey them, beginning in Letter 52, p. 359; John challenges this interpretation, beginning in Letter 53, p. 363.

241. Pope Pius XII, *Humani Generis*, no. 21; quoting Pope Pius IX.